Ready® | 5 Mathematics
TNCore
INSTRUCTION

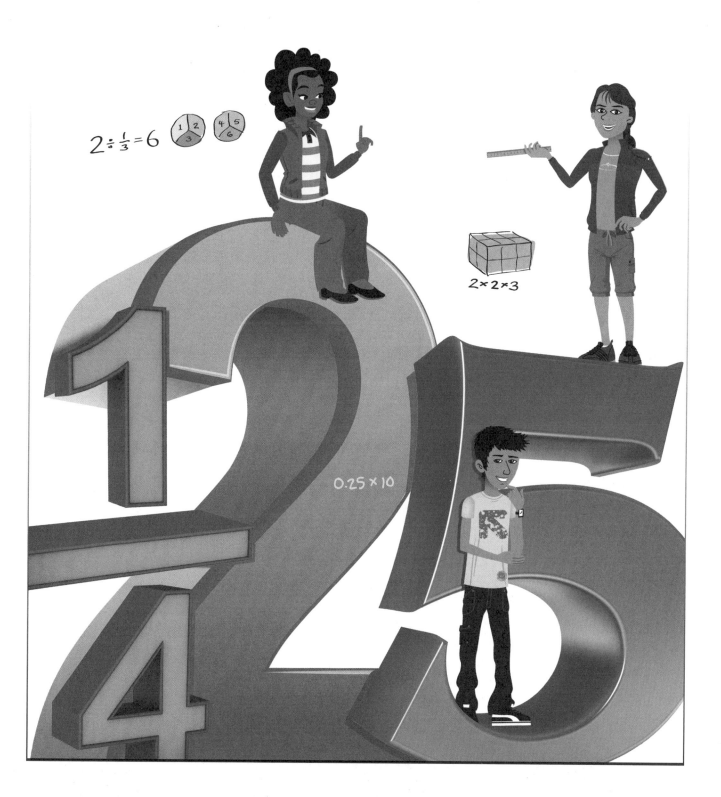

Vice President of Product Development: Adam Berkin
Editorial Director: Cindy Tripp
Project Manager: Grace Izzi
Executive Editor: Kathy Kellman
Supervising Editors: Pam Halloran, Lauren Van Wart
Cover Design and Illustrator: Matt Pollock
Book Design: Jeremy Spiegel

ISBN 978-1-4957-2338-4
©2016–Curriculum Associates, LLC
North Billerica, MA 01862

Table of Contents

Mathematical Practices Handbook . . . . SMPi

Unit 1 **Number and Operations in Base Ten** 1

Standards

Lesson

1 *Understand* Place Value 2   **5.NBT.A.1**

2 *Understand* Powers of Ten 8   **5.NBT.A.2**, 5.NBT.A.1

3 Read and Write Decimals 14   **5.NBT.A.3a**

4 Compare and Round Decimals 24   **5.NBT.A.3b, 5.NBT.A.4**

5 Multiply Whole Numbers 34   **5.NBT.B.5**

6 Divide Whole Numbers 42   **5.NBT.B.6**

7 Add and Subtract Decimals 50   **5.NBT.B.7**

8 Multiply Decimals 60   **5.NBT.B.7**

9 Divide Decimals. 70   **5.NBT.B.7**

MATH IN ACTION Use Whole Numbers and Decimals 82   5.NBT.A.1, 5.NBT.A.2, 5.NBT.A.3, 5.NBT.A.4, 5.NBT.B.5, 5.NBT.B.6, 5.NBT.B.7

Interim Assessment 90

Unit 2 **Number and Operations—Fractions** 93

Lesson

10 Add and Subtract Fractions 94   **5.NF.A.1**, 5.NF.A.2

11 Add and Subtract Fractions in Word Problems . . 104   **5.NF.A.2**, 5.NF.A.1

12 Fractions as Division 112   **5.NF.B.3**

Standards in boldface are the focus standards that address major lesson content.

Table of Contents continued

Unit 2	Number and Operations— Fractions continued		Standards

Lesson

13 *Understand* Products of Fractions	120	**5.NF.B.4a,** 5.NF.B.4b
14 Multiply Fractions Using an Area Model	126	**5.NF.B.4b,** 5.NF.B.4a
15 *Understand* Multiplication as Scaling	136	**5.NF.B.5a, 5.NF.B.5b**
16 Multiply Fractions in Word Problems	142	**5.NF.B.6**
17 *Understand* Division with Unit Fractions	152	**5.NF.B.7a, 5.NF.B.7b,** 5.NF.B.7c
18 Divide Unit Fractions in Word Problems	158	**5.NF.B.7c,** 5.NF.B.7a, 5.NF.B.7b
MATH IN ACTION Use Fractions	168	5.NF.A.1, 5.NF.A.2, 5.NF.B.4, 5.NF.B.6, 5.NF.B.7
Interim Assessment	176	

Unit 3	Operations and Algebraic Thinking	**179**	

Lesson

19 Evaluate and Write Expressions	180	**5.OA.A.1, 5.OA.A.2**
20 Analyze Patterns and Relationships	190	**5.OA.B.3**
MATH IN ACTION Expressions, Patterns, and Relationships	200	5.OA.A.1, 5.OA.A.2, 5.OA.B.3, 5.NBT.B.7, 5.NF.B.6
Interim Assessment	208	

Standards in boldface are the focus standards that address major lesson content.

Unit 4   Measurement and Data 211

Standards

Lesson

21 Convert Measurement Units 212   **5.MD.A.1**, 5.NF.B.7

22 Solve Word Problems Involving Conversions . . . 222   **5.MD.A.1**, 5.NF.B.7

23 Make Line Plots and Interpret Data 232   **5.MD.B.2**

24 *Understand* Volume 242   **5.MD.C.3a, 5.MD.C.3b**, 5.NBT.A.2

25 Find Volume Using Unit Cubes 248   **5.MD.C.4**, 5.MD.C.5a

26 Find Volume Using Formulas 256   **5.MD.C.5a, 5.MD.C.5b**, 5.MD.C.5c

27 Find Volume of Composite Figures. 264   **5.MD.C.5c**, 5.MD.C.5a, 5.MD.C.5b

MATH IN ACTION   Work with Measurement and Data. 272   5.MD.A.1, 5.MD.C.3a, 5.MD.C.3b, 5.MD.C.4, 5.MD.C.5a, 5.MD.C.5b, 5.MD.C.5c, 5.NBT.B.5

Interim Assessment 280

Unit 5   Geometry 283

Lesson

28 *Understand* the Coordinate Plane 284   **5.G.A.1**

29 Graph Points in the Coordinate Plane 290   **5.G.A.2**

30 Classify Two-Dimensional Figures 300   **5.G.B.4**

31 *Understand* Properties of
Two-Dimensional Figures 308   **5.G.B.3**

MATH IN ACTION   Work with Geometry and Coordinates 314   5.G.A.1, 5.G.A.2, 5.G.B.3, 5.G.B.4

Interim Assessment 322

Glossary 325

Standards, Grade 5 337

Standards in boldface are the focus standards that address major lesson content.

MATHEMATICAL PRACTICES HANDBOOK

We use our math thinking to figure out all kinds of problems, even hard problems from real life.

There are eight math habits that will help make your math thinking grow stronger.

Keep practicing! You'll be learning to think like a math pro. Then you'll be ready to take on any problem.

THE 8 MATH HABITS

1 Solve problems.
Keep looking for clues until you solve the problem.

2 Think and reason.
Make sense of the words and the numbers in a problem.

3 Show and explain.
Share your math ideas to help others understand you.

4 Use math in the real world.
Solve problems in real life.

5 Choose a tool.
Decide when to use tools like a diagram, a ruler, or mental math.

6 Be clear and precise.
Try to be exactly right in what you say and do.

7 Zoom in and zoom out.
Look for what's the same and what's different.

8 Use patterns.
Look for patterns in math to find shortcuts.

Read more about each math habit on the pages that follow.

MATH HABIT ①

Solve problems.

Keep looking for clues until you solve the problem.

For some math problems, you may not know where to start. Try different ways to find a solution and look for clues about which way works best. Then check that your answer makes sense.

To solve problems

Ask Yourself

- Can I say what the problem is asking for?
- Can I ask questions to understand it better?
- Can I think about what does or doesn't make sense?
- Can I try a different way if I need to?

Then, Discuss with a Partner

- I thought the problem didn't make sense until I asked …
- I know my answer makes sense because …

MATH HABIT ②

Think and reason.

Make sense of the words and the numbers in a problem.

Reasoning is a way of thinking that puts ideas together.
If you know one thing, then you know another thing.
Reasoning is using math rules and common sense together.

To use reasoning to solve a problem

Ask Yourself

- Can I show how whole numbers and decimals are related?
- When I see an equation, can I think of a situation that would go with it?
- When I read a problem, can I write an equation to find the answer?
- Can I try out my answer to see if it makes sense in the problem?

Then, Discuss with a Partner

- I turned the problem into numbers when I wrote …
- I think my answer makes sense because …

MATH HABIT ③

Show and explain.

Share your math ideas to help others understand you.

When you explain your math ideas to others, it helps you understand them even better. And that helps you solve other problems later. When you listen to other people, you get new ideas too.

To help explain your ideas or listen to others

Ask Yourself

- Can I use words to show how to solve the problem?
- Can I use pictures or act out the problem with objects?
- Can I ask questions to understand another person's ideas better?

Then, Discuss with a Partner

- I showed my ideas when I wrote …
- I explained my ideas when I said …

MATH HABIT ④

SMP 4 Model with mathematics.

Use math in the real world.

Solve problems in real life.

One of the best ways to use your math thinking is to solve real problems. Words tell the story for the problem. Math can turn the words into a model, such as a picture or an equation.

You can use models to solve problems about shopping, art projects, sports, cooking, or ... almost anything!

To solve a real-life problem

Ask Yourself

- Can I draw a picture, write an equation, or use a different model to show the math?
- Can I use my math model to solve the problem?
- Can I check that my answer makes sense?

Then, Discuss with a Partner

- I used a math model to show the problem when I ...
- I know my answer makes sense because ...

MATH HABIT ⑤

SMP 5 Use appropriate tools strategically.

Choose a tool.

Decide when to use tools like a diagram, a ruler, or mental math.

There are many tools to use in math. You can use a pencil to do a lot of math. Sometimes you need a ruler, or maybe a diagram. Often you can just do the math in your head.

To choose the best tools

Ask Yourself

- Can I do some problems in my head?
- Can I write the problem on paper?
- Can I make a table or a diagram?
- Can I use a ruler to solve the problem?

Then, Discuss with a Partner

- The tools I chose for this problem are …
- I chose these tools because …

MATH HABIT ⑥

SMP 6 Attend to precision.

Be clear and precise.

Try to be exactly right in what you say and do.

Everybody likes to be right when they do math. But sometimes people make mistakes. So it's good to check your work. And it's good say exactly what you mean when you talk about your math ideas.

To be exactly right

Ask Yourself

- Can I use words that will help everyone understand my math ideas?
- Can I ask questions to understand the meaning of math words I don't know?
- Can I find different ways to check my work when I multiply or add?
- Can I always think about whether my answer makes sense?

Then, Discuss with a Partner

- I was careful to use the right words when I …
- I checked my answer by …

MATH HABIT ⑦

Zoom in and zoom out.

Look for what's the same and what's different.

Math follows rules. Think about these equations:

$$3 \times 1 = 3$$
$$4 \times 1 = 4$$

You can *zoom out* to look at what's the *same* about problems.
They show that any number times 1 is that number.

You can also *zoom in* to see what's *different* about problems.
The number multiplied by 1 is different in each problem.

To zoom in and zoom out

Ask Yourself

- Can I see how decimals and fractions are both similar and different?
- Can I see how decimals and whole numbers are both similar and different?
- Can I see how shapes are different but are made from other shapes that are the same?

Then, Discuss with a Partner

- I zoomed out and used a math rule when I …
- I zoomed in and found a difference when I looked at …

MATH HABIT ⑧

Use patterns.

Look for patterns in math to find shortcuts.

It's important in math to pay close attention. You might
find a pattern or see a math idea.

Think about the pattern you see when you count by elevens:

11, 22, 33, 44, 55 …

You can use the pattern to make a good guess about
what comes next.

To use patterns

Ask Yourself

- Can I find a pattern in a math problem?
- Can I use clear math words to describe
  my pattern?
- Can I make a good guess about what
  is next?

Then, Discuss with a Partner

- I saw a pattern in this problem when
  I looked at …
- I made a good guess about the pattern
  when I …

Unit 1
Number and Operations in Base Ten

Let's learn about multiplying and dividing decimals.

Real-World Connection Knowing how to add, subtract, multiply, and divide whole numbers is important. But some situations do not involve whole numbers. You want to download 6 new songs that are $1.49 each. You just read that the beach you love to visit is wearing away at a rate of 17.2 centimeters each year. You have 11.5 meters of fabric and will be making 5 equal-sized table covers for the science fair.

In This Unit You will multiply and divide with whole numbers. You will also learn how to calculate with decimals. You will compare decimals, add them, subtract them, multiply them, and divide with them.

✓ Self Check

Before starting this unit, check off the skills you know below. As you complete each lesson, see how many more skills you can check off!

I can:

	Before this unit	After this unit
read and write decimals, for example: $80.63 = 8 \times 10 + 6 \times \frac{1}{10} + 3 \times \frac{1}{100}$.	☐	☐
compare decimals, for example: $3.47 > 3.096$.	☐	☐
round decimals, for example: 6.274 rounded to the nearest tenth is 6.3.	☐	☐
multiply whole numbers, for example: $410 \times 16 = 6,560$.	☐	☐
divide whole numbers, for example: $2,812 \div 38 = 74$.	☐	☐
add and subtract decimals, for example: $20.08 + 5.15 = 25.23$.	☐	☐
multiply decimals, for example: $7.25 \times 9.4 = 68.15$.	☐	☐
divide decimals, for example: $18.8 \div 4 = 4.7$.	☐	☐

Think It Through

How is place value related to the number 10?

We use a number system called **base ten**. This means that place value in any number is based on a pattern of tens.

Look at the following place-value models for whole numbers.

Thousands	Hundreds	Tens	Ones
1 thousand is **10 times** 1 hundred	1 hundred is **10 times** 1 ten	1 ten is **10 times** 1 one	1 one

1,000   +   100   +   10   +   1   =   1,111

Think Place value in decimals is just like place value in whole numbers.

Look at the following place-value models for decimal numbers.

Ones	Tenths	Hundredths
1 whole is **10 times** 1 tenth	1 tenth is **10 times** 1 hundredth	1 hundredth

1   +   0.1   +   0.01   =   1.11

In a decimal number, a digit in one place has ten times the value it would have in the place to its right.

×10   ×10   ×10   ×10   ×10

thousands   hundreds   tens   ones   tenths   hundredths

> **Circle** all of the numbers in the equation below the chart.

Think 1 hundredth is 10 times 1 thousandth.

If you break one hundredth into 10 equal parts, each part is
1 thousandth of the whole.

Look at the pattern in the chart.

0.001
0.01
0.1
1
10
100
1,000
10,000

$\times \frac{1}{10}$ ... $\times 10$

When you multiply a number by 10, the product is 10 times the number.

When the digit **1** moves one place to the left, its value is 10 times what it was.
When the digit **1** moves one place to the right, its value is $\frac{1}{10}$ what it was.

Look more closely at the first two numbers in the chart.

- One hundredth is 10 times one thousandth.
     $0.01 = 10 \times 0.001$

- One thousandth is one tenth of one hundredth.
     $0.001 = 0.01 \div 10$

To write the fraction one thousandth as a decimal, write a zero in the tenths and
hundredths places and a 1 in the thousandths place to the right of the decimal point.

$\frac{1}{1,000} = 0.001$

▶ Reflect

1 In which number does the digit 5 have a greater value, 0.05 or 0.005? How many
times as great is the value? Explain how you know.

_____

_____

_____

Think About ▶ Place-Value Patterns

Let's Explore the Idea Let's explore place-value patterns with another example using models. Each grid represents 1 whole.

A B C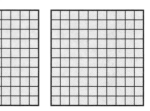

_____   _____   _____

2 Label models *A*, *B*, and *C* with a decimal to name the amount shaded.

3 The shaded region of Model *B* is how many times the shaded region of Model *A*?

_____

The shaded region of Model *C* is how many times the shaded region of Model *B*?

_____

4 Use the models above to complete the equations.

$0.03 \times 10 = $ _____

$0.3 \times 10 = $ _____

$0.3 \div 10 = $ _____

$3.0 \div 10 = $ _____

Now try these two problems.

5 Continue the ×10 pattern to fill in the blanks.

0.003   0.03   0.3   _____   _____   300

6 Use the ÷10 pattern to fill in the blanks.

500   _____   5   0.5   0.05   _____

Let's Talk About It
Now let's explore how 0.30 compares to 0.3.

7 Look at the models in problem 2 and the labels you wrote. Now shade some or all of the grids in the model below to show 30 hundredths. Each grid represents 1 whole.

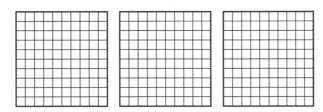

Find the model on the previous page that has the same shading as the model you shaded above. What label did you give that model on the previous page?

_____

8 Use the model you shaded in problem 7 to write a decimal for 30 hundredths.

thirty hundredths = _____

9 How do both shaded models show that 30 hundredths is the same as 3 tenths?

_____

_____

10 What equation can you write to represent "10 times 3 hundredths is 30 hundredths"?

_____

Try It Another Way

11 Imagine a model shaded to show 0.001. How much would be shaded?

_____

_____

12 How would you shade a model to show ten thousandths?

_____

_____

Connect **Ideas About Place-Value Patterns**

Talk through these problems as a class, then write your answers below.

13 Create Shade the models below to show how the value of 0.04 is related to the value of 0.4. Then write a division equation to represent the relationship.

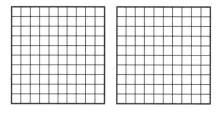

14 Analyze Kiran showed 0.08 with the model below.

What is wrong with Kiran's model? What can be done to her model to show 0.08?

_____

_____

_____

_____

15 Demonstrate A meter is one thousandth of a kilometer. Write an equation to show the relationship between 7 meters and 0.007 kilometer.

_____

_____

Apply Ideas About Place-Value Patterns

16 Put It Together Use what you have learned to complete this task.

> A small beetle has a mass of 0.002 kilogram. A bee has a mass of 0.02 kilogram. A small brick has a mass of 0.2 kilogram.

Part A Write each measurement in the place-value chart below.

Object	Tens	Ones	.	Tenths	Hundredths	Thousandths

Part B Shade the models to compare the mass of the bee to the mass of the brick.

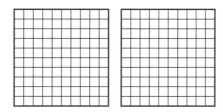

Part C Explain how many small beetles it would take to equal the mass of 1 small brick. Then write an equation using the measurements to show your answer.

_____

_____

_____

_____

Understand Powers of Ten

> ## Think It Through

What does it mean to multiply by 10, 100, or 1,000?

Numbers like 10, 100, or 1,000 that can be written as products of tens are sometimes called **powers of ten**. Multiplying and dividing by powers of ten is related to place value.

Look at the numbers 30, 300, and 3,000 in the place-value chart.

Thousands	Hundreds	Tens	Ones	
			3	
		3	0	$30 = 3 \times 10$
	3	0	0	$300 = 3 \times 100$
3	0	0	0	$3,000 = 3 \times 1,000$

Think Patterns can help you understand multiplying by powers of ten.

Look at the multiplication equations that use powers of ten next to the chart above.

$30 = 3 \times 10$

$300 = 3 \times \mathbf{100}$, or $3 \times \mathbf{10} \times \mathbf{10}$

$3,000 = 3 \times \mathbf{1,000}$, or $3 \times \mathbf{10} \times \mathbf{10} \times \mathbf{10}$

You can see a pattern when you compare the number of 0s in the factors to the number of 0s in the product. The pattern can help you multiply and divide with powers of 10.

Think Dividing by 10 "undoes" multiplying by 10.

If you multiply a number by 10 and then divide the result by 10, you end up with the number you started with. For example, $3 \times 10 = 30$ and $30 \div 10 = 3$. This happens because multiplication and division are **inverse operations**. They "undo" each other.

How many 0s would be in the product of $3 \times 10,000$?

Dividing by 100 is the inverse of multiplying by 100. Since 3×100 is 300, you know that $300 \div 100$ is the same as $3 \times 100 \div 100$, or 3.

Thousands	Hundreds	Tens	Ones	
3	0	0	0	
	3	0	0	$3,000 \div 10 = 300$
		3	0	$3,000 \div 100 = 30$
			3	$3,000 \div 1,000 = 3$

The patterns you find in dividing by powers of ten are similar to the patterns in multiplying by powers of ten.

$3,000 \div 10 = 300$ Check: $300 \times 10 = 3,000$
$3,000 \div 100 = 30$ Check: $30 \times 100 = 3,000$
$3,000 \div 1,000 = 3$ Check: $3 \times 1,000 = 3,000$

You can use the pattern when you divide by powers of ten. Notice how the number of zeros in the dividend and divisor are related to the number of zeros in the quotient.

▶ Reflect

1 How many 0s are in the product of 4×100? $4 \times 1,000$? $4 \times 10,000$? How do you know?

_____

_____

_____

_____

Think About ▷ **Working with Powers of Ten**

🔍 **Let's Explore the Idea** **Now explore patterns when multiplying or dividing a decimal by a power of ten.**

2 Compare the numbers 5.0 and 0.5. How many times 0.5 is 5? Use place value to explain how you know.

_____

_____

3 Compare the numbers 0.5 and 0.05. How many times 0.05 is 0.5? Use place value to explain how you know.

_____

_____

4 Now use place-value reasoning to fill in the blanks in the place-value chart below. Look for useful patterns as you work.

Ones	.	Tenths	Hundredths	Thousandths	
0	.	0	0	5	
	.				0.005×10
	.				$0.005 \times 10 \times 10$
	.				$0.005 \times 10 \times 10 \times 10$

Remember that division is the inverse of multiplication. Use understanding of division and place value to fill in the blanks in the place-value chart below. Look for useful patterns as you work.

Ones	.	Tenths	Hundredths	Thousandths	
7	.	0	0	0	
	.				$7 \div 10$
	.				$7 \div 100$
	.				$7 \div 1,000$

Let's Talk About It Find out what happens when a decimal is multiplied or divided by a power of ten.

5 How many places does the decimal point move when you multiply a number by 10? In which direction?

_____

6 How many places does the decimal point move when you divide a number by 10? In which direction?

_____

7 What pattern describes how the decimal point moves when you multiply a decimal by any power of ten?

_____

8 What pattern describes how the decimal point moves when you divide a decimal by any power of ten?

_____

▶ Try It Another Way

A shorthand for writing powers of ten can make it easier to use the patterns for multiplying and dividing. In the shorthand column of the table below, the small, raised number is called an **exponent**. The exponent in a power of ten tells how many times 10 is a factor.

Standard Form	Product of Tens	Shorthand	Read As
10	10	10^1	10 to the first power
100	10×10	10^2	10 to the second power
1,000	$10 \times 10 \times 10$	10^3	10 to the third power

9 What is 3×10^2? _____ What is 2.5×10^2? _____

What is the exponent in 10^2? _____ How many times do you multiply by 10? _____ How many places does the decimal point move? _____

10 What is 0.005×10^2? _____ What is 0.05×10^2? _____

Connect ▶ **Ideas About Powers of Ten**

Talk through these problems as a class, then write your answers below.

11 Compare Use this place-value chart to describe the relationship between $0.8 \div 10^2$ and 0.8×10^2.

Tens	Ones	.	Tenths	Hundredths	Thousandths	
8	0	.	0	0	0	0.8×10^2
	8	.	0	0	0	0.8×10^1
	0	.	8	0	0	0.8
	0	.	0	8	0	$0.8 \div 10^1$
	0	.	0	0	8	$0.8 \div 10^2$

12 Inspect Marisa said that multiplying 8.0 by 10^6 would increase the value of the 8 because there would be 6 more zeros to the right of the decimal point. Explain what is wrong in Marisa's statement.

13 Illustrate Show how $7,000 \div 10^3$ is the same as $7,000 \div 10 \div 10 \div 10$.

Apply > **Ideas About Powers of Ten**

14 **Put It Together** Use what you have learned to complete this task.

> Jaime claims that when you multiply a whole number by 100, the decimal point moves 2 places to the right. Salome argues that the decimal point only moves when you multiply a decimal number by 100. Salome says that when you multiply a whole number by 100, the product has 2 extra zeros.

Part A Explain each student's point of view, with examples.

_____

_____

_____

_____

_____

_____

_____

_____

_____

_____

Part B Which student is correct? Justify your answer.

_____

_____

_____

_____

_____

Ⓠ Use What You Know

You already know how to read and write whole numbers and fractions. Reading and writing decimals is similar.

> Jessica is reading aloud from a science website. She comes across the measurements 0.32 meter and 0.543 meter. How should she read 0.32?

Jessica can read 0.32 as 3 tenths and 2 hundredths, but it is easier to understand her if she says how many hundredths that is.

To read 0.32 as a number of hundredths:

a. Write 3 tenths as a fraction. _____

b. Rewrite 3 tenths as an equivalent fraction with a denominator of 100. _____

c. Write 2 hundredths as a fraction. _____

d. Complete the equation to add the like fractions for 3 tenths and 2 hundredths.

$$\frac{\square}{100} + \frac{\square}{100} = \frac{\square}{\square}$$

e. Write in words how Jessica should read the number 0.32. _____

_____

f. Explain how you can use place value and fractions to read a number with two digits to the right of the decimal point.

_____

_____

_____

_____

▷▷ Find Out More

You can read decimals as strings of digits, for example: *zero point three two*. But to give meaning to the amount a decimal represents, you name the place value of the smallest-sized unit and read the number to say how many of those units.

Ones	.	Tenths	Hundredths	Thousandths
0	.	3	2	

The least place value in 0.32 is hundredths, so you read the decimal by saying how many hundredths there are. Read 0.32 as *thirty-two hundredths*.

Now look at the same decimal with a zero in the thousandths place.

Ones	.	Tenths	Hundredths	Thousandths
0	.	3	2	0

In the decimal 0.320, the least place value is thousandths. Even though 0.320 is equal to 0.32, you read 0.320 to tell how many thousandths there are. Read 0.320 as *three hundred twenty thousandths*.

The chart below shows the decimal 0.543.

Ones	.	Tenths	Hundredths	Thousandths
0	.	5	4	3

The least place value in 0.543 is thousandths. You read the decimal to tell how many thousandths there are. Read 0.543 as *five hundred forty-three thousandths*.

When a decimal number includes a whole number, read it the way you read mixed numbers. You read the decimal point as *and*. You read $3\frac{5}{10}$ as *three and five tenths*. Read 3.5 as *three and five tenths*.

▶ Reflect

1 Write 1.005 as a mixed number. Then write how to read this number aloud.

_____

_____

Learn About ▶ Reading a Decimal

Read the problem below. Then explore different ways to represent decimals.

> Josh has been tracking the growth of his dog since it was a puppy. He uses a meter stick to measure the dog's height and records the height as 0.604 meter. Josh's mom asks, "How tall is your dog?" What does Josh tell his mom?

▶ **Model It** **You can use place-value understanding to write the expanded form of 0.604. You can also write it as a fraction.**

With decimals:

$$0.604 = 0.6 + 0.004$$
$$= 6 \times 0.1 + 4 \times 0.001$$

With fractions:

$$0.604 = 6 \times \frac{1}{10} + 4 \times \frac{1}{1,000}$$
$$= \frac{6}{10} + \frac{4}{1,000}$$
$$= \frac{600}{1,000} + \frac{4}{1,000}$$
$$= \frac{604}{1,000}$$

▶ **Model It** **You can write 0.604 in a place-value chart to show the place value of each digit.**

Ones	.	Tenths	Hundredths	Thousandths
0	.	6	0	4

The least place value of 0.604 is thousandths.

▶ **Connect It** **Now you will write the word form of the decimal on the previous page using both models.**

To read a decimal, you tell how many of the smallest fractional part it represents.

2 Look at the place-value chart. What are the names of the four place values in 0.604?

_____

Which of those places has the least value? _____

3 Look at the expanded form with fractions. How many thousandths are there altogether in 0.604? _____

4 What is the word form of 0.604?

_____

5 What is the word form of 1.604?

_____

6 Explain how reading the digits to the right of the decimal point and knowing the name of the least place value help you read a decimal number. Use the examples 0.604 and 1.604 in your explanation.

_____

_____

_____

_____

_____

_____

▶ **Try It** **Use what you just learned about identifying the least place value to read decimal numbers. Show your work on a separate sheet of paper.**

7 What is the word form of 0.44? _____

8 What is the word form of 1.057? _____

Learn About **Writing a Mixed Number as a Decimal**

Read the problem below. Then explore different ways to think about writing the numbers as decimals.

A school held a running race.

- Abha finished the race one and sixteen thousandths seconds ahead of Nadia.

- Brianne finished two and thirty-five hundredths seconds ahead of Chandra.

What decimals represent these measurements?

▶ **Model It** **Model the measurements with mixed numbers and expanded form.**

Write mixed numbers to show the number of whole seconds and the fraction of a second given by each measurement. Then expand.

one *and* sixteen thousandths

$1\frac{16}{1,000}$

$1 + \frac{16}{1,000}$

$1 + \frac{10}{1,000} + \frac{6}{1,000}$

$1 + \frac{1}{100} + \frac{6}{1,000}$

two *and* thirty-five hundredths

$2\frac{35}{100}$

$2 + \frac{35}{100}$

$2 + \frac{30}{100} + \frac{5}{100}$

$2 + \frac{3}{10} + \frac{5}{100}$

▶ **Model It** **Use a place-value chart to write the measurements.**

Ones	.	Tenths	Hundredths	Thousandths
1	.	0	1	6
2	.	3	5	

16 thousandths is
10 thousandths and 6 thousandths or
1 hundredth and 6 thousandths.

35 hundredths is
30 hundredths and 5 hundredths or
3 tenths and 5 hundredths.

Connect It Now you will use the models to write the numbers from the problem on the previous page as standard decimals.

9 Compare the mixed-number and the place-value representations of *one and sixteen thousandths*. How does each model show the number of whole seconds?

_____

_____

10 How does each representation of *one and sixteen thousandths* show the value of the fractional part of a second?

_____

_____

_____

11 How can you write *one and sixteen thousandths* as a decimal? _____

12 How does each representation of *two and thirty-five hundredths* show the value of the fractional part of a second?

_____

_____

_____

13 How can you write *two and thirty-five hundredths* as a decimal? _____

14 Explain how you can write the standard form of a decimal given in word form.

_____

_____

_____

Try It Use what you just learned to write numbers as decimals.

15 six and fifty-four thousandths _____

16 ten and seventy-five hundredths _____

Practice › Reading and Writing Decimals

Study the example below. Then solve problems 17–19.

Example

The height of Coach Roberts is two and fifty-four thousandths meters. Write this height as a decimal.

Look at how you could show your work using expanded form.

Two and fifty-four thousandths is $2\frac{54}{1,000}$.

$$\frac{54}{1,000} = \frac{50}{1,000} + \frac{4}{1,000}$$

$$= 5 \times \frac{10}{1,000} + 4 \times \frac{1}{1,000}$$

$$= 5 \times \frac{1}{100} + 4 \times \frac{1}{1,000}$$

$$= 5 \times 0.01 + 4 \times 0.001$$

Ones	.	Tenths	Hundredths	Thousandths
2	.	0	5	4

Solution _2.054 meters_

What place-value relationship lets me write $\frac{50}{1,000}$ as $\frac{5}{100}$?

Pair/Share
Why can you use fractions to represent a decimal number?

---

17 Aubrey runs the 100-meter dash in 14.895 seconds. What words could you use to read 14.895?

Show your work.

How can you write 14.895 as a mixed number?

 Pair/Share
Is there a different way to use words to represent 14.895?

Solution _____

18 Paulo measured the width of a sideline on a football field. It was one hundred two thousandths of a meter. Write this width as a fraction and as a decimal in expanded form.

Show your work.

How could you represent this number in a place-value chart?

Pair/Share
What other ways could you represent this number?

Solution _____

_____

---

19 Which of the following is a representation of 4.082? Circle the letter of the correct answer.

A $4 + \dfrac{8}{10} + \dfrac{2}{1,000}$

B four and eighty-two thousandths

C four and eight and two hundredths

D $4 + 8 \times \dfrac{1}{10} + 2 \times \dfrac{1}{100}$

Rachel chose **D** as the correct answer. How did she get that answer?

_____

_____

_____

_____

What are the place values of each digit in 4.082?

Pair/Share
Does Rachel's answer make sense?

Practice ▶ Reading and Writing Decimals

Solve the problems.

1 Daniel ran the 400-meter dash in 89.023 seconds. Which of the following expresses this time in words?

   A eighty-nine and twenty-three hundredths seconds

   B eighty-nine and two tenths and three thousandths seconds

   C eighty-nine and twenty-three thousandths seconds

   D eighty-nine thousand twenty three seconds

2 What decimal represents $6 \times 1{,}000 + 2 \times 10 + 3 \times \frac{1}{10} + 5 \times \frac{1}{1{,}000}$?

   A 6,020.305

   B 6,200.350

   C 6,020.035

   D 6,002.035

3 A guitar string that plays a very high note is eleven thousandths of an inch thick. A bass string that plays a very low note is ten times as thick. For each quantity, choose either *Yes* or *No* to tell whether it is equal to ten times eleven thousandths.

   a. $\frac{1}{100} + \frac{1}{1{,}000}$ ☐ Yes   ☐ No

   b. $\frac{1}{10} + \frac{1}{100}$ ☐ Yes   ☐ No

   c. 0.11   ☐ Yes   ☐ No

   d. eleven hundredths   ☐ Yes   ☐ No

   e. eleven ten thousandths   ☐ Yes   ☐ No

4 Which of the following correctly represent 57.036? Circle the letter for all that apply.

A $\quad 57 + \dfrac{3}{100} + \dfrac{6}{1,000}$

B $\quad 57 + 3 \times \dfrac{10}{1,000} + 6 \times \dfrac{10}{1,000}$

C $\quad 57 + 36 \times 0.01$

D $\quad 57 + 36 \times 0.001$

E $\quad$ fifty-seven and thirty-six hundredths

5 Represent 240.149 in two different ways. Then explain how each way shows the place value of the digits of the number.

_____

_____

_____

_____

_____

_____

_____

6 Alex wrote 103.903 in expanded form as $100 + 3 \times 1 + 9 \times \dfrac{1}{100} + 3 \times \dfrac{1}{1,000}$. Explain his mistake. Then tell how to correct it.

_____

_____

_____

_____

✓ **Self Check** **Go back and see what you can check off on the Self Check on page 1.**

Use What You Know

You already know how to compare and round whole numbers. In this lesson, you will use place-value understanding to compare and round decimals.

Grace has a collection of buttons in a jar. The blue buttons are 0.008 meter wide and the red buttons are 0.02 meter wide. Which color button is wider?

a. In the numbers 0.008 and 0.02, what are the place values of the 8 and the 2?

8 is in the _____ place.

2 is in the _____ place.

b. Compare those place values: There are _____ thousandths in 1 hundredth.

c. How do you know that 8 thousandths is less than 1 hundredth?

_____

d. Write an inequality statement using < or > to compare 0.008 and 0.01. _____

e. Now think about whether 0.02 is greater or less than 0.01. Then write an inequality statement to compare 0.008 and 0.02. _____

f. Explain how you know this inequality statement is correct.

_____

_____

_____

g. Which color of button is wider? _____

To compare decimals, you can think about how to express numbers in different ways. Each row in the table shows other ways to express the same number.

Words	Place Value	Fractions
10 hundredths is 1 tenth	$0.10 = 0.1$	$\frac{10}{100} = \frac{1}{10}$
10 thousandths is 1 hundredth	$0.010 = 0.01$	$\frac{10}{1,000} = \frac{1}{100}$
100 thousandths is 1 tenth	$0.100 = 0.1$	$\frac{100}{1,000} = \frac{1}{10}$

The decimal 0.008 is 8 thousandths. Since 8 thousandths is less than 10 thousandths, $0.008 < 0.010$.

Expressing numbers in different ways can also help you round decimals. To round 0.008 to the nearest hundredth is to determine whether it is closer to 0.00 or 0.01.

Just like you do with a whole number, you **round a decimal down** when it is **less than halfway** between two values. You always **round a decimal up** when it is **more than halfway, or exactly halfway**, between the two values.

But, what *is* halfway between 0 and 0.01, or halfway between 0.01 and 0.02?

Since half of 10 thousandths is 5 thousandths, halfway between 0 to 0.010 is **0.005**. Since 0.008 is more than halfway from 0 to 0.01, round 0.008 up to 0.01.

▶ Reflect

1 Look at the number line above. Is 0.013 more or less than halfway between 0.01 and 0.02? How do you know?

_____

_____

_____

Learn About ▷ **Comparing Decimals**

Read the problem. Then explore different ways to compare decimals.

Gary and Melissa compare the distances they walk each morning to get to school.

- Gary walks 3.275 kilometers.
- Melissa walks 3.24 kilometers.

Who walks farther to get to school?

▶ **Model It** **Express the two distances as mixed numbers with like denominators.**

Gary: $3.275 = 3\frac{275}{1,000}$ Melissa: $3.24 = 3\frac{24}{100}$

$3\frac{24}{100} = 3\frac{240}{1,000}$

$3\frac{275}{1,000} > 3\frac{240}{1,000}$, so Gary walks farther to get to school.

▶ **Model It** **Write the distances in a place-value chart.**

	Ones	.	Tenths	Hundredths	Thousandths
Gary	3	.	2	7	5
Melissa	3	.	2	4	0

Gary walks 3,275 thousandths kilometers to get to school.

Melissa walks 3,240 thousandths kilometers to get to school.

3,275 thousandths > 3,240 thousandths, so Gary walks farther to get to school.

Connect It Now you will use the two models on the previous page to explore the same problem. The first *Model It* shows $3\frac{24}{100}$ as $3\frac{240}{1,000}$. The second *Model It* shows 3.24 as 3.240.

2 Both *Model Its* change the way the fractional part or decimal part of 3.24 is represented. What is the same about how the denominator of the fraction and the place value of the decimal change? _____

_____

3 What is the same about how the numerator of the fraction and the digits to the right of the decimal point change? _____

_____

_____

4 How does rewriting the fractional part or decimal part of 3.24 make it easier to compare 3.24 to 3.275? _____

_____

_____

5 Explain how you can use what you know about comparing 240 and 275 to help you compare $3\frac{240}{1,000}$ with $3\frac{275}{1,000}$ or compare 3.240 with 3.275. _____

_____

_____

Try It Use what you just learned about comparing decimals to solve these problems. Show your work on a separate sheet of paper.

6 Heather's rabbit has a mass of 5.190 kilograms. Jeff's rabbit has a mass of 5.195 kilograms. Write an inequality statement comparing the masses of the rabbits. _____

7 Brayden and his cousin Kayla live twenty miles away from each other. On the same day, Brayden recorded 1.046 inches of rain at his house and Kayla recorded 1.062 inches of rain at her house. Whose house received fewer inches of rain that day? _____

Learn About ▷ **Rounding Decimals**

Read the problem. Then explore different ways to round the decimals.

Maura has a shelf that is 2.97 meters long. She is buying craft boxes that are 0.273 meter long. Maura wants to round these numbers to the nearest tenth to estimate how many boxes will fit on the shelf. About how many boxes will fit on the shelf?

▷ **Model It** **Place 0.273 on a number line to see its relationship to nearby tenths.**

0.273 is more than halfway from 0.2 to 0.3. It is closer to 0.3.

▷ **Model It** **Use a place-value chart to compare 2.97 to nearby tenths.**

Ones	.	Tenths	Hundredths
2	.	9	0
2	.	9	1
2	.	9	2
2	.	9	3
2	.	9	4
2	.	9	5
2	.	9	6
2	.	**9**	**7**
2	.	9	8
2	.	9	9
3	.	0	0

2.97 is more than halfway between 2.9 and 3.0, so it rounds up to 3.0.

Connect It Now compare the two ways to think about rounding numbers.

8 On the number-line model, how is the halfway point between the two nearby tenths shown? _____

_____

9 In the chart, how is the halfway point between the two nearby tenths shown?

_____

10 To the nearest tenth, how long is the shelf? _____

11 To the nearest tenth, how long is a craft box? _____

12 About how many boxes will fit on the shelf? How do you know?

_____

13 You can use the digit to the right of the place you want to round to tell if you should round up or down. Explain how.

_____

_____

14 Describe how each model can help you round a decimal. _____

_____

_____

15 When a number is exactly halfway between nearby tenths, you round it up. Round 0.25 to the nearest tenth. _____

Try It Use what you just learned about rounding decimals to solve these problems. Show your work on a separate sheet of paper.

16 A dropper holds 0.813 milliliter of fluid. What is this amount rounded to the nearest hundredth? _____

17 At the end of each month, Belinda earns $0.024 for every dollar in her savings account. Round this to the nearest hundredth to show about how many cents she earns for every dollar. _____

Practice ➤ **Comparing and Rounding Decimals**

Study the example below. Then solve problems 18–20.

Example

Makayla's mass at birth was 3.747 kilograms. Her brother John's mass at birth was 3.477 kilograms. Whose mass at birth rounded to the nearest whole kilogram was 4 kilograms?

Look at how you could show your work using a number line.

```
        3.477          3.747
  ◄──┼───┼───┼───┼───┼─●─┼───┼───┼─●─┼───┼───►
     3  3.1 3.2 3.3 3.4 3.5 3.6 3.7 3.8 3.9  4
```

The point representing Makayla's mass at birth is closer to 4 kilograms than to 3 kilograms. The point representing John's mass at birth is closer to 3 kilograms than to 4.

Solution _Makayla's mass at birth rounds to 4 kilograms._

> Rounding decimals is like rounding whole numbers.

Pair/Share
How do the masses at birth compare?

---

18 A grocery store charges to the nearest hundredth of pound for produce. If Landon purchased 2.386 pounds of tomatoes, what weight did the store charge for?

Show your work.

> How do I use place value to round whole numbers and decimals?

Pair/Share
About how many whole pounds of tomatoes did Landon purchase? About how many tenths of a pound did he purchase?

Solution _____

19 Ellie fills her car with 14.297 gallons of gas. Alivia fills her car with 14.209 gallons of gas. Write an inequality statement comparing the two gas purchases.

Show your work.

How do I use place value to compare numbers?

Solution _____

Pair/Share
How could you use rounding to compare the numbers?

20 Which of the following comparisons is NOT true? Circle the letter of the correct answer.

A 42.300 = 42.3

B 5.020 < 5.20

C 0.149 < 1.490

D 108.308 > 108.4

Ava chose **A** as the correct answer. How did she get that answer?

Do I compare the number of digits or compare the place value of the digits?

_____

_____

_____

_____

_____

Pair/Share
Does Ava's answer make sense?

Practice ▶ **Comparing and Rounding Decimals**

Solve the problems.

1 The weights of four similar packs of tomatoes are listed below.

> **Pack A:** 2.456 pounds
> **Pack B:** 2.457 pounds
> **Pack C:** 2.454 pounds
> **Pack D:** 2.459 pounds

Malcolm rounds the weights to the nearest hundredth pound. Which weight does NOT round to 2.46 pounds?

A 2.456 pounds

B 2.457 pounds

C 2.454 pounds

D 2.459 pounds

2 Which comparison is NOT true?

A $1.78 < 1.92$

B $1\frac{78}{100} < 1\frac{92}{100}$

C $1 + 7 \times \frac{1}{10} + 8 \times \frac{1}{100} < 1 + 9 \times \frac{1}{10} + 2 \times \frac{1}{100}$

D $1 + \frac{70}{10} + \frac{80}{100} < 1 + \frac{9}{10} + \frac{2}{100}$

3 Tori and Alvin use a stopwatch to record the amount of time it takes a marble to roll down a four-story ramp. Tori's marble takes 2.845 seconds, while Alvin's marble takes 2.835 seconds. Tell whether each sentence is *True* or *False*.

a. Rounded to the nearest tenth, both times are the same. ☐ True ☐ False

b. Rounded to the nearest hundredth, both times are the same. ☐ True ☐ False

c. Both times are closer to 2.8 than 2.9. ☐ True ☐ False

d. Both times are more than halfway between 2.84 and 2.85. ☐ True ☐ False

e. Alvin's marble was faster. ☐ True ☐ False

4 Lauren is going to have soup for dinner, but she doesn't want more than 0.92 gram of sodium. Decide if each brand of soup has less than, greater than, or exactly 0.92 gram of sodium. Write each brand in the correct category in the chart.

Brand A: 0.920 gram **Brand B:** 0.875 gram **Brand C:** 0.915 gram **Brand D:** 1.100 gram

Less than 0.92 gram	Equal to 0.92 gram	Greater than 0.92 gram

5 The weights of four packages of meat are shown below.

Package A	1.748 pounds
Package B	1.645 pounds
Package C	1.754 pounds
Package D	1.532 pounds

Part A Each package is priced by how much it weighs to the nearest tenth of a pound. Order the packages from greatest to least price.

Show your work.

Solution _____

Part B Explain how the order would change if you rounded the weights to the nearest hundredth.

_____

_____

_____

_____

 Self Check Go back and see what you can check off on the Self Check on page 1.

Lesson 5 👥 Introduction
Multiply Whole Numbers

⟳ Use What You Know

In grade 4, you multiplied two-digit numbers by two-digit numbers. Now you'll multiply three-digit numbers by two-digit numbers. Take a look at this problem.

A mall is designing an outdoor space. The available space is 127 feet by 46 feet. The plan is for a grassy section with a width of 40 feet. Next to the grass will be a cement sidewalk with a width of 6 feet. What is the area of the available space in square feet?

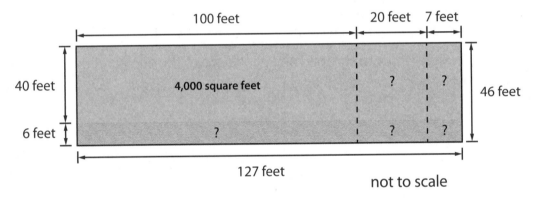

The area model above shows the length and width of each space.

a. What is the total length of the outdoor space? _____

What is the total width? _____

b. How is the area of each space found? _____

_____

c. How can you find the total area? _____

d. The product of 127 and 46 is the total area of the outdoor area. How can you find the area for grass? _____

How can you find the area for the sidewalk? _____

_____

e. What is the total area? _____

▶▶ Find Out More

One way to multiply multi-digit numbers is to find **partial products**. Break apart one of the factors into parts. Then multiply each of the parts by the other factor to get parts of the product, or partial products. Then, add the partial products to find the total product.

- **One way** to show using partial products to find 127×46:

  Break apart 46 into $(40 + 6)$: $127 \times \mathbf{46} = 127 \times (\mathbf{40 + 6})$

  Find each partial product.

  partial products

  Then find the sum of the two partial products.

  $\mathbf{5{,}080} + \mathbf{762} = 5{,}842$

- **Another way** to show using partial products to find 127×46:

$$
\begin{array}{r}
127 \\
\times\ \ 46 \\
\hline
762 \leftarrow \text{area for sidewalk} \\
+\ 5{,}080 \leftarrow \text{area for grass} \\
\hline
5{,}842 \leftarrow \text{total area}
\end{array}
$$

▶ Reflect

1 How is multiplying by a three-digit number similar to multiplying by a two-digit number?

_____

_____

_____

_____

Learn About ▷ Multiplying Three-Digit Numbers

Read the problem below. Then explore different ways to multiply a three-digit number by a two-digit number.

> There are 128 pens in a full box. How many pens are in 35 full boxes?

▶ Model It Use an area model to show partial products.

Sketch a rectangle with dimensions 128 by 35.

128×35

128 is **100 + 20 + 8**.

35 is **30 + 5**.

	100	+	20	+	8
30	$30 \times 100 = \mathbf{3{,}000}$		$30 \times 20 = \mathbf{600}$		$30 \times 8 = \mathbf{240}$
+ 5	$5 \times 100 = \mathbf{500}$		$5 \times 20 = \mathbf{100}$		$5 \times 8 = \mathbf{40}$

First row: $3{,}000 + 600 + 240 = 3{,}840$

Second row: $500 + 100 + 40 = 640$

So, $128 \times 35 = 3{,}840 + 640 = 4{,}480$.

▶ Model It Use the distributive property to find partial products and add them.

$128 \times 35 = 128 \times (30 + 5)$

$128 \times (30 + 5) = (128 \times 30) + (128 \times 5)$

$$
\begin{array}{r}
128 \\
\times\ \ 30 \\
\hline
240 \\
600 \\
+\ 3{,}000 \\
\hline
3{,}840
\end{array}
\quad
\begin{array}{l}
\rightarrow (30 \times 8) \\
\rightarrow (30 \times 20) \\
\rightarrow (30 \times 100) \\
\end{array}
\qquad
\begin{array}{r}
128 \\
\times\ \ 5 \\
\hline
40 \\
100 \\
+\ 500 \\
\hline
640
\end{array}
\quad
\begin{array}{l}
\rightarrow (5 \times 8) \\
\rightarrow (5 \times 20) \\
\rightarrow (5 \times 100) \\
\end{array}
$$

$3{,}840 + 640 = 4{,}480$

Connect It Now you will compare the two ways to multiply using partial products.

2 Why is the area model divided into six sections? _____

_____

_____

3 How do the three partial products in each multiplication equation in the second *Model It* relate to the three sections in each row of the area model? _____

_____

_____

4 Would the product change if 30 and 5 on the left side of the area model were changed to 20, 10, and 5? Explain. _____

_____

_____

_____

_____

5 List two different ways you could break up the factors in 239 × 64 to find the product. Explain why both ways would have the same product. _____

_____

_____

_____

_____

Try It Use what you just learned about multiplying numbers to solve this problem. Show your work on a separate sheet of paper.

6 A bookshelf at a library holds 156 books. There are 15 bookshelves in the children's section. How many children's books can the library place on the bookshelves?

_____

Study the example below. Then solve problems 7–9.

Example

There are 366 days in a leap year and 24 hours in a day. How many hours are in a leap year?

Look at how you could show your work.

$$
\begin{array}{r}
\overset{1\ 1}{\underset{2\ 2}{}}\ \ \ \\
366 \\
\times\ \ \ 24 \\
\hline
1{,}464 \\
+\ 7{,}320 \\
\hline
8{,}784
\end{array}
$$

Solution ___8,784 hours___

> Why does the product of 366 and 2 tens have a 0 in the ones place?

> **Pair/Share**
> How are the regrouped ones and tens used to find the partial products?

---

7 A certain dishwasher uses 29 kilowatts of energy per hour. If the dishwasher was used 156 hours last year, how many kilowatts of energy did the dishwasher use last year?

Show your work.

> What is the role of place value when multiplying two numbers?

> **Pair/Share**
> Show and explain how to solve this problem using a different method.

Solution _____

8 If 1 stamp costs 45 cents, what does a roll of 125 stamps cost in cents? What is this amount in dollars and cents?

Show your work.

How could I first estimate the answer to this problem?

Solution _____

Pair/Share
Why is multiplication used to solve this problem? What other operation is used?

---

9 Raquel can type 63 words every minute. Rick can type 73 words every minute. How many more words can Rick type than Raquel in 135 minutes? Circle the letter of the correct answer.

A 1,350

B 4,599

C 8,505

D 9,855

Jared chose **B** as the correct answer. How did he get that answer?

_____

_____

_____

_____

How can I use the difference in the number of words typed by Rick and Raquel every minute to solve this problem?

Pair/Share
Does Jared's answer make sense?

Practice ▶ **Multiplying Whole Numbers**

Solve the problems.

1 Mrs. Cady constructs a cube with 512 magnetic blocks. Students in her two classes will each make an identical cube. There are 28 students in one class and 25 students in the other class. How many blocks does she need for all her students?

A 5,120

B 12,800

C 14,336

D 27,136

2 What are the values of the regrouped amounts in the multiplication below?

$$\begin{array}{r} {\scriptstyle 2\,3} \\ 435 \\ \times\ \ 17 \\ \hline 3,045 \\ +\ 4,350 \\ \hline 7,395 \end{array}$$

A 2 and 3

B 20 and 3

C 200 and 30

D 2,000 and 300

3 Choose *Yes* or *No* to tell whether the expression is equivalent to 179×44.

		Yes	No
a.	$179 \times (4 + 4)$	☐	☐
b.	$(179 \times 40) + (179 \times 4)$	☐	☐
c.	$(100 \times 4) + (70 \times 4) + (9 \times 4)$	☐	☐
d.	$4,000 + 2,800 + 360 + 400 + 280 + 36$	☐	☐
e.	$(100 \times 44) + (70 \times 44) + (9 \times 44)$	☐	☐

4 Show two different ways to complete the multiplication problem.

$$
\begin{array}{r}
3\ 1\ 4 \\
\times\ \ \ \ \ \ 5\ \boxed{} \\
\hline
1\ \boxed{}\ \boxed{}\ 6
\end{array}
\qquad
\begin{array}{r}
3\ 1\ 4 \\
\times\ \ \ \ \ \ 5\ \boxed{} \\
\hline
1\ \boxed{}\ \boxed{}\ 6
\end{array}
$$

5 At the start of the day there are 78 boxes of DVDs in a warehouse. Each box has 116 DVDs. Then 19 of the boxes are shipped. Now how many DVDs are left in the warehouse?

Show your work.

Answer _____ DVDs

6 Use the distributive property two different ways to find the product of 127 and 32.

Show your work.

✔ **Self Check** Go back and see what you can check off on the Self Check on page 1.

Lesson 6 ·👥 Introduction
Divide Whole Numbers

⟳ Use What You Know

In the last lesson, you learned how to find products of two- and three-digit factors. Now you will learn how to divide with two-digit divisors.

There are 345 fifth graders enrolled at Wilson Middle School and 15 fifth-grade classrooms. How many students are in each class if each class has the same number of students?

a. What multiplication equation can you use to solve 345 ÷ 15? _____

b. Multiply 15 by multiples of 10. Fill in the blanks.

   15 × 10 = _____   15 × 20 = _____   15 × 30 = _____

c. Now estimate the quotient. The quotient will be between which two tens? _____

d. If 15 × 20 = 300, what number is left after you subtract this product from 345? _____

e. Divide what is left by 15. _____ ÷ 15 = _____

f. Use the information above to find 345 ÷ 15. Explain your thinking.

   _____

   _____

   _____

   _____

On the previous page, you used the relationship between multiplication and division along with properties of operations to divide.

You can also use an area model to show division. It is similar to an area model for multiplication. You can think of division as finding a missing factor. The dividend is the product, the divisor is the known factor, and the quotient is the unknown factor.

The area model shows $345 \div 15$.

Start with the greatest place and find the quotient place by place. On the previous page, you estimated the quotient to be between 20 and 30. So, **20** is the greatest ten that can be in the quotient.

- Start by multiplying **15** by **20**.

- Subtract the product from the dividend, 345.

- Write the difference, **45**, in the next section of the model.

- Think: **15 × ? = 45**. Multiply **15** by **3** and subtract this product from **45**.

- The difference is 0, so there is nothing left to divide.

▶ Reflect

1 How is dividing with an area model similar to multiplying with an area model? How is it different?

_____

_____

_____

_____

Learn About ▶ Dividing by Two-Digit Numbers

Read the problem below. Then explore different ways to divide by a two-digit divisor.

> A grocery store only sells eggs by the dozen. There are 12 eggs in 1 dozen eggs.
> If there are 624 eggs in stock, how many dozens of eggs are there?

▶ **Model It** **You can use the relationship between multiplication and division to estimate the quotient in a division problem with a two-digit divisor.**

$624 \div 12 = ?$ and $12 \times ? = 624$

Multiply 12 by multiples of 10. Make a table.

Number of dozens	10	20	30	40	50	60
Number of eggs	120	240	360	480	600	720

Since 624 is between **600** and **720**, the quotient is between **50** and **60**.

▶ **Model It** **You can use an area model to solve a division problem with a two-digit divisor.**

Connect It Now you will record the calculations from the model as partial quotients.

2 How many hundreds are in the dividend? _____

How many groups of 12 are in 600? _____

This partial quotient is written above the bar.

What equation in the area model shows this?

_____

```
      52 ← quotient
       2 ← partial quotient
      50 ← partial quotient
12)624
   − 600
     24
   − 24
      0
```

3 Why is 600 subtracted from 624?

_____

4 How does the area model relate to finding the second partial quotient?

_____

_____

5 Explain how to use the partial quotients to find 624 ÷ 12. _____

_____

6 Describe how to divide using partial quotients. _____

_____

_____

_____

_____

Try It Use what you just learned about dividing by a two-digit divisor to solve these problems. Show your work on a separate sheet of paper.

7 An elementary school has 1,134 seeds. The seeds will be planted in 27 rows. Each row will have the same number of seeds. How many seeds will be planted in each row? _____

8 Nathan writes an essay with a total of 583 words. Every line of his essay has 11 words. How many lines long is Nathan's essay? _____

Practice ▶ **Dividing Whole Numbers**

Study the example below. Then solve problems 9–11.

Example

Each package has 21 pieces of chalk. How many packages can be made with 1,701 pieces of chalk?

Look at how you could show your work using partial quotients.

$$
\begin{array}{r}
81 \\
1 \\
80 \\
21\overline{)1,701} \\
-\,1,680 \leftarrow 21 \times 80 \\
\overline{21} \\
-\,21 \leftarrow 21 \times 1 \\
\overline{0}
\end{array}
$$

Solution _81 packages_

Why is 80 a good number to use as a first partial quotient?

Pair/Share
How can you use multiplication to check that the quotient is correct?

---

9 A water cooler holds 1,284 ounces of water. How many more 6-ounce glasses than 12-ounce glasses can be filled from a full cooler?

Show your work.

You can first estimate how many glasses of each size can be filled.

 Pair/Share
Explain how you found your estimate.

Solution _____

10 Each student needs 35 craft sticks for an art project. The art teacher has 7,140 craft sticks. How many students can get crafts sticks from the teacher?

Show your work.

What numbers can I use to estimate the quotient?

Pair/Share
Explain how to check the answer to a division problem.

Solution _____

11 Harrison creates balloon animals for different events. He has 6,440 balloons. He wants to use the same number of balloons for each of 28 events. How many balloons can Harrison use at each event? Circle the letter of the correct answer.

A 23

B 203

C 230

D 2,030

What will be the greatest place in the quotient?

Tina chose **A** as the correct answer. How did she get that answer?

_____

_____

_____

_____

Pair/Share
Does Tina's answer make sense?

Lesson 6 Divide Whole Numbers

Practice ▶ **Dividing Whole Numbers**

Solve the problems.

1 Which equation can NOT be represented by the model below?

A 5,964 − ? = 42

B 5,964 ÷ ? = 42

C 42 × ? = 5,964

D 5,964 ÷ 42 = ?

2 Vera makes a table to help solve the problem 672 ÷ 16. Which is the best estimate of the quotient?

10	20	30	40	50	60
160	320	480	640	800	960

A a number between 30 and 40

B a number close to 40

C about 52

D a number between 50 and 60

3 Use the grid to draw a rectangle with an area of 1,125 square units and a side of 25 units.

4 Lisa's camera has 2,048 megabytes of memory for storing pictures. She has already used half this amount. A high-quality picture uses 16 megabytes of memory. How many high-quality pictures can Lisa store with the remaining memory?

_____

5 Mr. Kovich writes the problem $32 \times \triangle = 1{,}696$ on the board. Write a division equation that can be used to find the value of the triangle, and then find the value of the triangle.

Show your work.

Solution _____

6 Mr. Sullivan is organizing teams for the middle school's annual field day. There are eight classes at the school and 21 students in each class.

Part A What is the total number of students at the school?

Answer _____ students

Part B Mr. Sullivan wants to have 12 students on each team. How many teams will there be?

Answer _____ teams

Part C How many fewer students will be on each team if he decides to have 24 teams? Explain your answer using diagrams, pictures, mathematical expressions, and/or words.

Answer _____ fewer students

✔ **Self Check** Go back and see what you can check off on the Self Check on page 1.

Add and Subtract Decimals

5.NBT.B.7

🔄 Use What You Know

In grade 4, you learned to add whole numbers by adding the values of digits with the same place value. Now you'll add decimals the same way. Take a look at this problem.

> Sabrina and Christie are running in a relay. Sabrina runs 100 meters in 13.25 seconds, and Christie then runs the same distance in 12.2 seconds. What is their total time?

a. About how many seconds did the girls run altogether? _____ Explain your reasoning.

_____

_____

b. You can think of Sabrina's time as 1 ten + 3 ones + 2 tenths + 5 hundredths. Write Christie's time in the same way. _____

c. Combine Sabrina's and Christie's times. How many tens in all? _____ How many ones in all? _____ How many tenths in all? _____ How many hundredths in all? _____

d. Write the sum of the tens, ones, tenths, and hundredths as a decimal. _____

e. How does the sum compare to your estimate? Is your answer reasonable?

_____

f. Use words to explain how you could find Sabrina and Christie's total time.

_____

_____

You can use what you know about adding whole numbers to add decimals. To add 13.25 and 12.2, you combine like place values.

One way to add decimals is to stack the numbers vertically. Lining up the decimal points is a way to keep track of place values. Using a place-value chart can help.

	Tens	Ones	.	Tenths	Hundredths
	1	3	.	2	5
+	1	2	.	2	0
	2	5	.	4	5

$\frac{2}{10}$ is equivalent to $\frac{20}{100}$, so you can write a 0 in the hundredths column.

The total time is 25.45 seconds.

To find the difference between Sabrina's and Christie's times, subtract 12.20 from 13.25. You can use what you know about subtracting whole numbers to subtract decimals.

	Tens	Ones	.	Tenths	Hundredths
	1	3	.	2	5
−	1	2	.	2	0
	0	1	.	0	5

Christie was faster by 1.05 seconds.

▶ **Reflect**

1 If Christie's time were 13.26 seconds instead of 13.25 seconds, would that change your estimate for the total time? Explain. _____

_____

_____

_____

_____

Learn About ▸ **Adding Decimals to Hundredths**

Read the problem below. Then explore different ways to understand how to add decimals to solve the problem.

From his home, Tim rides the bus 3.82 miles. Then he walks 0.4 mile from the bus stop to school. How many miles does Tim travel from home to school?

▸ **Picture It** **You can picture adding two decimals on a number line.**

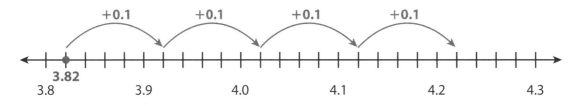

Starting at 3.82, you can make 4 jumps of 0.1 to the right to show the sum of 3.82 and 0.4.

▸ **Model It** **You can use a place-value chart to help you understand how to add decimals.**

	Ones	.	Tenths	Hundredths
Bus ride	3	.	8	2
Bus stop to school	0	.	4	0

$\frac{4}{10}$ is equivalent to $\frac{40}{100}$, so you can write a 0 in the hundredths column.

The sum is 3 ones + 12 tenths + 2 hundredths.

Connect It Now you will use the picture and the model to help you understand how to add decimals.

2 How can you use the number line in *Picture It* to figure out how many miles Tim travels from home to school? _____

_____

_____

3 Look at *Model It* on the previous page. What is another way to express 12 tenths?

_____

What is another way to express the sum? _____

4 You can add the decimals without a place-value chart by stacking them vertically. Line up the decimal points to keep track of place values.

$$\begin{array}{r} 3.82 \\ + 0.40 \\ \hline \end{array}$$

Why do you align the 8 in 3.82 with the 4 in 0.40? _____

5 The addition problem to the right is partially completed. Explain why there is a 1 above the ones place.

$$\begin{array}{r} \overset{1}{3.82} \\ + 0.40 \\ \hline .22 \end{array}$$

_____

_____

6 Complete the problem. How many miles does Tim travel from home to school?

_____

7 Explain how to add decimals.

_____

_____

_____

Try It Use what you just learned about adding decimals to solve this problem. Show your work on a separate sheet of paper.

8 Yana made a trail mix with 128.25 grams of dried fruit and 41.8 grams of almonds. How many grams of trail mix did Yana make? _____

Learn About > Subtracting Decimals to Hundredths

Read the problem below. Then explore different ways to subtract decimals.

> Marty cuts 2.05 ounces of cheese from a 4.6-ounce block of cheddar cheese. How many ounces of cheddar cheese are left in the block?

▶ **Picture It** **You can subtract decimals using base-ten models.**

Model 4 wholes and 6 tenths.

6 tenths = 60 hundredths

▶ **Model It** **You can subtract decimals using a place-value chart.**

Using a place-value chart helps you make sure the place values are lined up correctly.

	Ones	.	Tenths	Hundredths
Original amount	4	.	6	0
Amount cut	2	.	0	5

$\frac{6}{10}$ is equivalent to $\frac{60}{100}$, so you can write a 0 in the hundredths column.

Connect It Now you will use the base-ten models and the place-value chart to understand how to subtract decimals.

9 Look at the base-ten models on the previous page. Explain why parts of the models are crossed out. _____

_____

10 According to *Picture It*, how many ounces of cheddar cheese are left in the block?

_____

11 Look at the place-value chart in *Model It* on the previous page. Why can't you just subtract the 5 from the 6? _____

_____

_____

12 You can subtract the decimals without a place-value chart by stacking them vertically. Line up the decimal points to keep track of place values.

$$\begin{array}{r} 4.60 \\ -\ 2.05 \\ \hline \end{array}$$

13 Another way to express 6 tenths is _____ tenths + 10 hundredths. So you can rewrite the problem as

$$\begin{array}{r} \overset{5\ 10}{4.\cancel{6}0} \\ -\ 2.05 \\ \hline \end{array}$$

Complete the subtraction problem. There are _____ ounces of cheddar left.

14 Explain how to subtract two decimals and how to tell if your answer is reasonable.

_____

_____

_____

Try It Use what you just learned about subtracting decimals to solve this problem. Show your work on a separate sheet of paper.

15 Gwen is sending a box to a friend. The box weighs 23.5 pounds. Gwen removes a 4.47-pound book to decrease the shipping cost. What is the new weight of the box?

_____

Practice ▶ **Adding and Subtracting Decimals**

Study the example below. Then solve problems 16–18.

Example

Diana has 3 different beads on her necklace. The red bead is 0.68 centimeter long, the multi-colored bead is 1.22 centimeters long, and the blue bead is 0.8 centimeter long. What is the total length of the beads on Diana's necklace?

Look at how you could show your work using equations.

$$\begin{array}{r} \overset{1}{1}.22 \\ +\ 0.68 \\ \hline 1.90 \end{array} \qquad \begin{array}{r} \overset{1}{1}.90 \\ +\ 0.80 \\ \hline 2.70 \end{array}$$

$$0.68 + 1.22 + 0.8 = 2.7$$

Solution _2.7 centimeters_

The student needed two steps to solve the problem.

Pair/Share
Does it matter in what order you add the decimals?

---

16 On average, outdoor cats live 3.18 years and indoor cats live 16.7 years. How much longer does an average indoor cat live than an average outdoor cat?

Show your work.

How many hundredths are equivalent to 7 tenths?

Pair/Share
How do you know what operation to use to solve this problem?

Solution _____

17 Kenton is shopping for clothes at a twelfth anniversary sale. He buys a pair of jeans priced at $24.99 and a clearance-priced shirt for $5.25. The store reduces the amount of his entire purchase by $12.12. How much does Kenton pay for his clothes?

Show your work.

This problem takes more than one step to solve.

Pair/Share
Explain how to check if your answer is reasonable.

Solution _____

---

18 Three boxes of cereal have masses of 379.4 grams, 424.25 grams, and 379.37 grams. What is the difference between the box of cereal with the greatest mass and the box of cereal with the least mass?

A 44.15 grams

B 44.85 grams

C 44.88 grams

D 45.12 grams

What operation will solve this problem?

Cambria chose **D** as the correct answer. How did she get that answer?

_____

_____

_____

Pair/Share
How could Cambria have checked her answer?

_____

Practice ▶ **Adding and Subtracting Decimals**

Solve the problems.

1. Randy rode his bike 1.23 miles to school from his house. After school, he rode 0.9 mile farther to the library. Randy biked home along the same route, stopping at a park 1.05 miles from the library. How many miles is the park from Randy's house?

   A 3.18

   B 2.37

   C 1.08

   D 0.27

2. Tim tracked the change in outside temperature one afternoon. He recorded a temperature of 85.4°F at noon. The temperature then rose 3.85°F over the next 4 hours. At 5:00 PM, Tim recorded a temperature of 89.25°F. How did the temperature change between 4:00 PM and 5:00 PM?

   A The temperature increased 0.8°F.

   B The temperature decreased 0.2°F.

   C The temperature increased 1°F.

   D There was no change in temperature.

3. Tell whether each equation is *True* or *False*.

   a. $198.5 - 42.81 = 155.69$

   ☐ True ☐ False

   b. $73.27 + 251.6 = 98.43$

   ☐ True ☐ False

   c. $37.04 + 56.20 = 93.6$

   ☐ True ☐ False

   d. $70.64 - (9.3 + 29.36) = 90.7$

   ☐ True ☐ False

   e. $38.2 - (11.11 + 23.76) = 3.33$

   ☐ True ☐ False

4. The sum of three decimal numbers is 6. Exactly one of the numbers is less than 1. What could the numbers be?

   Show your work.

Solution _____

5 Choose all the models or expressions that represent the difference 3.7 − 1.02.

A

B

C   2 ones + 6 tenths + 8 hundredths

D

E

6 Ryan and Sarah are looking at cell phone plans. A group plan will cost $120.95 per month. An individual plan will cost $62.77 per month. Should Ryan and Sarah purchase a group plan or two individual plans? Justify your answer. How much money could they save?

Show your work.

✔ **Self Check** **Go back and see what you can check off on the Self Check on page 1.**

Multiply Decimals

 Use What You Know

You know how to multiply whole numbers by other whole numbers and by fractions. Now you'll learn how to multiply whole numbers by decimals. Take a look at this problem.

> Margo has 6 square tiles of equal size. Each side of each tile is 0.8 inch long.
> If Margo places all the tiles in a row with sides touching, how long is the row?
>
>

a. First, estimate the length of the side of each tile to the nearest inch. _____

b. Estimate the length of the row of 6 tiles using your answer. _____

c. Will the actual length be more or less than your estimate? _____

d. Why? _____

e. The length of the side of each tile is _____ tenths of an inch. There are _____ tiles in the row.

f. How many tenths of an inch long is the row of tiles? _____ tenths of an inch

g. Write the decimal equivalent:

   The length of the row is _____ inches.

h. Is your answer reasonable? Explain your thinking.

   _____

i. Use your own words to explain how you could find the length of the row of tiles.

   _____

   _____

On the previous page you saw that $6 \times 0.8 = 4.8$. How is this related to $6 \times 8 = 48$?

Notice that the digits of 6×0.8 are the same as the digits of 6×8. The digits of their products are also the same. Why is this?

In earlier lessons, you learned that dividing a number by 10 shifts the decimal point to the left so the value of the number decreases by a factor of 10. Dividing a number by 10 has the same result as multiplying the number by one tenth, or 0.1.

Look at the table below to see patterns when you multiply numbers by 0.1 and 0.01.

Expression	Equivalent Expressions	Product
6×8	$6 \times 8 \times 1.0$ 48×1.0	48.0
6×0.8	$6 \times 8 \times 0.1$ 48×0.1	4.8
6×0.08	$6 \times 8 \times 0.01$ $6 \times 8 \times 0.1 \times 0.1$ 48×0.01 $48 \times 0.1 \times 0.1$	0.48

Notice that the decimal point moves one place to the left each time you multiply by 0.1.

▶ **Reflect**

1 What is the product of 6×0.008? Explain your reasoning.

_____

_____

_____

_____

_____

_____

Learn About ▶ Multiplying Decimals by Whole Numbers

Read the problem below. Then explore different ways to understand multiplying by hundredths.

> Padma bought 3 pounds of grapes. Each pound of grapes costs $2.75. How much money did Padma spend on grapes?

▶ **Picture It** **You can use decimal grids to picture multiplying with hundredths.**

Think of 3 × $2.75 as 3 groups of 2.75.

▶ **Model It** **You can use partial products to multiply with hundredths.**

$$
\begin{array}{r}
2.75 \\
\times \quad 3 \\
\hline
\end{array}
$$

    15 ⟵ 3 ones × 5 hundredths   = 15 hundredths

  210 ⟵ 3 ones × 7 tenths = 21 tenths   = 210 hundredths

+ 600 ⟵ 3 ones × 2 ones = 6 ones   = 600 hundredths

825 hundredths = 8.25

Connect It Use what you know about decimals and place value to solve the problem.

2 To solve the problem, you need to find 3 × $2.75. Estimate the total cost of the grapes. Explain your thinking. _____

_____

3 Look at *Picture It*. How many full grids can you make? _____

How many squares would be shaded in the partially filled grid? _____

4 Look at *Model It*. How is multiplying with decimals like multiplying with whole numbers? _____

_____

_____

5 Complete the following:

825 hundredths = _____ tenths

825 hundredths = _____ ones

6 Both *Picture It* and *Model It* show that 3 × $2.75 = _____.

Is the product reasonable? Explain. _____

_____

7 Explain how to multiply a whole number by a decimal in the hundredths.

_____

_____

Try It Use what you have learned about multiplying by hundredths to solve these problems. Show your work on a separate sheet of paper.

8 Bananas cost $0.65 per pound. Sasha bought 4 pounds of bananas. How much did she pay for the bananas? _____

9 Brian creates a chain of 11 paper clips. Each paper clip is 2.48 centimeters long. How long is the chain of paper clips? _____

Learn About ▸ Multiplying Decimals with an Area Model

Read the problem below. Then explore different ways to multiply tenths by tenths.

> Hayden made a sign that is 1.4 meters long and 1.2 meters wide to post on the wall of his store. How many square meters of wall will the sign cover?

▶ **Picture It** **You can use an area model to multiply tenths by tenths.**

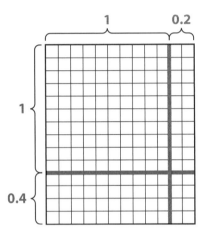

The rectangle measures **1.4 meters** by **1.2 meters**.

Each small square is 1 tenth of a meter by 1 tenth of a meter, or 0.1 meter by 0.1 meter.

The area of each small square is 0.1 meter × 0.1 meter = 0.01 square meter.

▶ **Model It** **You can also use partial products to multiply tenths by tenths.**

$$
\begin{array}{r}
1.2 \\
\times\, 1.4 \\
\hline
8 \\
40 \\
20 \\
+\,100 \\
\hline
168
\end{array}
$$

     8 ⟵ 4 tenths × 2 tenths   =   8 hundredths

 40 ⟵ 4 tenths × 1 one = 4 tenths = 40 hundredths

 20 ⟵ 1 one × 2 tenths = 2 tenths = 20 hundredths

+ 100 ⟵ 1 one × 1 one = 1 one   = 100 hundredths

 168 hundredths = 1.68

► **Connect It** Now you will use the model and properties of operations to solve the problem.

10 To solve the problem, you need to find 1.4×1.2. Estimate the area of wall that the sign will cover. Explain your thinking.

_____

11 Look at *Picture It*. Complete the area model below to find the area of each of the four sections of the rectangle.

$1 \times 1 =$ _____	$1 \times 0.2 =$ _____
$0.4 \times 1 =$ _____	$0.4 \times 0.2 =$ _____

12 Look at *Model It*. How do the partial products relate to the area model above?

_____

_____

13 Both *Picture It* and *Model It* show that $1.4 \times 1.2 =$ _____ square meters.
Is the product reasonable? Explain. _____

_____

_____

14 Explain what you know about the product when you multiply tenths by tenths.

_____

► **Try It** Use what you have learned about multiplying by tenths to solve these problems. Show your work on a separate sheet of paper.

15 Rosa filled her car's tank with 9.8 gallons of gas. Each gallon costs $3.85. How much did Rosa spend on gas? _____

16 Harry has 0.5 bottle of water in his game bag. The bottle holds 0.9 liter of water. How many liters of water does Harry have? _____

Practice ▶ Multiplying Decimals

Study the example below. Then solve problems 17–19.

Example

Liam ate 0.5 of a 1.25-ounce bag of raisins. How many ounces of raisins did Liam eat?

Look at how you could show your work using an area model.

	1	0.2	0.05
0.5	0.5 × 1 = 0.5	0.5 × 0.2 = 0.10	0.5 × 0.05 = 0.025

0.5 + 0.10 + 0.025 = 0.625

The student wrote 1.25 as 1 + 0.2 + 0.05 and used an area model to solve the problem.

Pair/Share
Solve the problem without a model.

Solution _0.625 ounce_

---

17 Gina rides her bike to work at an average of 10.4 miles per hour. She bikes 1.2 hours each day. How many miles does Gina ride each day?

Show your work.

I multiply tenths by tenths to solve this problem.

Pair/Share
What is a reasonable estimate for this problem? Explain your thinking.

Solution _____

18 If a person's hair grows 1.2 centimeters a month, how much would it grow in 9 months?

Show your work.

Will the product be in tenths or hundredths?

Pair/Share
Solve the problem using an area model.

Solution _____

19 What is the product of 1.05 and 0.7? Circle the letter of the correct answer.

A 73.5

B 7.35

C 0.735

D 0.0735

Will the product be greater than or less than 1.05?

Aaron chose **C** as the correct answer. How did he get that answer?

_____

_____

_____

_____

Pair/Share
Does Aaron's answer make sense?

Practice ▶ **Multiplying Decimals**

Solve the problems.

1 Which of the following has a product of 25.16?

   A 3.7 × 680

   B 3.7 × 68

   C 3.7 × 6.8

   D 3.7 × 0.68

2 Willa downloads 5 songs. Three of the song files are each 2.75 MB. Two song files are each 3.8 MB. How much space does Willa need for the songs she downloads?

   A 5.55 MB

   B 11.55 MB

   C 15.85 MB

   D 27.75 MB

3 Choose ALL the expressions that have the same value as the product of 0.11 and 4.5.

   A 0.495 × 0.01

   B 0.495 × 0.001

   C 49.5 × 0.01

   D 495 × 0.01

   E 495 × 0.001

4 The area model below can be used to represent the product of 2.8 and 1.3. Complete the model by writing each of the following numbers in the correct part of the model.

0.6   2   0.24   0.8

5 Tyrone said that 2.35 × 5 equals 1.175 because there is only one digit before the decimal point in 2.35, so there must be one digit before the decimal point in the product. Use pictures, numbers, or words to explain whether or not Tyrone is correct.

Show your work.

6 Each product below is missing a decimal point.

Part A Place the decimal point in each product so that the equation is correct.

$$12.53 \times 5 = 6\,2\,6\,5$$

$$4.28 \times 3.6 = 1\,5\,4\,0\,8$$

$$1.3 \times 0.89 = 1\,1\,5\,7$$

$$7 \times 6.12 = 4\,2\,8\,4$$

Part B Circle one of the equations. Explain how you decided where to place the decimal point in this equation.

✔ **Self Check** Go back and see what you can check off on the Self Check on page 1.

G Use What You Know

Now that you know how to multiply with decimals, you'll learn how to divide with decimals. Take a look at this problem.

Mr. Kovich is preparing materials for a craft project. He needs to cut 2 meters of string into pieces that are 0.2 meter long. How many 0.2-meter pieces can he cut from 2 meters of string?

a. You need to find how many lengths of 0.2 meter are in 2 meters. Look at the drawing below.

b. How many tenths of a meter are in 1 meter? _____

In 2 meters? _____

c. Circle lengths of 2-tenths meter on the drawing above.

How many lengths of 2-tenths meter are in 1 meter? _____

In 2 meters? _____

d. Explain how you could find how many 0.2-meter pieces can be cut from 2 meters of string.

_____

_____

_____

_____

▶▶ Find Out More

On the previous page, you saw that $2 \div 0.2 = 10$.
How is that similar to the division fact $2 \div 2 = 1$?
How is it different?

Look at the table below to see some patterns in division.

Expression	Expression in words	Quotient
$2 \div 2$	How many groups of 2 are in 2?	1
$2 \div 0.2$	How many groups of 0.2 are in 2?	10
$2 \div 0.02$	How many groups of 0.02 are in 2?	100

When the divisor is greater than 1, the quotient is less than the dividend.

When the divisor is less than 1, the quotient is greater than the dividend.

dividend		divisor		quotient
2	$\div$	2	$=$	1
2	$\div$	0.2	$=$	10
2	$\div$	0.02	$=$	100

▶ Reflect

1 Look at the table above. What do you think is the quotient of $2 \div 0.002$? Explain your reasoning.

_____

_____

_____

_____

_____

Learn About ⟩ **Dividing a Decimal by a Whole Number**

Read the problem below. Then explore different ways to understand dividing a decimal by a whole number.

> Coach Ann is setting up a 2.7-kilometer race. She uses flags to mark off 9 equal sections of the race. How far apart should she space the flags to mark off the sections?

▶ **Picture It** **You can draw a bar model to represent the problem.**

You know the **number of kilometers to be divided** into equal groups.

You know the **number of equal groups**.

2.7 kilometers

?

You do not know the **number of kilometers in each group**.

▶ **Model It** **You can use the relationship between multiplication and division to understand the problem.**

To find **2.7 ÷ 9**, think **9 × ? = 2.7**.

2.7 = 27 tenths

Use words:

9 × ? tenths = 27 tenths

Connect It Now use your understanding of division and place value to solve the problem.

2 Look at *Picture It*. Why is the bar divided into 9 equal parts?

_____

What do you need to find? _____

3 Look at *Model It*. How does the division expression 2.7 ÷ 9 relate to the bar model?

_____

_____

_____

_____

4 Explain how you know that 2.7 = 27 tenths.

_____

_____

5 How far apart should Coach Ann space the flags? _____ tenths kilometer.

Write that answer as a decimal: _____ kilometer

6 Explain how you could divide a decimal by a whole number.

_____

_____

_____

_____

Try It Use what you have learned about dividing a decimal by a whole number to solve these problems. Show your work on a separate sheet of paper.

7 How much will each person receive if $20.35 is split equally among 5 people? _____

8 What is 0.99 ÷ 11? _____

Learn About ▶ Dividing by Tenths

Read the problem below. Then explore different ways to divide by tenths.

> Grant has 3.6 pounds of pretzels. He puts the pretzels into bags that each hold 0.3 pound. How many bags does Grant use to hold the pretzels?

▶ **Picture It** **You can picture dividing by tenths with decimal grids.**

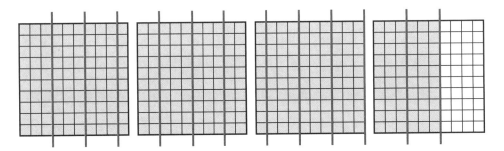

Each large square represents 1 pound of pretzels.

You know the amount to be shared in equal groups and the size of each group.

▶ **Model It** **You can use the relationship between multiplication and division to understand the problem.**

To find 3.6 ÷ 0.3, think 0.3 × ? = 3.6.

   3.6 = 36 tenths

Use words:

   3 tenths × ? = 36 tenths

► **Connect It** Now use your understanding of division and place value to solve the problem.

9 Look at *Picture It*. How do you decide what to shade?

_____

_____

_____

10 Why are the grids separated into groups of 3 columns?

_____

_____

_____

11 Look at *Model It*. How do you know this is a division problem?

_____

_____

_____

12 Explain why 3.6 = 36 tenths. _____

_____

13 Both *Picture It* and *Model It* tell me that Grant uses _____ bags of pretzels.

14 Explain how to divide tenths by tenths. _____

_____

_____

► **Try It** Use what you have learned about dividing by tenths to solve these problems. Show your work on a separate sheet of paper.

15 How many dimes are there in a jar of dimes worth $2.70? _____

16 What is 42 ÷ 0.7? _____

Learn About ▷ Dividing by Hundredths

Read the problem below. Then explore different ways to divide by hundredths.

Fiona has $1.20 with which to buy some elastic tape. The elastic tape is on sale for $0.08 per foot. How many feet of elastic tape can Fiona buy?

▶ **Picture It** **You can picture the division problem using a bar model.**

You know the **total amount of money** and the **size of one group**.

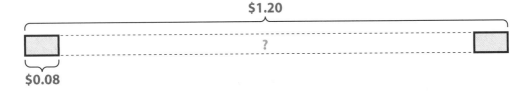

$1.20

$0.08

You do not know the **number of groups**.

▶ **Model It** **You can use the relationship between multiplication and division to understand the problem.**

To find 1.20 ÷ 0.08, think 0.08 × ? = 1.20.

1.20 = 120 hundredths

Use words:

8 hundredths × ? = 120 hundredths

Use your understanding of division and place value to solve the problem.

17 Look at *Picture It*. What are you trying to find in this problem?

_____

18 What operation will solve this problem? How do you know?

_____

_____

_____

19 Explain why 1.20 = 120 hundredths. _____

_____

20 Write a division expression for the problem. _____

21 How many feet of elastic tape can Fiona buy? Show your work.

_____

_____

22 Check your answer using the decimals in a multiplication equation.

_____ feet of elastic tape × $ _____ = $ _____ .

Fiona can buy _____ feet of elastic tape.

23 Explain how to divide by a decimal in the hundredths. _____

_____

_____

_____

▶ **Try It** **Use what you have learned about dividing by hundredths to solve these problems. Show your work on a separate sheet of paper.**

24 How many quarters are in a jar of quarters worth $9.75? _____

25 What is 16 ÷ 0.16? _____

Practice ▶ **Dividing Decimals**

Study the model below. Then solve problems 26–28.

Example

Nancy ran a total of 35 miles to train for a race. She ran 2.5 miles each day. How many days did Nancy run to train for the race?

Look at how you could show your work using equations.

$$2.5 \times \boxed{} = 35$$

$$2.5 = 25 \text{ tenths}, \ 35 = 350 \text{ tenths}$$

$$25 \times \boxed{} = 350$$

$$350 \div 25 = 14$$

Solution _Nancy ran 14 days to train for the race._

The student wrote a related multiplication equation to solve the problem.

 Pair/Share
Can you solve the problem in another way?

---

26 What number multiplied by 8 will give a product of 9.6? Write an equation and solve.

Show your work.

What is a good estimate for your answer?

 Pair/Share
How could you model this problem with a number line?

Solution _____

27 The width of a math textbook is 0.75 inch. How many math textbooks can be placed standing up on a shelf that is 18 inches wide?

Show your work.

Will the answer be greater than or less than 18?

Pair/Share
Explain how you decided what operation to use to solve the problem.

Solution _____

---

28 What is 6.5 ÷ 0.5? Circle the letter of the correct answer.

A 3.25

B 6

C 7

D 13

I could draw a model to represent this problem.

Gwen chose **A** as the correct answer. How did she get that answer?

_____

_____

_____

_____

Pair/Share
Does Gwen's answer make sense?

Practice ▶ **Dividing Decimals**

Solve the problems.

1 Jordan has $11.40 to spend at the used book store. Each book costs $2.85. How many books can Jordan buy?

   A   3

   B   4

   C   5

   D   6

2 Keith bought 3.4 pounds of peanuts on Monday, 2.5 pounds on Tuesday, and 4 pounds on Wednesday. He is going to divide the peanuts equally between himself and two friends. How many pounds of peanuts will each friend get?

   A   99 pounds

   B   33 pounds

   C   9.9 pounds

   D   3.3 pounds

3 A sticker is 1.2 centimeters wide. How many stickers will fit edge to edge on a strip of paper that is 108 centimeters long?

_____ stickers

4 If you put 0.7 on the blank for each equation below, does it make the equation true? Select *Yes* or *No* for each equation.

   a. _____ $\times 5.2 = 36.4$ ☐ Yes   ☐ No

   b. $49 \div$ _____ $= 70$ ☐ Yes   ☐ No

   c. _____ $\div 3.5 = 0.02$ ☐ Yes   ☐ No

   d. $9.1 \times$ _____ $= 6.37$ ☐ Yes   ☐ No

5 Jamie has 5 jars to fill with beads for a carnival game. She has 7.5 cups of multi-colored beads. Jamie wants to put an equal amount of beads in each jar. How many cups of beads can she place into each jar?

Part A Use pictures to solve the problem.

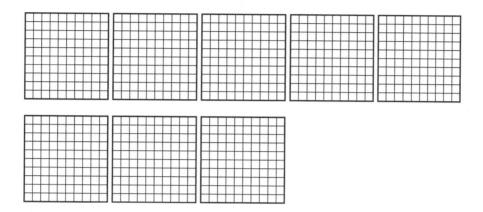

Answer _____ cup

Part B Justify your answer.

✓ **Self Check** Go back and see what you can check off on the Self Check on page 1.

Lesson 9 Divide Decimals   **81**

Use Whole Numbers and Decimals

Study an Example Problem and Solution

In this lesson, you will work with whole numbers and decimals to solve real-world problems. Look at this problem and one solution.

Dog Collars

Alex is organizing a pet fair. Money from the fair will be donated to the local pet shelter. Alex's friend Bella will have a booth at the fair. Here is Bella's sign.

Adorable Dog Collars	
Small $8.99	
Medium . . . $9.99	
Large $10.99	

Supplies to make a small collar cost $1.50. Bella estimates that the supplies for each size collar cost $0.50 more than the next smaller size. Bella hopes to make at least $200 for the pet shelter by selling collars.

• Find how much Bella makes on each collar after paying for supplies.

• Show a way to make at least $200 by selling collars.

• Include at least 5 collars of each size in your plan.

Read the sample solution on the next page. Then look at the checklist below. Find and mark parts of the solution that match the checklist.

✏️ Problem-Solving Checklist

☐ Tell what is known.

☐ Tell what the problem is asking.

☐ Show all your work.

☐ Show that the solution works.

a. Circle something that is known.

b. Underline something that you need to find.

c. Draw a box around what you do to solve the problem.

d. Put a checkmark next to the part that shows the solution works.

Alex's Solution

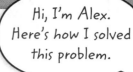

▷ **I know the selling price** of each collar. **I need to find the cost** to make each size collar and subtract it from the price.

Size	Price	Cost of Supplies	Amount left to Donate
Small	$8.99	$1.50	$7.49
Medium	$9.99	$1.50 + $0.50	$7.99
Large	$10.99	$2.00 + $0.50	$8.49

I used a table to organize my information.

▷ **I'll round the donation amounts so that I can estimate.**
I can multiply each rounded amount by 5 since I have to include at least 5 of each size collar.

$7.49 ⟶ $7 and $7 × 5 = $35
$7.99 ⟶ $8 and $8 × 5 = $40
$8.49 ⟶ $8 and $8 × 5 = $40
                              $115

By rounding and estimating first, I avoid some computing with decimals.

▷ **I can see** that I need almost $90 more to get to $200. I can try to make about $30 with each of the three collar sizes.

$7 × 4 = $28 $8 × 4 = $32 $8 × 4 = $32

▷ **Now I can find the actual amounts from 5 + 4 small collars, 5 + 4 medium collars, and 5 + 4 large collars.**

$7.49 × 9 = (7 × 9) + (0.4 × 9) + (0.09 × 9) and 63 + 3.6 + 0.81 = 67.41
$7.99 × 9 = (7 × 9) + (0.9 × 9) + (0.09 × 9) and 63 + 8.1 + 0.81 = 71.91
$8.49 × 9 = (8 × 9) + (0.4 × 9) + (0.09 × 9) and 72 + 3.6 + 0.81 = 76.41
                                                                  215.73

If Bella sells 9 of each size collar
she will be able to donate $215.73.

This is my final answer.

The solution works because it includes at least 5 collars of each size and it makes more than $200.

Try ▸ **Another Approach**

There are many ways to solve problems. Think about how you might solve the Dog Collars problem in a different way.

Dog Collars

Alex is organizing a pet fair. Money from the fair will be donated to the local pet shelter. Alex's friend Bella will have a booth at the fair. Here is Bella's sign.

Adorable Dog Collars

Small $8.99

Medium . . . $9.99

Large $10.99

Supplies to make a small collar cost $1.50. Bella estimates that the supplies for each size collar cost $0.50 more than the next smaller size. Bella hopes to make at least $200 for the pet shelter by selling collars.

- Find how much Bella makes on each collar after paying for supplies.
- Show a way to make at least $200 by selling collars.
- Include at least 5 collars of each size in your plan.

▶ **Plan It** Answer these questions to help you start thinking about a plan.

A. How can you use estimation to help find a solution?

_____

_____

B. How can you use the sample solution to plan how to find a different solution?

_____

_____

► **Solve It** **Find a different solution for the Dog Collars problem.**
Show all your work on a separate sheet of paper.

You may want to use the problem-solving tips to get started.

Problem-Solving Tips

- **Models** You may want to use . . .
  - partial products.
  - area models.

- **Word Bank**

round	multiply	greater than
estimate	product	decimal

- **Sentence Starters**
  - I can round _____
  - If I multiply _____

► **Reflect**
Use Mathematical Practices As you work through the problem, discuss these questions with a partner.

- **Use Models** How can you use an area model to help find a solution?

- **Repeated Reasoning** If you are multiplying by 0.99, how can you multiply by a whole number and use subtraction to find the product?

Discuss ▸ **Models and Strategies**

Read the problem. Write a solution on a separate sheet of paper.
Remember, there can be lots of ways to solve a problem!

Petting Zoo

The zoo where Alex works has agreed to bring some animals to the pet fair.
Guests can pay to feed and play with the animals. Alex has to decide which
animals to bring and how much food they will need.

Petting Zoo Notes

· Include 2 or 3 different kinds
  of animals.

· Include more than 10 but fewer
  than 20 animals.

· Have enough food to feed each
  animal a day's worth of food.

Alex reads the keeper's notes to find about how much an average
animal eats in a day.

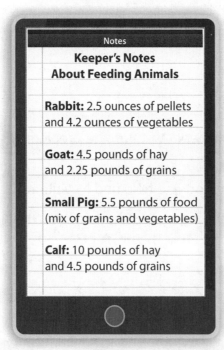

Notes
Keeper's Notes About Feeding Animals
Rabbit: 2.5 ounces of pellets and 4.2 ounces of vegetables
Goat: 4.5 pounds of hay and 2.25 pounds of grains
Small Pig: 5.5 pounds of food (mix of grains and vegetables)
Calf: 10 pounds of hay and 4.5 pounds of grains

How much food should Alex bring to the pet fair?

▶ Plan It and Solve It Find a solution to the Petting Zoo problem.

Write a detailed plan for Alex. Be sure to include:

- which animals and how many of each to bring to the pet fair.
- a list of the food she will need to feed all the animals for 1 day, including amounts of each kind of food.
- reasons for the choices you made.

Problem-Solving Tips

- **Questions**
  - How does the size of the animal affect your choice?
  - Which animals eat some of the same kind of food?

- **Sentence Starters**
  - I would bring _____
  - Alex needs about _____

Problem-Solving Checklist

Make sure that you . . .
- ☐ tell what you know.
- ☐ tell what you need to do.
- ☐ show all your work.
- ☐ show that the solution works.

▶ Reflect

Use Mathematical Practices As you work through the problem, discuss these questions with a partner.

- **Make Sense of Problems** What will you do first? Why?
- **Make an Argument** How can you justify the choices you made?

Persevere ▸ **On Your Own**

Read the problems. Write a solution on a separate sheet of paper. Remember, there are many different ways to solve a problem!

Robot Area

Alex asked her friend Beau to bring his robots to the fair. Guests can buy tickets to play with the robots. Beau needs to rope off an area of the fairgrounds to keep his robots in sight. Read his notes.

Robot Area Notes

· The area should be rectangular.

· It needs to be more than 100 feet long and less than 100 feet wide.

· The area needs to be between 7,500 and 10,000 square feet.

What dimensions should the robot area have?

▶ **Solve It** **Describe an area that Beau can rope off for his robots.**

• Give the length and width of the area.

• Give the area in square feet.

• Explain why your measurements work.

▶ **Reflect**

Use Mathematical Practices After you complete the task, choose one of these questions to discuss with a partner.

• **Use Structure** How did you use place value ideas to think about numbers that would work?

• **Persevere** Did you try different combinations of numbers before deciding on a final answer? Explain.

Barely Used

Alex's friend Brandi has a collection of used books, CDs, and DVDs that people have given her. She will sell them at a booth at the pet fair. Brandi thinks she can sell enough items to make at least a $100 donation to the pet shelter. Look at Brandi's prices.

| Paperback Books $0.95 | Hardcover Books $3.75 | DVDs $3.25 | CDs $1.95 |

What items can Brandi sell to make at least $100?

▶ **Solve It** **Find a combination of items that Brandi needs to sell to meet her goal.**

• Include some of all four items.

• For each item, tell how many Brandi needs to sell and how much money she will make.

• Give the total amount Brandi will make selling all the items on your list.

• Explain why this total works.

▶ **Reflect**

Use Mathematical Practices After you complete the task, choose one of these questions to discuss with a partner.

• **Use Models** What equations or expressions did you use to find your solution?

• **Persevere** What were all of the steps you took to find a solution?

Solve the problems.

1 Which number is equivalent to 0.15×10^3?

A 0.015

B 0.15

C 15

D 150

2 The driving distance between Buffalo, NY, and Rochester, NY, is 117.456 kilometers. What is this distance rounded to the nearest tenth?

A 117 kilometers

B 117.5 kilometers

C 117.46 kilometers

D 120 kilometers

3 Julie likes to ride her bike during summer vacation. In June, she rode her bike 104.78 miles. In July, she rode 129.53 miles. In August, she rode 61.05 miles. Which statement is true? Circle the letter for all that apply.

A Julie rode more than twice as many miles in July as in August.

B Julie rode a total of 295.36 miles during summer vacation.

C Julie rode 43.73 miles more in June than in August.

D Julie rode more miles in June than in July.

4 The table shows the lengths of the five keys that Paco has on his keychain.

Key Label	Length (centimeters)
T	6.104
G	5.793
W	6.079
H	5.785
S	6.106

Choose *True* or *False* for each inequality.

a. $T > S$ ☐ True ☐ False

b. $W < G$ ☐ True ☐ False

c. $G > H$ ☐ True ☐ False

d. $S < W$ ☐ True ☐ False

e. $W > H$ ☐ True ☐ False

5 Which equation is true? Circle the letter for all that apply.

A $61 \times 5 = 3{,}050 \div 10$

B $381 \times 27 = 1{,}143 \div 9$

C $854 \times 63 = 53{,}802$

D $562 \times 42 = 23{,}604$

6 Ben is learning about place value in his math class.

Part A Ben writes the number 74,443. The value of the digit 4 in the hundreds place is 10 times the value of the digit 4 in what place value?

Solution _____

Part B Ben's teacher asks him to write a three-digit number that uses the digit 3 once and the digit 6 twice. The value of one 6 needs to be $\frac{1}{10}$ the value of the other 6. What number can Ben write?

Solution _____

7 Coach Miller is having a cookout at the park for his baseball team.

Part A Coach Miller bought 5.15 pounds of ground beef to make burgers. The cost of ground beef is $3.40 for each pound. What was the total cost for all of the ground beef?

Show your work.

Solution _____

Part B Coach Miller is using all the ground beef to grill 17 burgers. What is the cost for each burger?

Show your work.

Solution _____

Performance Task

Answer the questions and show all your work on separate paper.

You have a movie theater gift card worth $40, so you invite a friend to go to the movies with you. Your friend challenges you to spend the exact value of the gift card. Find at least one way to do so by choosing from the items listed below.

Item	Price
2D movie ticket	$7.25
3D movie ticket	$8.50
Small Popcorn	$3.25
Medium Popcorn	$5.50
Large Popcorn	$7.75
Bottle of Water	$2.50
1 Ounce of Snack Mix	$0.50

Checklist

Did you . . .

☐ organize your choices?

☐ check your calculations?

☐ use words and numbers to complete the task?

▶ Reflect

Use Mathematical Practices After you complete the task, choose one of the following questions to answer.

- **Persevere** What strategies did you use? If a strategy did not work, what did you do?

- **Model** How did you use equations to solve this problem?

Unit 2
Number and Operations—Fractions

Let's learn about multiplying and dividing fractions.

Real-World Connection Some situations require sharing. Suppose you and a friend make a batch of 24 cookies to share equally with your families. Dividing the batch into two groups allows you each to have 12 cookies. But you might decide that since your friend has a large family, your friend should get $\frac{2}{3}$ of the batch. How many cookies does your friend get? If your friend gets $\frac{2}{3}$ of the batch of cookies, can you also get $\frac{2}{3}$ of the batch? In order to decide, you need to know how to multiply by a fraction and how to add fractions.

In This Unit You will learn how to add, subtract, multiply, and divide fractions. You will also see how fractions are used in many real-world situations.

✓ Self Check

Before starting this unit, check off the skills you know below. As you complete each lesson, see how many more skills you can check off!

I can:	Before this unit	After this unit
add and subtract fractions with unlike denominators, for example: $\frac{3}{5} + \frac{1}{4} = \frac{17}{20}$.		
estimate sums or differences of fractions, for example: $2\frac{3}{8} + 5\frac{1}{2}$ is a little less than 8.		
multiply fractions, for example: $\frac{2}{3} \times \frac{5}{6} = \frac{10}{18}$ or $\frac{5}{9}$.		
divide with unit fractions, for example: $4 \div \frac{1}{7} = 28$.		

Lesson 10 👥 Introduction
Add and Subtract Fractions

G Use What You Know

In Grade 4, you learned that adding and subtracting fractions is similar to adding and subtracting whole numbers. Take a look at this problem.

Emiliano needs $\frac{1}{2}$ stick of butter to make corn bread. He also needs $\frac{1}{4}$ stick of butter to make apple muffins. How many sticks of butter does he need?

$\frac{1}{2}$ stick of butter

$\frac{1}{4}$ stick of butter

a. Does Emiliano need more than 1 stick of butter or less than 1 stick of butter for the corn bread and the apple muffins? _____

b. How do you know? _____

_____

c. Do $\frac{1}{2}$ and $\frac{1}{4}$ have like denominators? _____

d. How do you find equivalent fractions? _____

_____

e. 4 is a multiple of both 2 and 4. Write an equivalent fraction for $\frac{1}{2}$ using fourths.

$$\frac{1}{2} = \frac{\square}{4}$$

f. You now have fractions that have same-size parts. How many fourths of a stick of butter does Emiliano need?

$\frac{1}{2} + \frac{1}{4} =$ _____ $+ \frac{1}{4} =$ _____ . So he needs _____ stick of butter.

To add fractions, the size of the parts that make up the whole must be the same. Because $\frac{1}{2}$ and $\frac{1}{4}$ use different-size parts, you rewrote $\frac{1}{2}$ as the equivalent fraction $\frac{2}{4}$. Since $\frac{1}{4}$ and $\frac{2}{4}$ both use fourths, you combined $\frac{2}{4}$ and $\frac{1}{4}$ to get the sum $\frac{3}{4}$.

The same idea works for subtracting fractions. Here is a similar problem: $\frac{3}{4} - \frac{1}{2}$.
Write $\frac{1}{2}$ as the equivalent fraction $\frac{2}{4}$.

$$\frac{3}{4}$$

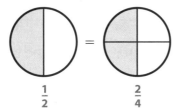
$$\frac{1}{2} \qquad \frac{2}{4}$$

To subtract $\frac{2}{4}$ from $\frac{3}{4}$, you can take 2 shaded parts away from the 3 shaded parts. You have 1 shaded part left.

$$\frac{3}{4} - \frac{2}{4} = \frac{1}{4}$$

Before adding or subtracting fractions, the fractions must be built from the same-size part of a whole. This means the fractions must have the same denominator, or a **common denominator**.

▶ Reflect

1 Write a multiplication equation that shows how the denominators of $\frac{3}{4}$ and $\frac{1}{2}$ are related. Explain how this equation helps you write $\frac{1}{2}$ as an equivalent fraction with a denominator of 4.

_____

_____

_____

Learn About > **Adding Fractions with Unlike Denominators**

Read the problem below. Then explore different ways to add fractions with unlike denominators.

> Jenna spent $1\frac{2}{3}$ hours mowing the back yard. After taking a break, she spent $\frac{3}{4}$ hour mowing the front yard. How much time did she spend mowing the whole yard?

▶ **Picture It** **You can picture the fractions in the problem using models.**

The shaded parts represent time spent on the back yard, $1\frac{2}{3}$ hours, and the front yard, $\frac{3}{4}$ hour.

$1\frac{2}{3}$ hours $\qquad +\qquad$ $\frac{3}{4}$ hour

The sections need to be divided into same-size parts to add. Use dashed lines to divide the fraction models into 12 equal parts. This works because 12 is a multiple of both 3 and 4.

$1\frac{8}{12}$ hours $\qquad +\qquad$ $\frac{9}{12}$ hour

▶ **Model It** **You can use a number line to add fractions.**

The number line is divided into twelfths with a point at $1\frac{2}{3}$.

0 $\quad \frac{1}{4} \quad$ 1 $\quad 1\frac{2}{3}$ 2 $\qquad$ 3

$\frac{1}{4} = \frac{3}{12}$, so $\frac{3}{4} = \frac{3}{12} + \frac{3}{12} + \frac{3}{12}$.

$\frac{3}{12} + \frac{3}{12} + \frac{3}{12} = \frac{9}{12}$

Start at $1\frac{2}{3}$ and jump right $\frac{9}{12}$.

Connect It Now you will solve the problem from the previous page using equivalent fractions and addition.

2 Are $1\frac{2}{3}$ and $\frac{3}{4}$ made up of same-size parts? Justify your answer.

_____

_____

_____

3 Look at the models on the previous page. What is a common denominator of $1\frac{2}{3}$ and $\frac{3}{4}$? _____

4 You can find this common denominator without a model. Write a multiplication equation that shows how the denominators 3 and 4 are related to 12.

_____

5 Use this common denominator to find equivalent fractions for $1\frac{2}{3}$ and $\frac{3}{4}$.

$1\frac{2}{3} = 1$ _____ $\frac{3}{4} =$ _____

6 Using the equivalent fractions, what is the sum of $1\frac{2}{3}$ and $\frac{3}{4}$? _____

7 Explain how to add two fractions with unlike denominators. _____

_____

_____

_____

Try It Use what you just learned about adding fractions with unlike denominators to solve these problems. Show your work on a separate sheet of paper.

8 What is $1\frac{1}{6} + 2\frac{3}{8}$? _____

9 Hank practices $\frac{2}{5}$ of the words on his spelling list on Monday. He practices another $\frac{1}{2}$ of his list on Tuesday. How much of his spelling list has Hank practiced so far? _____

Learn About ▷ **Subtracting Fractions with Unlike Denominators**

Read the problem below. Then explore different ways to subtract fractions with unlike denominators.

> Gavin's water bottle has $1\frac{3}{8}$ cups of water. He drinks $\frac{1}{2}$ cup. How much water is left in the bottle?

▷ **Picture It** **You can use a picture to model subtracting fractions.**

The water bottle is shaded to show that it has 1 cup $+ \frac{3}{8}$ cup of water in it. 1 cup is equivalent to $\frac{8}{8}$ cup. The bottle has 11 eighths shaded.

Gavin drinks $\frac{1}{2}$ **cup**, or $\frac{4}{8}$ **cup**. So take away 4 shaded parts of the bottle to show how much is left.

There are 7 parts of the bottle left with water in it.

▷ **Model It** **You can use a number line to model subtracting fractions.**

The number line below is divided into $\frac{1}{8}$s with a point at $1\frac{3}{8}$.

$\frac{1}{2}$ is equivalent to $\frac{4}{8}$. $\frac{4}{8}$ is four $\frac{1}{8}$ units on the number line. Start at $1\frac{3}{8}$ and jump left $\frac{4}{8}$.

Connect It Now you will solve the problem from the previous page using equivalent fractions and a subtraction equation.

10 Estimate the amount of water left in Gavin's bottle. _____

How did you get your estimate? _____

_____

11 Look at *Picture It* and *Model It* on the previous page. Why is $\frac{1}{2}$ rewritten as $\frac{4}{8}$?

_____

_____

12 Use the number line on the previous page to rewrite $1\frac{3}{8}$ as a fraction greater than 1. Then use it to write a subtraction equation with equivalent fractions.

_____ − _____ = _____

13 Why was it helpful to rewrite $1\frac{3}{8}$ as a fraction greater than 1? _____

_____

_____

14 Explain how to subtract two fractions with unlike denominators. _____

_____

_____

Try It Use what you just learned about subtracting fractions with unlike denominators to solve these problems. Show your work on a separate sheet of paper.

15 What is $\frac{7}{8} - \frac{1}{2}$? _____

16 Emily's living room window is $2\frac{5}{6}$ feet wide. The window in her bedroom is $1\frac{1}{3}$ feet wide. How much wider is the living room window than her bedroom window? _____

Practice ▶ **Using Fractions with Unlike Denominators**

Study the example below. Then solve problems 17–19.

Example

Chapter 1 of Henry's book is $5\frac{2}{3}$ pages long. Chapter 2 is $8\frac{2}{5}$ pages long. How much longer is Chapter 2 than Chapter 1?

Look at how you could show your work using an equation.

$$5\frac{2}{3} = 5 + \left(\frac{2 \times 5}{3 \times 5}\right) = 5\frac{10}{15}$$

$$8\frac{2}{5} = 8 + \left(\frac{2 \times 3}{5 \times 3}\right) = 8\frac{6}{15} = \left(7 + \frac{15}{15}\right) + \frac{6}{15} = 7\frac{21}{15}$$

$$\begin{array}{r} 7\frac{21}{15} \\ - \ 5\frac{10}{15} \\ \hline 2\frac{11}{15} \end{array}$$

Solution _$2\frac{11}{15}$ pages longer_____

I need to find a common denominator before I subtract fractions.

 Pair/Share
Explain why the model regrouped $8\frac{6}{15}$ as $7\frac{21}{15}$.

---

17 What is $1\frac{1}{2} + 1\frac{2}{3}$?
Show your work.

I think this sum is a little more than 3. I can use this estimate to check if my answer is reasonable.

 Pair/Share
Explain why you chose the type of model you did to solve this problem.

Solution _____

18 Michael rode his bike $2\frac{2}{3}$ miles on Saturday. He rode another $1\frac{5}{6}$ miles on Sunday. How many miles did Michael ride his bike on both days combined?

Show your work.

How are the denominators 3 and 6 related?

Pair/Share
How did you decide what operation to use to solve this problem?

Solution

---

19 Cara's bathroom floor has an area of $2\frac{2}{3}$ square yards. She lays down a rug that has an area of $1\frac{1}{4}$ square yards. What area of floor is NOT covered by the rug? Circle the letter of the correct answer.

A 1 square yard

B $1\frac{1}{12}$ square yards

C $1\frac{5}{12}$ square yards

D $1\frac{3}{7}$ square yards

What equivalent mixed numbers could I subtract?

John chose **D** as the correct answer. How did he get that answer?

_____

_____

 Pair/Share
Does a denominator of 7 make sense?

_____

Practice ▷ **Using Fractions with Unlike Denominators**

Solve the problems.

1 The model below represents the expression $1\frac{5}{8} + 2\frac{1}{3}$.

Which of the following could NOT be represented by the model?

A $1 + 2 + \frac{6}{11}$

B $1\frac{15}{24} + 2\frac{8}{24}$

C $1 + 2 + \frac{23}{24}$

D $\frac{39}{24} + \frac{56}{24}$

2 Mackenzie's footprint is $\frac{7}{12}$ foot long. Her dad's footprint is $1\frac{1}{6}$ feet long. Which equation can be used to find how much longer Mackenzie's dad's footprint is than Mackenzie's? Select *Yes* or *No* for each equation.

a. $1\frac{2}{12} - \frac{7}{12} = ?$ ☐ Yes   ☐ No

b. $\frac{7}{12} + 1\frac{1}{6} = ?$ ☐ Yes   ☐ No

c. $1\frac{1}{6} - \frac{2}{3} = ?$ ☐ Yes   ☐ No

d. $\frac{14}{12} - \frac{7}{12} = ?$ ☐ Yes   ☐ No

3 Find two fractions in the list below that can be added using the denominator 18. Write those two fractions in the box.

$$\frac{1}{4} \qquad \frac{5}{6} \qquad \frac{7}{12} \qquad \frac{1}{8} \qquad \frac{4}{9}$$

Like denominator = 18

4 Lucy is making a smoothie by following the recipe below.

Recipe

Sunshine Smoothie

$1\frac{1}{3}$ cups banana

$\frac{1}{2}$ cup yogurt

1 cup strawberries

$\frac{3}{4}$ cup orange juice

Place ingredients in blender.

Blend until smooth.

Part A Explain whether the recipe will make enough for Lucy and 3 friends to each have at least 1 cup of smoothie. If it doesn't make enough, explain how to change the recipe to make enough.

_____

_____

_____

_____

Part B How much smoothie remains after Lucy gives each of her friends $\frac{3}{4}$ cup of smoothie?

Show your work.

Answer _____ cups

 Self Check Go back and see what you can check off on the Self Check on page 93.

Lesson 10 Add and Subtract Fractions   **103**

Add and Subtract Fractions in Word Problems

G Use What You Know

Now that you can add and subtract fractions with different denominators, you can use this skill to solve word problems. Take a look at this problem.

Aleena has a 1-gallon watering can that is full of water. She uses $\frac{3}{8}$ gallon to water her roses and $\frac{1}{3}$ gallon to water her geraniums. How much water did Aleena use to water both the roses and geraniums?

a. Does Aleena use more than $\frac{1}{2}$ gallon or less than $\frac{1}{2}$ gallon of water? _____

b. How do you know? _____

_____

_____

c. Estimate how much water Aleena used. _____

_____

d. Write an equation with equivalent fractions to find the amount of water Aleena used.

_____

e. Is this answer reasonable based on your estimate? Explain. _____

_____

_____

The number line below shows the location of **benchmark fractions** between 0 and 2. You can use these fractions to estimate sums and differences.

There are different ways to estimate the sums or differences of fractions. The examples below show two ways to think about fractions to find estimates for the amount of water Aleena used to water her flowers.

$$\frac{3}{8} + \frac{1}{3} = ?$$

Student A

$\frac{3}{8}$ and $\frac{1}{3}$ are both less than $\frac{1}{2}$, or $\frac{4}{8}$.

So the sum must be less than 1.

Student B

$\frac{3}{8}$ is a little greater than $\frac{1}{4}$. $\frac{1}{3}$ is a little greater than $\frac{1}{4}$.
I know $\frac{1}{4} + \frac{1}{4}$ is $\frac{2}{4}$, or $\frac{1}{2}$.

So, I estimate the sum is greater than $\frac{1}{2}$.

▶ Reflect

1 Both estimates above model correct thinking. Which estimate makes more sense to you? Why?

_____

_____

_____

_____

Learn About Solving Word Problems with Fractions

Read the problem below. Then explore different ways to estimate and solve problems with fractions.

> Frankie purchases a $3\frac{1}{2}$-pound bag of chicken. He uses $1\frac{1}{3}$ pounds of chicken for fajitas. How many pounds of chicken are left?

▶ **Picture It** **You can picture the problem using a fraction strip.**

The fraction strip below represents $3\frac{1}{2}$ pounds of chicken. It is separated into sections representing the $1\frac{1}{3}$ pounds used for fajitas and the unused amount.

$1\frac{1}{3}$ pounds for fajitas

unused amount

total amount of chicken

The model shows the difference $3\frac{1}{2} - 1\frac{1}{3}$.

▶ **Model It** **You can model the problem with a number line.**

Since $2 \times 3 = 6$, the fractions in the problem, $3\frac{1}{2}$ and $1\frac{1}{3}$, can be rewritten using a common denominator of 6. $3\frac{1}{2} = 3\frac{3}{6}$ and $1\frac{1}{3} = 1\frac{2}{6}$.

The number line below is divided into sixths. It shows starting with a total of $3\frac{1}{2}$ pounds, with two jumps to the left representing the $1\frac{1}{3}$ pounds of chicken used.

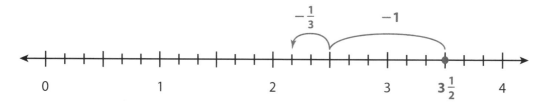

You can rewrite the difference $3\frac{1}{2} - 1\frac{1}{3}$ as $3\frac{3}{6} - 1\frac{2}{6}$.

Connect It Now you will estimate and then solve the problem from the previous page using benchmark fractions and an equation.

2 Identify the closest half on either side of $1\frac{1}{3}$.

$1\frac{1}{3}$ is greater than _____ and less than _____.

3 Why are halves a good choice for benchmark fractions for $1\frac{1}{3}$?

_____

4 The difference $3\frac{1}{2}$ minus $1\frac{1}{3}$ must be between _____ and _____.

Estimate $3\frac{1}{2} - 1\frac{1}{3}$ and explain your estimate.

_____

_____

5 Find the actual difference. _____

There are _____ pounds of chicken remaining.

6 Is this a reasonable answer based on your estimate? Explain. _____

_____

7 Explain how you can check if a fraction sum or difference is reasonable.

_____

_____

Try It Use what you just learned about estimating with benchmark fractions to solve this problem. Show your work on a separate sheet of paper.

8 Tim's bean sprout grew $3\frac{3}{8}$ inches. Teegan's bean sprout grew $2\frac{3}{4}$ inches. How many more inches did Tim's bean sprout grow than Teegan's? First, estimate the difference and explain your reasoning. Then find the actual difference.

_____

_____

Practice ▶ **Solving Word Problems with Fractions**

Study the example below. Then solve problems 9–11.

Example

The blue field of stars on a flag has an area of $1\frac{3}{5}$ square yards. The red stripes have a combined area of $2\frac{3}{10}$ square yards. What is the difference between the area of the blue field of stars and the area of the red stripes?

Look at how you could show your work using fraction strips.

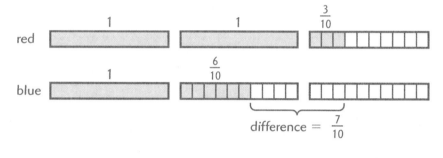

Solution $\frac{7}{10}$ square yard

> What common denominator was used to subtract these fractions?

> **Pair/Share**
> What benchmark fractions could you use to estimate the answer?

---

9 Parker mixes $3\frac{1}{2}$ ounces of blue paint with $1\frac{2}{5}$ ounces of yellow paint to create green paint to use for the leaves of a tree. How many ounces of green paint did Parker create?

Estimate, and then compute. Explain how you know your result is reasonable.

Show your work.

> Will there be a little more than $4\frac{1}{2}$ ounces or a little less than $4\frac{1}{2}$ ounces of green paint?

> **Pair/Share**
> Was your estimate more than or less than the actual answer? By how much?

Solution _____

10 Jose's football weighs $\frac{7}{8}$ pound. His football helmet weighs $5\frac{1}{6}$ pounds. Estimate how much more the helmet weighs than the football. Explain your estimate.

What benchmark fractions could I use to estimate the difference in weight?

Solution _____

Pair/Share
How does an estimate help you tell if your answer is reasonable?

---

11 Which is a reasonable estimate for the difference $5\frac{1}{2} - 3\frac{5}{9}$? Circle the letter of the correct answer.

A between $\frac{1}{2}$ and 1

B between 1 and $1\frac{1}{2}$

How can I use benchmark fractions to estimate the difference?

C between $1\frac{1}{2}$ and 2

D between 2 and $2\frac{1}{2}$

Elise chose **D** as the correct answer. How did she get that answer?

_____

_____

_____

_____

Pair/Share
Does Elise's answer make sense?

_____

Practice ▶ **Solving Word Problems with Fractions**

Solve the problems.

1 William compares monthly rainfall amounts for the summer months using the table below.

Month	Monthly Rainfall
June	$3\frac{3}{10}$ inches
July	$3\frac{3}{4}$ inches
August	$3\frac{1}{2}$ inches

About how much more rain fell in July than in June?

A $\frac{1}{4}$ inch

B $\frac{1}{2}$ inch

C 1 inch

D $1\frac{1}{2}$ inches

2 Several expressions are shown. Decide if the value of each expression is less than $1\frac{1}{2}$, between $1\frac{1}{2}$ and 2, or greater than 2. Write each expression in the correct category in the chart.

$$2\frac{1}{2} - 1\frac{1}{8} \qquad 1\frac{5}{11} + \frac{3}{4} \qquad 3\frac{4}{5} - 1\frac{1}{3} \qquad \frac{3}{8} + \frac{9}{10}$$

Less than $1\frac{1}{2}$	Between $1\frac{1}{2}$ and 2	Greater than 2

3 The table below shows the thickness of coins.

Coin	Thickness
quarter	$1\frac{3}{4}$ millimeters
dime	$1\frac{7}{20}$ millimeters
nickel	$1\frac{19}{20}$ millimeters
penny	$1\frac{1}{2}$ millimeters

Hailey stacks a dime on top of a penny. She estimates the thickness of the two coins to be less than 3 millimeters.

Write a symbol ($<$, $>$, or $=$) in the box to make the statement true. Then use the statement to tell whether Hailey's estimate is correct.

$$1\frac{1}{2} + 1\frac{7}{20} \,\square\, 1\frac{1}{2} + 1\frac{1}{2}$$

Is Hailey's estimate correct? _____

4 Jimmy says $3\frac{4}{9} - 2\frac{5}{6}$ is $1\frac{1}{3}$.

Part A Without finding the actual difference, explain why Jimmy's difference is or is not reasonable.

_____

_____

Part B Find the actual difference.

Show your work.

Solution _____

✓ **Self Check** **Go back and see what you can check off on the Self Check on page 93.**

Use What You Know

You know that division is used for equal sharing and that fractions represent a number of equal parts. In this lesson, you will learn how division and fractions are related. Take a look at this problem.

Mrs. Tatum needs to share 4 fluid ounces of red paint equally among 5 art students. How much red paint will each student get?

1 ounce   1 ounce   1 ounce   1 ounce

PAINT

4 ounces

a. Start with 1 ounce of paint. What fraction is represented by 1 ounce of paint shared equally among 5 students?

1 ounce of paint shared equally among 5 students = _____ ounce per student

b. Look at the model above. Write a multiplication expression that represents a student getting $\frac{1}{5}$ of each of 4 ounces of paint.

_____

c. What fraction is represented by the product? _____

d. 4 ounces of paint ÷ 5 students = _____ ounce of paint per student

What if Mrs. Tatum wants to share 8 fluid ounces of paint equally among the 5 students? How much will each student get? You can think about this quotient two ways.

One way: Each student will get $\frac{1}{5}$ ounce of paint if 1 ounce of paint is shared among 5 students. There are 8 ounces to share.

1 ounce ÷ 5 students = $\frac{1}{5}$ ounce for each student

1 ounce   1 ounce   1 ounce   1 ounce   1 ounce   1 ounce   1 ounce   1 ounce

8 ounces ÷ 5 students = $\frac{8}{5}$ ounces per student

Another way: Think of 8 ounces as 5 ounces + 3 ounces. Each student will receive 1 full ounce of paint because there are 5 students. This leaves 3 ounces to divide.

5 ounces   **3 ounces**

1 ounce   1 ounce   1 ounce   1 ounce   1 ounce   1 ounce   1 ounce   1 ounce

5 ounces ÷ 5 students = **1 ounce** for each student   3 ounces ÷ 5 students =
$\frac{3}{5}$ **ounce** for each student

Each student will receive 1 ounce plus $\frac{3}{5}$ ounce of paint.

8 ounces ÷ 5 students = **1** $\frac{3}{5}$ ounces per student

▶ Reflect

1 Describe in words a problem that could be represented by the quotient $\frac{2}{5}$. Use the situation about sharing paint among art students.

_____

_____

_____

Learn About ▶ **Finding Fraction Quotients**

Read the problem below. Then explore different ways to understand fractions as quotients.

> Jared, Monica, and Heather have 5 hallways to decorate for the student council. If they share the work equally, how much will each student decorate?

▶ **Picture It** **You can use a rectangle to represent the quotient.**

There are 5 hallways for 3 students to decorate, which is $5 \div 3$.

If they share the work equally, each student can decorate $\frac{1}{3}$ of each hallway.

$\frac{1}{3} \times 5 = \frac{5}{3}$

$5 \div 3 = \frac{5}{3}$

▶ **Model It** **You can use a number line to represent the quotient.**

The number line is numbered from 0 to 5 because there are 5 hallways. It is divided into thirds because each student can decorate one third of each hallway.

5 divided into 3 equal sections is five thirds, or $\frac{5}{3}$.

Connect It Now you will solve the problem from the previous page by thinking about division as equal sharing.

2 How many thirds of a hallway are there to decorate in 5 hallways? _____ thirds

3 How many thirds of a hallway will each student decorate if the thirds are shared equally? _____ thirds

Write this as a fraction. _____ of a hallway

Here is another way to think of the problem.

4 How many whole hallways can each student decorate? _____

How many hallways remain after these are done? _____

If 5 hallways are shared equally by 3 students, there will be _____ whole hallway per student and _____ hallways remaining.

5 How much of 2 remaining hallways will each student decorate? _____

5 hallways ÷ 3 students = _____ whole and _____ hallway per student

Write this as a mixed number. _____ hallways

6 Write two division equations, one using the fraction and one using the mixed number, to represent the quotient.

_____

7 How does the bar in a fraction represent division? _____

_____

Try It Use what you just learned about fractions as quotients to solve these problems. Show your work on a separate sheet of paper.

8 Five friends are equally sharing 3 packs of football cards. How much of a pack will each friend get? _____

9 Mary made 18 ounces of apple chips. She evenly portions the apple chips between 4 containers. How many ounces of apple chips are in 1 container? Write a division expression to represent the problem and solve. _____

Practice ▶ **Fractions as Division**

Study the example below. Then solve problems 10–12.

Example

Luke, Carter, and Ava have 2 quarts of juice. They want to share it evenly. How many quarts of juice will each of them get?

Look at how you could show your work using a model.

$$\frac{1}{3} \times 2 = \frac{2}{3}$$

Solution $\frac{2}{3}$ quart

2 quarts are shared by 3 friends, so I know that each friend will have less than 1 quart of juice. That means the quotient is a fraction.

Pair/Share

Model the problem for 3 quarts of juice divided evenly among Luke, Carter, Ava, and Ava's little brother.

10 Erica has 7 square feet of garden space to plant carrots, beans, peppers, and lettuce. Suppose she gives each vegetable an equal amount of space. How much space will each vegetable get?

Show your work.

Each vegetable will get at least 1 square foot of garden space. How will the rest of the space be divided up?

Pair/Share

What are some ways you can check your solution?

Solution _____

11 Daniel needs to make 6 pizza crusts. He has 20 ounces of dough and wants to use the same amount of dough for each crust. He weighs a portion of dough for 1 crust on a scale. The weight, in ounces, should fall between what two whole numbers?

Show your work.

How many whole ounces of dough will each crust get? What will happen with the remaining ounces?

Pair/Share

Create a different division story to represent $\frac{20}{6}$.

Solution _____

12 Jonas is doing a science experiment with his class. The teacher has 21 fluid ounces of pond water to share equally with 10 pairs of students. How much pond water will Jonas and his science partner receive? Circle the letter of the correct answer.

A $\frac{10}{21}$ fluid ounce

B $1\frac{1}{10}$ fluid ounces

C 2 fluid ounces

D $\frac{21}{10}$ fluid ounces

Olivia chose **A** as the correct answer. How did she get that answer?

_____

_____

_____

_____

About how much water will each pair of students receive? Will it be more or less than 2 fluid ounces?

 Pair/Share

Does Olivia's answer make sense?

Practice ▶ **Fractions as Division**

Solve the problems.

1 Teddy makes 32 fluid ounces of hot cocoa. He pours equal amounts of cocoa into 5 cups. The amount of hot cocoa in each cup will fall between which two amounts?

    A 3 and 4 fluid ounces

    B 4 and 5 fluid ounces

    C 5 and 6 fluid ounces

    D 6 and 7 fluid ounces

2 Pierce swims 10 laps in a pool in 8 minutes. He spent the same amount of time on each lap. How much time did each lap take him?

    A $\frac{2}{10}$ minute

    B $\frac{8}{10}$ minute

    C $\frac{10}{8}$ minutes

    D $1\frac{2}{8}$ minutes

3 Dani needs 8 equal sections from a board that is 13 meters long. Does the expression represent the largest possible length of 1 section of the board, in meters? Select *Yes* or *No* for each expression.

    a. $1\frac{5}{8}$ ☐ Yes   ☐ No

    b. $\frac{8}{13}$ ☐ Yes   ☐ No

    c. $\frac{13}{8}$ ☐ Yes   ☐ No

    d. $8 \div 13$ ☐ Yes   ☐ No

    e. $13 \times \frac{1}{8}$ ☐ Yes   ☐ No

4 Which situation is represented by $\frac{25}{9}$? Circle the letter for all that apply.

   A   Melanie equally shares 25 meters of paper to create 9 banners.

   B   Quill gives away 9 baseball cards from a pack of 25 cards.

   C   George invites 25 kids and 9 adults to his birthday party.

   D   Becca creates 9 rows with 25 buttons each.

   E   Joe makes 9 equal servings from a 25-ounce bag of peanuts.

5 Paco is trying to explain to his friend that $7 \div 2 = \frac{7}{2}$.

   Part A Draw a model or number line showing $7 \div 2 = \frac{7}{2}$.

   Part B Explain the equivalence of $7 \div 2$ and $\frac{7}{2}$ using words.

   _____

   _____

   _____

   _____

   Part C Describe in words a situation that can be represented by $7 \div 2$ or $\frac{7}{2}$.

   _____

   _____

   _____

   _____

✔ **Self Check**   **Go back and see what you can check off on the Self Check on page 93.**

5.NF.B.4a

Think It Through

What does it mean to multiply a fraction by a whole number?

The ruler below shows three $\frac{1}{2}$-inch segments. You can represent this as $3 \times \frac{1}{2}$.

You have learned different ways to think about fractions and also about multiplication. Below are other ways to think about $3 \times \frac{1}{2}$ inch.

- Three $\frac{1}{2}$-inch sections is $\frac{3}{2}$ inches.
- Three $\frac{1}{2}$-inch sections is 1 whole inch plus $\frac{1}{2}$ inch, or $1\frac{1}{2}$ inches.
- $\frac{3}{2}$ inches is 3 times as long as $\frac{1}{2}$ inch.

Think What does it mean to multiply a whole number by a fraction?

The ruler below shows a 3-inch segment divided into 2 equal parts. That's the same as multiplying 3 by $\frac{1}{2}$. You can represent this as $\frac{1}{2} \times 3$.

Below are ways to think about $\frac{1}{2} \times 3$.

- When 3 is divided into 2 equal parts, $\frac{1}{2} \times 3$ is one part.
- When 3 is divided into 2 equal parts, each part is $1\frac{1}{2}$ or $\frac{3}{2}$.
- $\frac{1}{2} \times 3 = 1\frac{1}{2}$

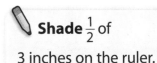

Shade $\frac{1}{2}$ of 3 inches on the ruler.

Think What happens when a fraction is multiplied by a fraction?

Find $\frac{1}{4}$ of a $\frac{1}{2}$-inch line segment, or $\frac{1}{4} \times \frac{1}{2}$.

The ruler below shows that $\frac{1}{2}$ inch is half of the whole 1 inch.

$\frac{1}{2}$ of 1 inch

If I say "find one fourth of," it means to divide by 4 or multiply by $\frac{1}{4}$.

To find $\frac{1}{4}$ of $\frac{1}{2}$ inch, you divide the half inch into 4 equal parts. Remember that one-half inch is already part of the whole 1 inch. Divide the other half inch into 4 equal parts, and the whole will have 8 equal parts. So, $\frac{1}{4}$ of $\frac{1}{2}$ inch is 1 of 8 parts of the whole 1 inch: $\frac{1}{8}$ inch.

What if you need to find $\frac{3}{4}$ of a $\frac{1}{2}$-inch line segment? Above, you found that $\frac{1}{4}$ of $\frac{1}{2}$ inch is $\frac{1}{8}$ inch. Now you need to find three $\frac{1}{4}$s of $\frac{1}{2}$ inch.

$\frac{3}{4} \times \frac{1}{2}$

If $\frac{1}{4} \times \frac{1}{2}$ is $\frac{1}{8}$, then $\frac{3}{4}$ of $\frac{1}{2}$ is three $\frac{1}{8}$s, or $\frac{3}{8}$.

So, $\frac{3}{4} \times \frac{1}{2} = \frac{3}{8}$.

▶ Reflect

1 Based on the two problems above, what do you expect is the product of $\frac{2}{4} \times \frac{1}{2}$? Explain.

_____

_____

_____

_____

Think About ▷ **Multiplying a Fraction by a Fraction**

🔍 **Let's Explore the Idea** **Find the product of $\frac{3}{4} \times \frac{2}{3}$ with an area model.**

2 Look at the model on the left above.

Each column is what fraction of the whole? _____

Each row is what fraction of the whole? _____

3 The dark blue part shows $\frac{1}{4}$ of $\frac{1}{3}$.

How many parts are in the whole? _____

So, $\frac{1}{4} \times \frac{1}{3}$ is what fraction of the whole? _____

4 Look at the model on the right above.

Two columns are what fraction of the whole? _____

Three rows are what fraction of the whole? _____

5 The dark blue parts show $\frac{3}{4}$ of $\frac{2}{3}$.

What fraction of the whole is $\frac{3}{4} \times \frac{2}{3}$? _____

6 What is the product of $\frac{3}{4} \times \frac{2}{3}$? _____

Let's Talk About It

Complete these problems as a group.

7 Use the area model on the previous page to fill in the products in the table below.

$\frac{1}{4} \times \frac{1}{3} =$	$\frac{2}{4} \times \frac{1}{3} =$	$\frac{3}{4} \times \frac{1}{3} =$	$\frac{4}{4} \times \frac{1}{3} =$
$\frac{1}{4} \times \frac{2}{3} =$	$\frac{2}{4} \times \frac{2}{3} =$	$\frac{3}{4} \times \frac{2}{3} =$	$\frac{4}{4} \times \frac{2}{3} =$

8 Look at the numerators of each factor pair. How do these numbers relate to the numerator of the product? Now look at the denominators of each factor pair. How do these denominators relate to the denominator of the product?

_____

_____

_____

▶ Try It Another Way Work with your group to connect the model to the multiplication expression.

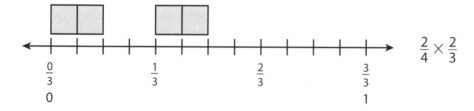

$\frac{2}{4} \times \frac{2}{3}$

9 Each third on the number line is divided into how many equal parts? _____

Each of these parts is what fraction of the whole? _____

10 How many fourths of the first $\frac{1}{3}$ are shaded? _____

How many fourths of the second $\frac{1}{3}$ are shaded? _____

11 How many twelfths of the whole are shaded? _____

12 Explain how the model shows $\frac{2}{4} \times \frac{2}{3}$. What is the product? _____

_____

_____

Connect ▸ Ideas About Multiplying Fractions

Talk through these problems as a class. Then write your answers below.

13 Describe Tell what multiplication problem the model shows.
Explain why. _____

_____

_____

_____

_____

_____

14 Explain Landon said that $\frac{2}{3} \times \frac{1}{6} = \frac{5}{6}$. Tell how Landon found his product, and then
explain how to find the correct product. _____

_____

_____

_____

_____

15 Create Complete the multiplication table for the unit fractions $\frac{1}{2}$, $\frac{1}{3}$, and $\frac{1}{4}$. Identify
two patterns in the table.

×	$\frac{1}{2}$	$\frac{1}{3}$	$\frac{1}{4}$
$\frac{1}{2}$			
$\frac{1}{3}$			
$\frac{1}{4}$			

_____

_____

16 Put It Together Use what you have learned to complete this task.

Part A Start with a sheet of paper. Fold it in half, then fold it in half again. Continue folding the paper in half. As you do, fill in the blanks to tell what fraction of the whole each equal part is.

$\frac{1}{2} \times 1 = $ _____

$\frac{1}{2} \times \frac{1}{2} = $ _____

$\frac{1}{2} \times$ _____ $= $ _____

$\frac{1}{2} \times$ _____ $= $ _____

Part B Write the products as the terms of a pattern. Then look at the denominators of the fractions. Each time you multiply by $\frac{1}{2}$, what happens to the denominator?

_____

_____

_____

Without folding the paper, what do you think the next fraction in the pattern will be? Why?

_____

_____

_____

Part C Now look at the sizes of the equal parts of the folded paper. Each time you fold the paper in half, what happens to the size of the parts?

_____

_____

_____

🔄 Use What You Know

In Lesson 13, you learned about multiplying fractions. Now you will use area models to multiply fractions. Take a look at this problem.

Mr. Thompson has a 1-meter-square whiteboard. He creates a square with $\frac{5}{10}$-meter sides on his whiteboard to post a weekly puzzle. How many square meters of whiteboard space does he use for the weekly puzzle?

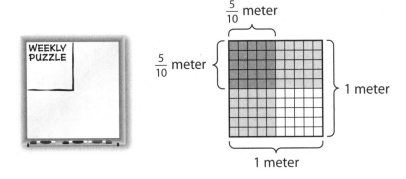

a. Write a multiplication equation for the area of the square with side lengths of 1 meter.

_____

b. What expression can you write for the area of the smaller square with side lengths

of $\frac{5}{10}$ meter? _____

c. The square with the darker shading is 5 units wide and 5 units long. How many square units is this? _____

d. What is the total number of small squares in the large square? _____

e. What fraction of the whole square is the part with the darker shading? _____

f. The area of the square with the darker shading is _____ square meter.

The area of a square with sides $\frac{5}{10}$ meter represents the product $\frac{5}{10} \times \frac{5}{10}$.

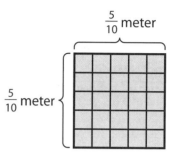

$\frac{5}{10}$ meter

$\frac{5}{10}$ meter

- The length of each unit is $\frac{1}{10}$ meter. The length and the width of the blue square are both 5 units, or $\frac{5}{10}$ meter.

- The area of one square unit is $\frac{1}{100}$ square meter. The area of the blue square is 25 square units, or $\frac{25}{100}$ square meter.

$$\frac{5}{10} \text{ meter} \times \frac{5}{10} \text{ meter} = \frac{25}{100} \text{ square meter}$$

You can also think about multiplying $\frac{5}{10} \times \frac{5}{10}$ another way.

$\frac{5}{10}$ is $5 \times \frac{1}{10}$.   Rewrite.

$$\frac{5}{10} \times \frac{5}{10} = \left(5 \times \frac{1}{10}\right) \times \left(5 \times \frac{1}{10}\right)$$

Change the order of the factors.

$$= 5 \times 5 \times \frac{1}{10} \times \frac{1}{10}$$

Then multiply.

$$= 25 \times \frac{1}{100} \text{, or } \frac{25}{100}$$

▶ **Reflect**

1 Look at the models on these pages. Explain why multiplying the numerators tells you the number of parts in the product.

_____

_____

_____

Learn About ▸ **Multiplying Unit Fractions to Find Areas**

Read the problem below. Then explore different ways to understand multiplying two unit fractions.

Titus has a square sheet of paper measuring 1 foot on each side. He folds the paper in half vertically and then folds it into fourths horizontally. Titus unfolds the paper as shown below. What is the area of each part?

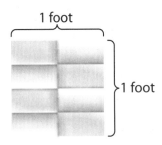

1 foot

1 foot

▶ **Picture It** **You can understand the problem by picturing parts of the unfolded paper.**

The folding created 8 equal sections.

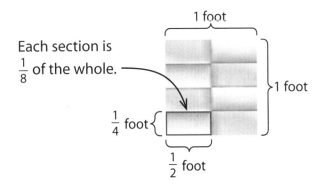

Each section is $\frac{1}{8}$ of the whole.

1 foot

1 foot

$\frac{1}{4}$ foot

$\frac{1}{2}$ foot

Each section is $\frac{1}{2}$ foot long and $\frac{1}{4}$ foot wide.

▶ **Model It** **You can model the problem with an equation.**

Each equal part of the paper has a length of $\frac{1}{2}$ foot and width of $\frac{1}{4}$ foot.

$$\text{area} = \frac{1}{2} \text{ foot} \times \frac{1}{4} \text{ foot}$$

$$\frac{1}{2} \text{ foot} \times \frac{1}{4} \text{ foot} = \frac{1 \times 1}{2 \times 4} \text{ square foot}$$

Connect It Now you will solve the problem from the previous page by connecting the model to the equation.

2 Explain why each part of the paper is $\frac{1}{2}$ foot long. _____

_____

_____

3 Explain why each part of the paper is $\frac{1}{4}$ foot wide. _____

_____

_____

4 What expression do you use to find the area of 1 part of the paper? _____

5 Multiply the denominators of these fractions. How does the product relate to the size of the units compared to the size of the whole model? _____

_____

_____

6 Multiply the numerators of these fractions. How does the product relate to the number of outlined parts of the model? _____

_____

_____

7 Explain how to find the area of one part of the sheet of paper.

_____

_____

_____

Try It Use what you just learned about multiplying unit fractions to solve this problem. Show your work on a separate sheet of paper.

8 What is the area of a paper strip with a width of $\frac{1}{3}$ yard and length of $\frac{1}{6}$ yard?

_____

Learn About ▷ Multiplying Fractions Greater than One

Read the problem below. Then explore different ways to understand multiplying fractions greater than 1.

A postage stamp has a width of $\frac{3}{4}$ inch and length of $\frac{3}{2}$ inches. What is the area of the stamp in square inches?

▶ **Picture It** You can picture the problem using the area of a rectangle.

The first area model shows $\frac{1}{4}$ inch $\times \frac{1}{2}$ inch $= \frac{1}{8}$ square inch. The second model uses the same $\frac{1}{8}$-square-inch parts to show an area that is $\frac{3}{4}$ inch $\times \frac{3}{2}$ inches.

$$\frac{1}{4} \times \frac{1}{2}$$

$$\frac{3}{4} \times \frac{3}{2}$$

▶ **Model It** You can model the problem with an equation.

The dimensions of the stamp are $\frac{3}{4}$ inch and $\frac{3}{2}$ inches, so multiply the fractions to find the area.

$$\text{area} = \frac{3}{4} \times \frac{3}{2} = \frac{3 \times 3}{4 \times 2}$$

Connect It Now you will solve the problem from the previous page by connecting the model to the equation.

9 Look at the area model for $\frac{3}{4} \times \frac{3}{2}$. Explain why each part shows $\frac{1}{8}$ square inch.

_____

_____

10 What is the total width of the three $\frac{1}{2}$-inch columns? _____

What is the total height of the three $\frac{1}{4}$-inch rows? _____

11 How many $\frac{1}{8}$-square-inch parts are shaded purple? _____ parts

Write the area of the purple section as a fraction greater than 1. _____ square inches

12 Now look at the equation in *Model It*. Multiply the numerators, multiply the denominators, and write the fraction. How does this product compare with the one shown by the area model?

_____

_____

_____

13 How do you multiply fractions greater than 1?

_____

_____

_____

_____

Try It Use what you just learned about multiplying fractions to solve this problem. Show your work on a separate sheet of paper.

14 Bernice's math workbook is $\frac{2}{3}$ foot wide and $\frac{5}{6}$ foot long. What is the area of a

page in the workbook? _____

Practice ▶ **Multiplying Fractions to Find Area**

Study the example below. Then solve problems 15–17.

Example

Rachel is designing a newspaper ad. The ad will include a piece of art whose dimensions are $\frac{5}{8}$ inch long and $\frac{1}{2}$ inch wide. How many square inches of space will the art cover?

Look at how you could show your work using an area model.

$$\frac{5}{8} \times \frac{1}{2} = \frac{5 \times 1}{8 \times 2} = \frac{5}{16}$$

Solution _____ $\frac{5}{16}$ square inch

$\frac{1}{8}$ inch $\times$ $\frac{1}{2}$ inch is $\frac{1}{16}$ square inch. How many sixteenth square inches are shown in the model?

💬 **Pair/Share**

How can you write $\frac{5}{8} \times \frac{1}{2}$ as a product of unit fractions and whole numbers?

---

15 What is the area of a rectangle with a length of $\frac{1}{2}$ yard and a width of $\frac{11}{6}$ yards? Write an equation to represent your solution.

Show your work.

How can I represent a fractional side length with an area model?

💬 **Pair/Share**

Find the area of a rectangle with side lengths of $\frac{3}{4}$ yard and $\frac{6}{5}$ yards. How is the model different?

Solution _____

16 Brent is designing a poster that has an area of 1 square foot. He is going to paste a photo collage on a section of the poster that is $\frac{1}{3}$ foot wide and $\frac{3}{5}$ foot long. What part of a square foot will the photo collage cover?

Show your work.

If I draw a square to represent a square foot, how can I represent thirds and fifths on the square?

Pair/Share
Write an equation to represent your model. Explain the meaning of the numerators.

Solution _____

17 What is the area of the square?
Circle the letter of the correct answer.

 $\frac{6}{7}$ yd

A $\frac{36}{49}$ square yard

B $\frac{12}{14}$ square yard

C $\frac{49}{36}$ square yards

D $\frac{12}{7}$ square yards

 $\frac{6}{7}$ yd

Think about the size of the two fractions. Will the product of the fractions be greater than 1 or less than 1?

Ollie chose **D** as the correct answer. How did he get that answer?

_____

_____

_____

Pair/Share
Does Ollie's answer make sense?

Practice ▷ **Multiplying Fractions to Find Area**

Solve the problems.

1 The square below represents 1 square unit.

Which expression represents the area of the dark blue section?

A $\frac{7}{3} \times \frac{3}{1}$ square units

B $\frac{3}{7} \times \frac{1}{3}$ square units

C $\frac{1}{7} \times \frac{1}{3}$ square units

D $\frac{7}{3} \times \frac{1}{3}$ square units

2 Fill in the missing numbers to make the equation true. Then complete the area model to check your answer.

$$\frac{1}{6} \times \frac{\Box}{\Box} = \frac{1}{24}$$

3 Which products could you find by shading the model below? Circle the letter for all that apply.

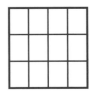

A $\frac{3}{4} \times \frac{1}{3}$

B $\frac{1}{3} \times \frac{1}{6}$

C $\frac{2}{3} \times \frac{1}{4}$

D $\frac{5}{3} \times \frac{1}{4}$

E $\frac{3}{4} \times \frac{3}{4}$

4 Draw an area model to represent the expression $\frac{5}{4}$ inches $\times$ $\frac{4}{5}$ inch.

5 Explain how to find the area of the model you drew in problem 4, then find the area .

_____

_____

_____

_____

6 Write the dimensions of a different rectangle that has the same area as the rectangle you drew in problem 4. Show how you know the area is the same.

_____

_____

_____

_____

_____

✓ **Self Check** Go back and see what you can check off on the Self Check on page 93.

Understand Multiplication as Scaling

Think It Through

What does scaling mean?

Think of how you use words and phrases such as "double," "triple," "half of," or "take one tenth." These words and phrases describe **scaling,** or changing the size of a quantity. *Stretching* and *shrinking* are two different ways to scale a quantity.

The table below shows some ways that a quantity of 6 can be scaled.

	Words	Symbols
stretching	6 **doubled** is 12.	$2 \times 6 = 12$
	6 **tripled** is 18.	$3 \times 6 = 18$
shrinking	**Half of** 6 is 3.	$\frac{1}{2} \times 6 = 3$
	A tenth of 6 is $\frac{6}{10}$.	$\frac{1}{10} \times 6 = \frac{6}{10}$

Think How can you use models to show what scaling means?

Below is a rectangle with an area of 6 square units.

The model for 2×6 has an area that is double the size of the original rectangle.

The model for $\frac{1}{2} \times 6$ has an area that is half the size of the original rectangle.

> ✏️ **Circle** the factor that describes how the rectangle is being stretched or shrunk.

Think How does the size of the factors affect the product?

Products aren't always greater than their factors. The table below shows products of different factors multiplied by 6.

Factor	$\frac{1}{10}$	$\frac{1}{3}$	$\frac{1}{2}$	$\frac{5}{6}$	1	$\frac{4}{3}$	2	$2\frac{1}{2}$	3
Product of factor and 6	$\frac{6}{10}$	2	3	5	6	8	12	15	18

Look at the products that are less than 6, then look at those that are greater than 6. What do you notice about the factors?

Notice that the products are sometimes less than 6, sometimes greater than 6, and sometimes equal to 6.

What do the **products less than 6** have in common? The other factor is less than 1.

What do the **products greater than 6** have in common? The other factor is greater than 1.

- If you multiply 6 by a factor less than 1, the product will be less than 6.

- If you multiply 6 by a factor greater than 1, the product will be greater than 6.

- If you multiply 6 by 1, or a factor equivalent to 1, the product will be 6.

▶ Reflect

1 Describe the products you get if you multiply 8 by factors less than 1. Describe the products you get if you multiply 8 by factors greater than 1. Give some examples that justify your answers.

_____

_____

_____

_____

_____

Think About ▷ **Comparing Factors and Products**

🔍 **Let's Explore the Idea** A number line can help you see what happens when a fraction is multiplied by a factor less than 1.

2 You can show $\frac{1}{3} \times \frac{3}{4}$ on a number line. If you break up $\frac{3}{4}$ into 3 equal parts, each part is $\frac{1}{4}$.

$\frac{1}{3} \times \frac{3}{4} = \underline{\hspace{2cm}}$

Is the product *less than, greater than,* or *equal to* $\frac{3}{4}$? $\underline{\hspace{4cm}}$

3 Show $\frac{2}{3} \times \frac{3}{4}$ on a number line. If you break up $\frac{3}{4}$ into 3 equal parts, each part is $\frac{1}{4}$. Since you multiply by $\frac{2}{3}$, you need 2 of those parts. Shade and label $\frac{2}{3}$ of $\frac{3}{4}$.

$\frac{2}{3} \times \frac{3}{4} = \underline{\hspace{2cm}}$

Is the product *less than, greater than,* or *equal to* $\frac{3}{4}$? $\underline{\hspace{4cm}}$

4 You multiplied $\frac{3}{4}$ by two different factors. How do both factors relate to the number 1? What happens when you multiply a given fraction by a factor less than 1?

$\underline{\hspace{12cm}}$

$\underline{\hspace{12cm}}$

$\underline{\hspace{12cm}}$

Let's Talk About It A number line can also help you see what happens when a fraction is multiplied by a factor greater than 1.

5 Shade the number line to show $\frac{4}{3} \times \frac{3}{4}$.

$\frac{4}{3} \times \frac{3}{4} =$ _____

Is the product *less than, greater than,* or *equal to* $\frac{3}{4}$? _____

6 Shade and label the number line to show $\frac{7}{3} \times \frac{3}{4}$.

$\frac{7}{3} \times \frac{3}{4} =$ _____

Is the product *less than, greater than,* or *equal to* $\frac{3}{4}$? _____

7 Think about how each of your answers compared to $\frac{3}{4}$. What can you say about the product of a given fraction and a factor greater than 1?

_____

▶ **Try It Another Way** Explore multiplying $\frac{3}{4}$ by a fraction using an area model.

The model to the right represents $\frac{3}{4}$.

8 Show $\frac{1}{2} \times \frac{3}{4}$ using the area model.

9 $\frac{1}{2} \times \frac{3}{4} =$ _____

10 Is the product *less than, greater than,* or *equal to* $\frac{3}{4}$? _____

11 Could you have answered problem 10 without drawing a model? Explain.

_____

_____

Talk through these problems as a class, then write your answers below.

12 Analyze Use reasoning to order the following expressions from least to greatest. Don't calculate any of the products. Explain your reasoning.

$$\frac{7}{9} \times 348{,}980 \qquad \frac{12}{11} \times 348{,}980 \qquad \frac{50}{50} \times 348{,}980$$

13 Explain Gillian said that the product of a given number and a fraction is always less than the given number. Explain what is wrong with Gillian's statement and give an example that does not follow her rule.

14 Compare Represent the expression $\frac{4}{4} \times \frac{8}{5}$ with a model. Write a sentence comparing the product with $\frac{8}{5}$. Explain your reasoning.

15 **Put It Together** You can compare the size of a product to the size of the factors in a multiplication equation if you know whether the factors are greater than, less than, or equal to 1.

Part A Write a multiplication equation (different from any in this lesson) in which the product is greater than both of the factors. Draw a model to support your answer.

Part B Write a multiplication equation (different from any in this lesson) in which both the factors are fractions and the product is less than both of the factors. Draw a model to support your answer.

Part C Write a multiplication equation (different from any in this lesson) in which the product is equal to one of the factors.

Multiply Fractions in Word Problems

Ⓖ Use What You Know

Now that you have learned how to multiply fractions, take a look at this problem.

> Grayson lives $\frac{4}{5}$ mile from the park. He has already walked $\frac{3}{4}$ of the way to the park. How far has Grayson walked?

a. You can draw a model to help you solve the problem. Locate a point on the number line below to show what fraction of a mile Grayson lives from the park.

b. Label the point to show the distance to the park.

c. Shade the segment that shows one fourth of the distance to the park. One fourth of

the distance to the park is _____ mile. Label this distance.

d. Two fourths of the distance to the park is _____ mile.

e. Three fourths of the distance to the park is _____ mile.

f. Explain how you can use the model to show how far Grayson has already walked.

_____

_____

_____

_____

▶▶ Find Out More

Consider the problem from the previous page. The distance you need to find is a fraction of a fraction: $\frac{3}{4}$ of $\frac{4}{5}$ mile. On the previous page you used a model to find this distance. You can also use an equation.

Finding $\frac{3}{4}$ of a number is the same as multiplying the number by $\frac{3}{4}$.

$\frac{3}{4}$ of $\frac{4}{5}$ means $\frac{3}{4} \times \frac{4}{5}$.

To multiply two fractions, multiply the numerators to get the numerator of the product, and multiply the denominators to get the denominator of the product.

$$\frac{3}{4} \times \frac{4}{5} = \frac{3 \times 4}{4 \times 5} = \frac{12}{20}$$

The fraction $\frac{12}{20}$ is equivalent to $\frac{3}{5}$. To find equivalent fractions, multiply or divide the numerator and the denominator of the fraction by the same number.

$$\frac{12}{20} = \frac{12 \div 4}{20 \div 4} = \frac{3}{5}$$

Grayson has walked $\frac{3}{5}$ mile.

The product, $\frac{3}{5}$, is less than $\frac{4}{5}$, so it is reasonable. When you multiply $\frac{4}{5}$ by a factor less than 1, the product should be less than $\frac{4}{5}$.

▶ Reflect

1 Which method, *drawing a model* or *writing an equation*, made more sense to you for solving this problem? Why?

_____

_____

_____

_____

| Learn About ▶ | **Multiplying Fractions in Word Problems** |

Read the problem below. Then explore different ways to understand how to find a fraction of a fraction.

Brandon's mother left $\frac{3}{4}$ of a pizza on the counter. If Brandon eats $\frac{2}{3}$ of it, how much of the whole pizza did Brandon eat?

▶ **Picture It** **You can draw a picture to help you understand the problem.**

Show $\frac{3}{4}$ of a pizza.

Since Brandon eats $\frac{2}{3}$ of what is left, outline 2 of the 3 pieces that are left. You can see from the outlined parts how much of the whole pizza Brandon ate.

▶ **Model It** **You can write an equation to help you understand the problem.**

You need to find a fraction of a fraction: $\frac{2}{3}$ of $\frac{3}{4}$ of a pizza.

$\frac{2}{3}$ of $\frac{3}{4}$ means $\frac{2}{3} \times \frac{3}{4}$.

$$\frac{2}{3} \times \frac{3}{4} = \frac{2 \times 3}{3 \times 4}$$

Connect It Now you will solve the problem from the previous page using both strategies.

2 Look at *Picture It*. Why did you outline 2 of the 3 parts of the pizza?

_____

3 How much of the whole pizza did Brandon eat? Explain your reasoning.

_____

_____

4 Look at *Model It*. How do you know that you should multiply $\frac{2}{3} \times \frac{3}{4}$?

_____

_____

5 What is $\frac{2 \times 3}{3 \times 4}$? _____

Is this product the same as your answer to problem 3? Explain.

_____

6 What strategies can you use to solve a word problem that involves multiplying fractions? _____

_____

_____

Try It Use what you just learned about finding products of fractions to solve these problems. Show your work on a separate sheet of paper.

7 Lewis walked $\frac{9}{10}$ of a mile. His friend walked $\frac{2}{5}$ of the way with him. How many miles did Lewis's friend walk with him? _____

8 Jamie worked $\frac{5}{6}$ hour filing papers for her mother. She listened to music for $\frac{2}{5}$ of the time she spent filing. How much time did Jamie spend listening to music?

_____

Learn About ▸ **Multiplying Mixed Numbers in Word Problems**

Read the problem below. Then explore different ways to understand multiplying fractions and mixed numbers.

Janie has $2\frac{3}{4}$ yards of yellow ribbon. She uses $\frac{1}{2}$ of the ribbon to decorate bookmarks for her cousins. How many yards of ribbon did Janie use for the bookmarks?

▸ **Picture It** **You can use an area model to help you understand the problem.**

The purple shaded region of the area model shows **half** of $2\frac{3}{4}$.

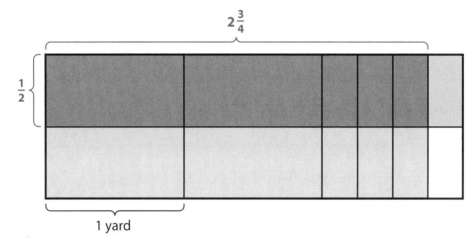

$2\frac{3}{4}$

$\frac{1}{2}$

1 yard

▸ **Model It** **You can write an equation to help you understand the problem.**

You can write $2\frac{3}{4}$ as a fraction.

$$2\frac{3}{4} = 2 + \frac{3}{4}$$
$$= \frac{8}{4} + \frac{3}{4}$$
$$= \frac{11}{4}$$

You need to find a fraction of a fraction: $\frac{1}{2}$ of $\frac{11}{4}$ yards of ribbon.

$\frac{1}{2}$ of $\frac{11}{4}$ means $\frac{1}{2} \times \frac{11}{4}$.

$$\frac{1}{2} \times \frac{11}{4} = \frac{1 \times 11}{2 \times 4}$$

Connect It Now you will solve the problem from the previous page comparing the two strategies.

9 Does Janie use more or less than $2\frac{3}{4}$ yards of ribbon for the bookmarks? Explain.

_____

_____

10 How many yards of ribbon did Janie use? _____ Explain how you can use the picture to answer the question. _____

_____

11 How do you know that you should multiply to solve the problem? _____

_____

_____

12 How can you multiply $2\frac{3}{4}$ by $\frac{1}{2}$? _____

_____

13 What is $\frac{1}{2} \times 2$? _____ What is $\frac{1}{2} \times \frac{3}{4}$? _____

Add the two products. _____ + _____ = _____

Is this result the same as your answer to problem 10? _____

14 Suppose Janie had $2\frac{1}{4}$ yards of ribbon and used $\frac{1}{2}$ of the ribbon for bookmarks. Explain how you could find how many yards of ribbon she used. _____

_____

_____

Try It Use what you just learned about multiplying fractions and mixed numbers to solve this problem. Show your work on a separate sheet of paper.

15 Izzy has $3\frac{1}{2}$ yards of rope. She uses $\frac{3}{5}$ of the rope to attach a tire swing to a tree in the yard. How many yards of rope does Izzy use for the tire swing? _____

Practice ▸ **Multiplying Fractions in Word Problems**

Study the example below. Then solve problems 16–18.

Example

Chris is $4\frac{1}{4}$ feet tall. His mom is $1\frac{1}{2}$ times as tall as Chris. How tall is Chris's mom?

Look at how you can solve this problem using an equation.

$$4\frac{1}{4} \times 1 = 4\frac{1}{4}$$

$$4\frac{1}{4} \times \frac{1}{2} = \left(4 \times \frac{1}{2}\right) + \left(\frac{1}{4} \times \frac{1}{2}\right) = 2 + \frac{1}{8}$$

$$4\frac{1}{4} + 2 + \frac{1}{8} = 6\frac{1}{4} + \frac{1}{8} = 6\frac{2}{8} + \frac{1}{8} = 6\frac{3}{8}$$

Solution $6\frac{3}{8}$ feet

> The student wrote and solved an equation to solve the problem.

> **Pair/Share**
> How does the product compare to $4\frac{1}{4}$ feet?

---

16 Josh exercises at the gym $3\frac{3}{4}$ hours a week. He spends $\frac{2}{5}$ of his time at the gym lifting weights. How many hours a week does Josh spend lifting weights at the gym?

Show your work.

> How do I know what operation to use to solve this problem?

> **Pair/Share**
> What is a reasonable estimate for the number of hours Josh lifts weights each week?

Solution

17 A field is in the shape of a rectangle $\frac{5}{6}$ mile long and $\frac{3}{4}$ mile wide. What is the area of the field?

Show your work.

What model can I use to help understand this problem?

Pair/Share
Can you solve this problem in another way?

Solution _____

18 Ari had $\frac{3}{4}$ of a bag of popcorn. His friends ate $\frac{1}{2}$ of his popcorn. What fraction of the whole bag of popcorn did Ari's friends eat?

Circle the letter of the correct answer.

What equation can I write to solve this problem?

A $\frac{1}{4}$

B $\frac{3}{8}$

C $\frac{5}{4}$

D $\frac{3}{2}$

Kayla chose **A** as the correct answer. How did she get that answer?

_____

_____

_____

Pair/Share
Does Kayla's answer make sense?

Practice ▶ Multiplying Fractions in Word Problems

Solve the problems.

1 On Sunday, Kristen bought a carton of 24 bottles of water.

- On Monday, Kristen drank $\frac{1}{6}$ of the bottles in the carton.

- On Tuesday, Kristen drank $\frac{1}{4}$ of the bottles that remained in the carton after Monday.

Which picture represents the number of bottles of water remaining in the carton after Kristen drank her water on Tuesday?

A

C

B

D

2 Milo's pancake recipe makes 9 servings. It calls for $\frac{3}{4}$ cup milk. Milo wants to make 6 servings. How much milk will he need?

Answer _____ cup

3 Look at the rectangle below.

$2\frac{2}{5}$ in.

$4\frac{1}{8}$ in.

What is the area of the rectangle? _____ or _____ square inches

4 Lily designed the letters of her name on the computer and printed them on paper. The table below shows the width and height of the printed letters.

Letter	Width	Height
L	$2\frac{1}{2}$ in.	4 in.
I	$1\frac{3}{4}$ in.	4 in.
Y	$1\frac{2}{3}$ in.	4 in.

She used a copier to change the size of the letters to $\frac{3}{4}$ of the original size. Make a table to show the new dimensions of each letter.

Show your work.

✓ **Self Check** Go back and see what you can check off on the Self Check on page 93.

Lesson 16 Multiply Fractions in Word Problems

Understand Division with Unit Fractions

💭 Think It Through

How is dividing with fractions related to multiplying with fractions?

You know that multiplication and division are related. Dividing 8 by 4, for example, gives the same result as multiplying 8 by $\frac{1}{4}$.

$$8 \div 4 = 2$$

$$8 \times \frac{1}{4} = 2$$

Dividing with unit fractions works the same way. You can solve a division problem involving fractions by multiplication.

Think What does dividing a unit fraction by a whole number mean?

Mrs. Cook wants to share $\frac{1}{4}$ pound of fish equally among 3 cats.

That means she needs to divide $\frac{1}{4}$ into 3 equal parts. You can draw an area model to represent the problem.

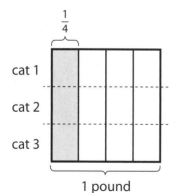

$$\frac{1}{4} \div 3 = \frac{1}{12}$$

If $\frac{1}{4}$ pound of fish is divided into 3 equal parts, each cat will receive $\frac{1}{3}$ of the $\frac{1}{4}$ pound of fish.

$$\frac{1}{3} \times \frac{1}{4} = \frac{1}{12}$$

> ✏️ **Circle** the multiplication equation that solves the division situation.

Think What does dividing a whole number by a unit fraction mean?

Mr. Putnam wants to cut a 3-foot rope into $\frac{1}{4}$-foot sections.

To figure out how many sections he will get, Mr. Putnam thinks, "How many fourths are in 3?"

Look at the answer to this division problem. It is greater than 3, the number I started with!

You can draw a number line to represent the 3 feet of rope. There are three 1-foot sections.

You can mark fourths on the number line to represent $\frac{1}{4}$ foot. You can see there are twelve $\frac{1}{4}$-foot sections in 3 feet.

$$3 \div \frac{1}{4} = 12$$

You can also write a multiplication equation to show how many fourths are in 3. There are 4 fourths in each whole foot. To find the number of fourths in 3 feet, you can multiply.

$$3 \times 4 = 12$$

When you divide 3 by $\frac{1}{4}$, you are dividing 3 into parts smaller than 1. So there will be more than 3 of those parts.

▶ Reflect

1 Explain what it means to divide 5 by $\frac{1}{4}$.

_____

_____

Think About ▷ **Using Unit Fractions in Division**

🔍 **Let's Explore the Idea** Explore dividing a whole number by a unit fraction with the problem below.

Jemma made 5 cups of pancake batter. She uses a scoop measuring $\frac{1}{3}$ cup to pour batter onto the skillet to make large pancakes. How many pancakes can Jemma make?

The 5 rectangles below represent the 5 cups of pancake batter.

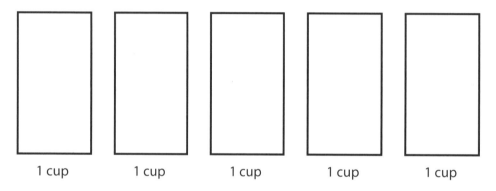

1 cup   1 cup   1 cup   1 cup   1 cup

2 You need to find out how many _____ there are in _____ .

3 The scoop holds $\frac{1}{3}$ cup of batter. How many scoops are in 1 cup? _____

4 Divide each of the 5 rectangles into sections to show your answer to problem 3.

5 How many scoops are in 5 cups? _____

6 $5 \div \frac{1}{3} =$ _____

7 What multiplication equation will also solve this problem? _____

8 How is 5×3 related to $5 \div \frac{1}{3}$? _____

_____

_____

_____

Let's Talk About It

Solve the problems below as a group.

Suppose Jemma wanted to divide $\frac{1}{3}$ cup of pancake batter to make 4 mini pancakes. What fraction of a cup of batter will each pancake get?

9 The rectangle to the right shows 1 cup divided into 3 equal sections. How much does each section represent?

_____

10 Shade $\frac{1}{3}$ of the rectangle to show $\frac{1}{3}$ cup.

11 You need to divide $\frac{1}{3}$ cup equally to make 4 pancakes.

Divide each third of the rectangle vertically into 4 equal parts.

Then shade $\frac{1}{4}$ of the rectangle to show 1 of the 4 pancakes.

12 The overlapping section shows the fraction of a cup of batter that each pancake

will get. What is this fraction? _____

13 $\frac{1}{3} \div 4 =$ _____

14 What multiplication equation also solves $\frac{1}{4}$ of $\frac{1}{3}$? _____

15 How is $\frac{1}{3} \div 4$ related to $\frac{1}{3} \times \frac{1}{4}$? _____

_____

▶ Try It Another Way Explore dividing by a unit fraction using a common denominator.

Another way to think about dividing unit fractions is to write equivalent fractions with a common denominator. What is $5 \div \frac{1}{2}$?

16 Write 5 as a fraction with a denominator of 2. _____

17 Divide $\frac{10}{2}$ into equal groups of $\frac{1}{2}$. How many groups can you make? _____

18 $5 \div \frac{1}{2} =$ _____

Talk through these problems as a class. Then write your answers below.

19 **Compare** Draw a model to represent $\frac{1}{4} \div 4$ and a model to represent $\frac{1}{4} \times \frac{1}{4}$. Explain the relationship between the two expressions.

_____

_____

20 **Analyze** Helena said that $12 \div \frac{1}{3}$ is 4. Draw a model and use words to explain why Helena's statement is not reasonable.

_____

_____

21 **Justify** Show that $\frac{1}{2} \div 3 = \frac{1}{6}$ by using a model. Explain why the result is less than the number you started with, $\frac{1}{2}$.

_____

_____

Apply ▷ **Ideas About Dividing with Unit Fractions**   157

22 **Put It Together** Use what you have learned to complete this task.

Choose one of the following problems to solve. Circle the problem you choose.

> Drew wants to run at least 6 miles this month. He plans to run $\frac{1}{4}$ mile each day. How many days will it take Drew to run 6 miles?

> Maya made $\frac{1}{2}$ quart of strawberry jam. She plans to share it equally among 4 friends. How much jam will each friend get?

Part A Draw a model to represent the problem.

Part B Write a division equation and a multiplication equation that represent the problem.

_____

_____

_____

Lesson 17 *Understand* Division with Unit Fractions   **157**

Divide Unit Fractions in Word Problems

Use What You Know

Now that you understand what it means to divide with unit fractions, take a look at this problem.

> Micah is running a 6-mile race. There are water stops every $\frac{1}{2}$ mile, including at the 6-mile finish line. How many water stops are there?

WATER

a. You want to find how many groups of $\frac{1}{2}$ there are in 6. Write a division expression that represents the problem. _____

b. You can use a number line to help you solve the problem. Finish labeling the number line below from 0 to 6.

0   6

c. Draw points on the number line to show the location of all the water stops.

d. How many $\frac{1}{2}$s are in 1? _____

e. How many $\frac{1}{2}$s are in 6? _____

f. Explain how you can use the number line to find the number of water stops there are. _____

_____

_____

_____

You can find how many half miles are in 6 miles in different ways.

- You can find $6 \div \frac{1}{2}$ by drawing a model.

  You can start by drawing 6 rectangles to represent the 6 miles.

  Start   Finish

  Then show the halves and count.

  Start   Finish

  first   last
  stop   stop

  There are 12 halves, so there are 12 water stops.

- You can also find $6 \div \frac{1}{2}$ by writing a related multiplication equation.

  $6 \div \frac{1}{2} = ?$

  $? \times \frac{1}{2} = 6$

  $12 \times \frac{1}{2} = 6$

  So, $6 \div \frac{1}{2} = 12$.

▶ **Reflect**

1 Suppose the problem is changed so that there are water stops every $\frac{1}{4}$ mile, including the finish line. Explain why you would model this by dividing each rectangle into fourths instead of halves.

_____

_____

_____

_____

Learn About **Dividing a Fraction by a Whole Number**

Read the problem below. Then explore different ways to understand dividing a unit fraction to solve word problems.

> Piper used $\frac{1}{5}$ meter of ribbon to create a border around a triangle. If each side of the triangle is the same length, how much ribbon did Piper use for each side?

▶ **Picture It** **You can draw a picture to help understand the problem.**

Draw a **1-meter** length of ribbon, then draw and label a $\frac{1}{5}$-meter length.

Divide the $\frac{1}{5}$-meter length into **3 equal parts** that represent the 3 sides of the triangle.

▶ **Model It** **You can use a model to help understand the problem.**

Draw and shade $\frac{1}{5}$ of a rectangle.

Divide the rectangle into 3 equal parts. Then shade one of the thirds of the shaded $\frac{1}{5}$.

Connect It Now you will solve the problem from the previous page using your understanding of unit fractions and the models.

2 Look at *Picture It* on the previous page. What information in the problem does the first diagram show?

_____

_____

3 Why does the second diagram show each bar divided into 3 equal parts?

_____

_____

4 When you divide $\frac{1}{5}$ meter into 3 equal parts, how long is each part? _____ meter

How do you know? _____

_____

5 How much ribbon did Piper use for each side of the triangle? _____

6 What division expression represents this problem? _____

7 What is $\frac{1}{5} \div 3$? _____

8 Describe how *Model It* on the previous page shows dividing a unit fraction by a

whole number. _____

_____

_____

Try It Use what you just learned about dividing unit fractions to solve this problem. Show your work on a separate sheet of paper.

9 Tate has $\frac{1}{4}$ of a pizza. He wants to share the pizza equally with a friend. How much of the original whole pizza will each of them get? Draw a model and write an equation to represent and solve the problem.

_____

_____

Learn About ▶ Dividing a Whole Number by a Fraction

Read the problem below. Then explore different ways to understand dividing a whole number by a unit fraction.

> Alex makes 2 pounds of bread dough. He separates the dough into $\frac{1}{4}$-pound loaves before baking them in the oven. How many loaves does he make?

▶ **Picture It** You can draw a model to help understand the problem.

Draw 2 rectangles to represent the 2 pounds of bread dough.

Show each pound divided into fourths.

1 pound   1 pound

▶ **Model It** You can use a number line to help understand the problem.

Draw a number line and label it to show the 2 pounds of bread dough.

Mark the number line to divide each whole into fourths.

Connect It Now you will solve the problem from the previous page using the models.

10 Write a division expression that represents the problem. _____

11 How many fourths are in one whole? _____

How many fourths are in two wholes? _____

12 Use the information in problem 11 to solve the problem from the previous page.

Using words: There are _____ fourths in 2.

Using numbers: $2 \div \dfrac{1}{4} =$ _____

Alex makes _____ loaves of bread.

13 What multiplication equation could you write to check your answer? _____

14 Describe a model you can use to divide a whole number by a unit fraction.

_____

_____

_____

Try It Use what you just learned about dividing whole numbers by unit fractions to solve this problem. Show your work on a separate sheet of paper.

15 Stacy has 4 sheets of paper to make cards. Each card requires $\dfrac{1}{2}$ sheet of paper. How many cards can Stacy make? Choose a model to solve the problem. Then explain why you chose that model.

_____

_____

Practice ▶ **Dividing Unit Fractions in Word Problems**

Study the example below. Then solve problems 16–18.

Example

Sierra has a photo album with 3 empty pages. Each photo uses $\frac{1}{6}$ of an album page. How many photos can Sierra put on the empty pages?

Look at how you could show your work using rectangles.

6 photos will fit on one page, so 18 photos will fit on 3 pages.

Solution ___18 photos___

> The student used a model to visualize the problem.

> **Pair/Share**
> What related equations can you write to represent the problem?

---

16 Corrine picked $\frac{1}{4}$ gallon of blackberries. She poured the berries equally into 4 containers. What fraction of a gallon is in each container?

Show your work.

> Can I draw a model to help understand the problem?

> **Pair/Share**
> How will the answer compare to $\frac{1}{4}$ gallon?

Solution _____

17 Cooper's USB drive is $\frac{1}{2}$ full with 5 video files. Each video file is the same size. What fraction of the USB drive does 1 video file use?

Show your work.

How could I represent this problem using an equation?

Pair/Share
How can you check your answer?

Solution _____

---

18 Devonte is studying for a history test. He uses $\frac{1}{8}$ of a side of one sheet of paper to write notes for each history event. He fills 2 full sides of one sheet of paper. Which expression could be used to find how many events Devonte makes notes for? Circle the letter of the correct answer.

Is this problem like any problem I've seen before?

A $2 \times \frac{1}{8}$

B $2 \div \frac{1}{8}$

C $\frac{1}{8} \times 2$

D $\frac{1}{8} \div 2$

Barry chose **D** as the correct answer. How did he get that answer?

_____

_____

_____

_____

Pair/Share
Does Barry's answer make sense?

Practice ▷ Dividing Unit Fractions in Word Problems

Solve the problems.

1 Elise picks 6 pounds of apples. She uses $\frac{1}{2}$ pound of apples to make 1 container of applesauce. How many containers of applesauce can Elise make with all the apples?

A 12 containers

B $6\frac{1}{2}$ containers

C $5\frac{1}{2}$ containers

D 3 containers

2 Students are running in a relay race. Each team will run a total of 3 miles. Each member of a team will run $\frac{1}{3}$ mile.

How many students will a team need to complete the race? Circle the correct number below.

$\frac{1}{9}$ 3 9 12 36

You may use the number line to help find your answer.

3 Mr. Bernstein will cut 8 pies into pieces that are each $\frac{1}{6}$ of the whole. After he cuts the 8 pies, how many pieces will Mr. Bernstein have? _____ pieces

4 Marina has a pattern to make bows that requires $\frac{1}{4}$ yard of ribbon for each bow.

Part A Fill in the table to show how many bows she can make from a given length of ribbon.

Ribbon Length (yards)	Number of Bows
1	
2	
3	
4	

Part B Use words or an equation to describe a rule to find the number of bows Marina can make if you know how many yards of ribbon she has.

_____

_____

Part C Use your rule to find how many bows Marina can make if she has 18 yards of ribbon.

Answer _____ bows

✓ **Self Check** Go back and see what you can check off on the Self Check on page 93.

Study an Example Problem and Solution

In this lesson, you will use what you know about fractions to solve real-world problems. Look at this problem and one solution.

Solar Lights

G.O. and his neighbors are taking steps to save energy and water. G.O.'s street is $1\frac{1}{2}$ miles long. They plan to install solar lights along the sidewalk. Read G.O.'s plan.

Solars Light Plan
- Install the lights at equal intervals.
- Use a fraction of the whole length to choose the interval length.
- Use a fraction greater than $\frac{1}{8}$ but less than $\frac{1}{2}$.

Choose an appropriate fraction. Find the length of the interval. Tell how many solar lights are needed and where along the street the lights should be located.

Read the sample solution on the next page. Then look at the checklist below. Find and mark parts of the solution that match the checklist.

✏️ Problem-Solving Checklist
- ☐ Tell what is known.
- ☐ Tell what the problem is asking.
- ☐ Show all your work.
- ☐ Show that the solution works.

- **a. Circle** something that is known.
- **b. Underline** something that you need to find.
- **c. Draw a box around** what you do to solve the problem.
- **d. Put a checkmark** next to the part that shows the solution works.

G.O.'s Solution

▷ **I know the length of the street.** I have to use the length and a fraction between $\frac{1}{8}$ and $\frac{1}{2}$ to find the distance between the lights.

▷ **I can use $\frac{1}{4}$.** The fractions $\frac{1}{8}$, $\frac{1}{4}$, and $\frac{1}{2}$ all have the same numerator, so I can look at the denominators to compare.

Since 4 is < 8, $\frac{1}{4} > \frac{1}{8}$.

Since 4 is > 2, $\frac{1}{4} < \frac{1}{2}$.

▷ **I know that** the distance is a fraction of the whole length, so I multiply $\frac{1}{4}$ by $1\frac{1}{2}$.

"Fraction of" means multiply by a fraction.

$1\frac{1}{2} = \frac{3}{2}$ and $\frac{1}{4} \times \frac{3}{2} = \frac{3}{8}$

The interval length is $\frac{3}{8}$ mile.

▷ **Now I can** make a number line to find where the lights will go and how many are needed. It represents the street, so it goes to $1\frac{1}{2}$.

I divided the number line into eighths so I can count by $\frac{3}{8}$.

$$0 \qquad \frac{3}{8} \qquad \frac{6}{8} \qquad 1 \quad \frac{9}{8} \qquad \frac{12}{8}$$

▷ **I put a light at 0**, which is one end of the street. Then I marked each $\frac{3}{8}$ mile along the number line.

▷ **The number line shows** that there will be 5 lights installed at intervals of $\frac{3}{8}$ mile. The locations are at:

0 miles, $\frac{3}{8}$ mile, $\frac{6}{8}$ mile, $\frac{9}{8}$ ($1\frac{1}{8}$ miles), and $\frac{12}{8}$ ($1\frac{1}{2}$ miles).

My answer makes sense because it fits the information in the problem.

▷ There are 5 lights but only 4 intervals. Each interval is $\frac{3}{8}$ mile long and $4 \times \frac{3}{8} = \frac{12}{8}$. That's the same as $1\frac{1}{2}$ miles.

There are many ways to solve problems. Think about how you might solve the Solar Lights problem in a different way.

Solar Lights

G.O. and his neighbors are taking steps to save energy and water. G.O.'s street is $1\frac{1}{2}$ miles long. They plan to install solar lights along the sidewalk. Read G.O.'s plan.

Solar Light Plan

· Install the lights at equal intervals.

· Use a fraction of the whole length to choose the interval length.

· Use a fraction greater than $\frac{1}{8}$ but less than $\frac{1}{2}$.

Choose an appropriate fraction. Find the length of the interval. Tell how many solar lights are needed and where along the street the lights should be located.

▶ **Plan It** Answer these questions to help you start thinking about a plan.

A. What are some other fractions that you can use?

_____

_____

B. What can you do if you want to use more lights? Fewer lights?

_____

_____

▶ Solve It   Find a different solution for the Solar Lights problem.
Show all your work on a separate sheet of paper.

You may want to use the problem-solving tips to get started.

Problem-Solving Tips

- **Models**

- **Word Bank**

fraction	numerator	multiply
interval	denominator	product

- **Sentence Starters**

  • I can multiply _____

  • Each interval _____

**Problem-Solving
Checklist**

Make sure that you . . .

☐ tell what you know.

☐ tell what you need
   to do.

☐ show all your work.

☐ show that the
   solution works.

▶ Reflect

Use Mathematical Practices   As you work through the problem, discuss these questions with a partner.

- **Persevere** What is your first step? What will you do next?

- **Repeated Reasoning** How can you use what you know about the denominators of unit fractions to find an appropriate fraction?

**Read the problem. Write a solution on a separate sheet of paper.
Remember, there can be lots of ways to solve a problem!**

Plant Shrubs

The neighborhood has a small piece of
common land that is now covered with
grass. To save water, the neighbors will
plant shrubs on part of the common area.
Read G.O.'s notes.

Planting Notes

· Plant shrubs on a rectangular area
a little more than half of the
common land area.

· One side of the shrub section has
a length greater than 8 feet and
less than 9 feet.

10 feet

Common Land | 10 feet

What is the area of the part where G.O. and his neighbors will plant shrubs?

▶ Plan It and Solve It Find a solution to the Plant Shrubs problem.

Find the length, width, and area of the part of the common land that will be used to plant shrubs.

- Find the area of the common land.
- Find a length and width of a rectangle that will create an area that is a little more than half the area of the common land.

Problem-Solving Tips

- ### Questions
  - What are some fractions equivalent to $\frac{1}{2}$?
  - What are some fractions that are a little more than $\frac{1}{2}$?

- ### Word Bank

area	multiply	numerator
fraction	product	denominator

Problem-Solving Checklist
Make sure that you . . .
- ☐ tell what you know.
- ☐ tell what you need to do.
- ☐ show all your work.
- ☐ show that the solution works.

▶ Reflect

Use Mathematical Practices As you work through the problem, discuss these questions with a partner.

- **Reason Mathematically** How can you compare fractions to find a fraction a little more than $\frac{1}{2}$?
- **Use Models** What models can you use to help you visualize the problem?

Read the problems. Write a solution on a separate sheet of paper.
Remember, there are many different ways to solve a problem.

Water Shrubs

G.O. and his neighbors clear an area $8\frac{1}{2}$ feet by $6\frac{1}{4}$ feet to plant the shrubs.
Now they have to decide how many shrubs to plant and how much water to
use on the shrubs. Read G.O.'s planting instructions.

Shrub Planting Instructions

· Each shrub needs an area of about
  2 square feet.
· Each shrub will need about $1\frac{1}{4}$ gallons
  of water a week.

How many shrubs should G.O. plant?

How much water will the shrubs need?

▶ **Solve It** Help G.O. make a plan for planting shrubs.

• Tell how many shrubs G.O. should plant and why you chose this number.
• Find the amount of water this number of shrubs will need in a week.

▶ **Reflect**

Use Mathematical Practices After you complete the task, choose one
of these questions to discuss with a partner.

• **Reason Mathematically** How did you decide the number of shrubs that
  G.O. should plant?

• **Make an Argument** How could you justify the number of shrubs that
  you suggested?

Use Compost

A local nursery hears about the shrub planting project that G.O. and his neighbors are planning. The nursery gives them 50 pounds of compost to use. G.O. reads about using compost on a website.

About how many shrubs can G.O. plant with the compost that the nursery gave him?

Using Compost to Plant

When you plant a shrub, it can help to mix the soil with some compost. You can use a scoop of compost for each shrub. An average scoop of compost is between $\frac{1}{4}$ and $\frac{1}{2}$ pound.

▶ **Solve It** Help G.O. estimate how many shrubs he can plant with the compost.

- Decide on a fraction of a pound to use as the weight of an average scoop.
- Show how to use this fraction to find the number of shrubs that can be planted. Explain.

▶ **Reflect**

Use Mathematical Practices After you complete the task, choose one of these questions to discuss with a partner.

- **Make Sense of Problems** How did you use each of the numbers given in the problem?

- **Persevere** Why might you try using different fractions before giving your final answer? Explain.

Interim Assessment

Solve the problems.

1 What is the area of the rectangle shown below?

$\frac{7}{8}$ ft

$\frac{3}{5}$ ft

A $\frac{40}{21}$ square feet

B $\frac{10}{13}$ square foot

C $\frac{24}{35}$ square foot

D $\frac{21}{40}$ square foot

2 Look at the equations below. Choose *True* or *False* for each equation.

a. $3\frac{4}{5} + 6\frac{2}{10} = 10$

☐ True ☐ False

b. $22\frac{7}{9} - 16\frac{1}{4} = 6\frac{19}{36}$

☐ True ☐ False

c. $\frac{2}{3} \times \frac{1}{6} = \frac{4}{6}$

☐ True ☐ False

d. $6 \div \frac{1}{5} = \frac{6}{5}$

☐ True ☐ False

3 Classify each product below as less than $\frac{3}{7}$, equal to $\frac{3}{7}$, or greater than $\frac{3}{7}$ by writing each expression in the correct box.

$\frac{3}{7} \times \frac{1}{10}$ $\frac{3}{7} \times \frac{9}{4}$ $\frac{3}{7} \times 2$

$\frac{3}{7} \times \frac{2}{3}$ $\frac{3}{7} \times 1\frac{1}{8}$ $\frac{3}{7} \times \frac{5}{5}$

Less than $\frac{3}{7}$	Equal to $\frac{3}{7}$	Greater than $\frac{3}{7}$

4 Look at each fraction. Can it be placed in the box to make a true inequality? Choose *Yes* or *No* for each fraction.

$$\frac{4}{11} \times \boxed{} < \frac{4}{11}$$

a. $\frac{5}{3}$ ☐ Yes ☐ No

b. $\frac{3}{3}$ ☐ Yes ☐ No

c. $\frac{1}{3}$ ☐ Yes ☐ No

5 How many pounds of peanuts will each person get if 3 people share $\frac{1}{5}$ pound of peanuts equally?

Part A Write and solve a division equation to represent the problem.
Show your work.

Answer _____ pound

Part B Write a multiplication equation that explains why your division equation solved the problem.

Solution _____

6 Two students painted murals on canvas for a school play.

Part A José painted a square-shaped mural. The length of each side of the canvas is $1\frac{1}{3}$ yards.

What is the area of the mural in square yards?

Answer _____ square yards

Part B Lori painted a rectangular mural with the same area as José's mural. Her mural is not square-shaped.

What could be the dimensions of Lori's mural, in yards?

Length = _____ yards   Width = _____ yards

Performance Task

Answer the questions and show all your work on separate paper.

The Drama Club is painting sets for their next play. Blue and green paint is on sale at the hardware store, so the students have sketched the design for a set that will use only those two paint colors. How much of each color will they need to buy in order to paint the set?

Checklist

Did you . . .

☐ use the information in the diagram and the notes?

☐ organize your information?

☐ check the accuracy of your solution?

Notes

1 pint turquoise = $\frac{2}{3}$ pint green and $\frac{1}{3}$ pint blue

1 pint of paint covers about 40 square feet.

▶ Reflect

Use Mathematical Practices After you complete the task, choose one of the following questions to answer.

- **Persevere** What was your first step in solving this problem?

- **Model** How did you use fractions to help you solve this problem?

Unit 3
Operations and Algebraic Thinking

Let's learn about expressions and relationships between numbers.

Real-World Connection Sometimes you can solve a problem by completing the steps in any order. Other times you need to complete the steps in a certain order. For example, consider making a pizza with a vegetable mixture and pepperoni. You could first put the vegetable mixture on the pizza, and then top with pepperoni. Or you could first put on the pepperoni and then top with the vegetable mixture. Either way, the pizza will be tasty! Suppose you are given the math problem "double 8 + 12, then add 43." The order in which you complete the steps is important. The expressions $2 \times 8 + 12 + 43$ and $2 \times (8 + 12) + 43$ have different values. You must follow the steps in a certain order to find the correct value.

In This Unit You will write numerical expressions and find their value. You will also identify and create number patterns, describe the relationships between numbers in the patterns, and plot the numbers on a graph.

✔ Self Check

Before starting this unit, check off the skills you know below. As you complete each lesson, see how many more skills you can check off!

I can:	Before this unit	After this unit
evaluate expressions, for example: $48 \div (6 + 10)$ has a value of 3.	☐	☐
write expressions, for example: "subtract 5 from 12, then multiply by 4" can be written as $(12 - 5) \times 4$.	☐	☐
find the relationship between two number patterns, for example: Pattern A: 0, 2, 4, 6, 8, . . . Pattern B: 0, 8, 16, 24, 32, . . . Each term in Pattern B is 4 times the corresponding term in Pattern A.	☐	☐
list ordered pairs for two number patterns and graph the relationship on the coordinate plane, for example: ordered pairs for Patterns A and B above are (0, 0), (2, 8), (4, 16), (6, 24), (8, 32).	☐	☐

Use What You Know

You know about the order of operations. Now you will see how using parentheses in an expression can change the value of the expression. Take a look at this problem.

> Maria and her friend go to a movie. At the snack stand, they each get a drink that costs $5 and a popcorn that costs $8. Maria pays for her friend. How much does Maria pay altogether?

a. What operation do you use to find the cost of a drink and a popcorn for one person?

_____

b. Write an expression for the cost of a drink and popcorn for one person. _____

c. How does the cost for two people compare to the cost for one person?

_____

d. Explain how you can find the cost for two people. What do you need to do first?

_____

_____

e. How much does Maria pay for a drink and popcorn for two people? _____

f. Maria thought she could use the equation $2 \times 5 + 8 = 18$ to find the cost. Explain why she is not correct.

_____

_____

▶▶ Find Out More

To **evaluate** an expression means to find its value. To evaluate the expression $2 \times 5 + 8$, you first multiply 2×5, then add 8. But what if you wanted to add 5 and 8 and then multiply by 2? You could use **parentheses** in the expression to tell which operation to do first.

Parentheses are a type of grouping symbol. Grouping symbols tell which operation to do first. Fraction bars are another type of grouping symbol.

Parentheses	$2 \times (5 + 8)$	First, add $5 + 8$ because it is inside the parentheses. Then multiply by 2.
Fraction Bar	$\dfrac{2 + 8}{11 - 6}$	The fraction bar groups the numerator separately from the denominator. First evaluate the numerator and the denominator. Then divide.

Look at the problem on the previous page. Maria wants to first find the cost of a drink and popcorn for 1 person, then double it to find the cost for 2 people. Maria could write the expression $2 \times (5 + 8)$ or $(5 + 8) \times 2$.

One way to read $2 \times (5 + 8)$ is "2 times the sum of 5 and 8." Another way is "twice the sum of 5 and 8." You can also think of $2 \times (5 + 8)$ as "adding 5 and 8, then multiplying by 2."

Adding parentheses into an expression can change its value. The expressions $2 \times 5 + 8$ and $2 \times (5 + 8)$ do not have the same value.

$2 \times 5 + 8$ $2 \times (5 + 8)$

$10 + 8$ 2×13

18   26

▶ Reflect

1 What should you look for to indicate a group? How do you evaluate an expression if you see a grouping symbol?

_____

_____

_____

_____

_____

Learn About ▸ Evaluating Expressions

Read the problem below. Then explore how to evaluate expressions that use grouping symbols.

> There were 24 students on a field trip to the aquarium. There were also 8 adults on the trip. The expression $0.50 \times (24 + 8)$ represents the cost in dollars to buy everyone a 50-cent souvenir eraser. What is the total cost of the erasers?

▶ **Picture It** You can use a picture to help understand the problem.

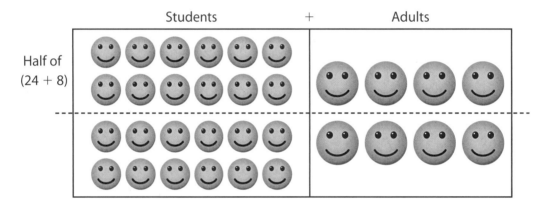

Students   +   Adults

Half of $(24 + 8)$

▶ **Model It** You can use words to help understand the problem.

0.50	×	$(24 + 8)$
↑	↑	↑
Half	of	the sum of the number of students and the number of adults

Connect It Now you will solve the problem from the previous page using the picture and words.

2 Describe one way you could read the expression $0.50 \times (24 + 8)$.

_____

3 How could you use *Picture It* on the previous page to evaluate $0.50 \times (24 + 8)$?

_____

_____

4 Evaluate $0.50 \times (24 + 8)$ to find the cost in dollars of the erasers. _____

5 Morgan sees a different way to evaluate $0.50 \times (24 + 8)$. She finds half of 24 and half of 8, and then adds those numbers together. Why does her method work?

_____

_____

6 The expression $3 \times$ (number of students + number of adults) represents the cost in dollars for another group to go to the dolphin show at the aquarium. Describe how the cost compares to the total number of students and adults.

_____

_____

Try It Use what you just learned about evaluating expressions to solve these problems. Show your work on a separate sheet of paper.

7 Describe what happens when you multiply a sum by 2.

_____

8 Sara buys a shirt that regularly costs $12 and a pair of pants that regularly costs $26. They are on sale, so she only needs to pay half the regular cost. Evaluate the expression $\frac{1}{2} \times (12 + 26)$ to find Sara's cost in dollars. _____

Learn About ▶ **Writing Expressions**

Read the problem below. Then explore how to write numerical expressions.

Write a numerical expression to represent the following phrase.

15 minus the sum of 6 and 7

▶ **Picture It** **You can use a picture to help understand the problem.**

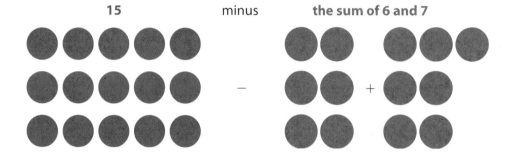

▶ **Model It** **You can think about what the words mean to help understand the problem.**

15   minus   the sum of 6 and 7
              ↓   ↓
         Minus means   A sum is the
         to subtract.   result of
                             addition. So
                             add 6 and 7.

Connect It Now you will solve the problem from the previous page using the picture and words.

9 In the expression "15 minus the sum of 6 and 7," do you add or subtract first? Why?

_____

_____

10 When you write a numerical expression, how can you show what operation to do first?

_____

_____

11 Write a numerical expression for "15 minus the sum of 6 and 7." _____

12 Harper wrote the expression $15 - 6 + 7$ to represent "15 minus the sum of 6 and 7." Evaluate $15 - 6 + 7$ and then explain why Harper's expression is incorrect.

_____

_____

_____

13 Omar wrote $3 + (4 \times 6)$ to represent the phrase "3 more than the product of 4 and 6." Did Omar need to use a grouping symbol? Explain.

_____

_____

_____

Try It Use what you just learned about writing numerical expressions to solve these problems. Show your work on a separate sheet of paper.

14 Write a numerical expression to represent "2 times the difference of 8 and 1." Then evaluate your expression. _____

15 Write a numerical expression to represent "15 divided by the sum of 1 and 4." Then evaluate your expression.

_____

Practice ▶ **Writing and Evaluating Expressions**

Study the example below. Then solve problems 16–18.

> **Example**
>
> Insert parentheses to make the following equation true.
>
> 15 − 7 − 2 = 10
>
> **Look at how you could show your work.**
>
> $$(15 - 7) - 2 = 8 - 2 = 6$$
> $$6 \neq 10$$
>
> $$15 - (7 - 2) = 15 - 5 = 10$$
> $$10 = 10$$
>
> **Solution** $\underline{15 - (7 - 2) = 10}$

The student used trial and error to answer the question.

Pair/Share
How many different ways can you group the numbers?

---

16 Carol sells bracelets and pairs of earrings at a craft fair. Each item sells for $8. Write and evaluate an expression to show how much money Carol will make if she sells 23 bracelets and 17 pairs of earrings.

Show your work.

How many items will Carol sell altogether?

Pair/Share
What other ways could you solve the problem?

Solution _____

17 Write numerical expressions for "the product of 3 and 2, plus 5" and "3 times the sum of 2 and 5." Which expression has a greater value?

Show your work.

The comma is a clue to where to put the grouping symbol. In this case, group the math that comes before the comma.

Pair/Share
When do you use parentheses in an expression?

Solution _____

18 Which expression represents "the quotient of 10 and 2, plus 3"? Circle the letter of the correct answer.

A $10 \div (2 + 3)$

B $\dfrac{10}{2 + 3}$

C $(10 \times 2) + 3$

D $\dfrac{10}{2} + 3$

What does the word "quotient" mean?

Jason chose **A** as the correct answer. How did he get that answer?

_____

_____

_____

_____

_____

Pair/Share
Is Jason's answer reasonable?

Lesson 19 Evaluate and Write Expressions

Practice ▶ **Writing and Evaluating Expressions**

Solve the problems.

1 Kris ran 3 miles each day for 7 days in a row. One day, she ran an extra $\frac{1}{2}$ mile. Which expression represents how many miles Kris ran altogether?

A $3 + 7 + \frac{1}{2}$

B $3 \times 7 + \frac{1}{2}$

C $3 \times 7 + 3\frac{1}{2}$

D $\left(3 + \frac{1}{2}\right) \times 7$

2 Which expression does NOT represent the statement "divide the difference of 20 and 8 by the sum of 1 and 3"?

A $\frac{20 - 8}{1 + 3}$

B $(20 - 8) \div (1 + 3)$

C $\frac{20}{1 + 3} - \frac{8}{1 + 3}$

D $(20 - 8) \div 1 + 3$

3 Which expression has a value of 8? Circle the letter for all that apply.

A $3 \times 8 \div 4 + 2$

B $3 \times (8 \div 4) + 2$

C $(3 \times 8) \div (4 + 2)$

D $(3 \times 8) \div 4 + 2$

E $3 \times 8 \div (4 + 2)$

4 Adam is 2 years old. His sister Lina is 1 year less than three times his age. Write a numerical expression for Lina's age. _____

5 Several expressions are shown below. Decide if the value of the expression is less than, equal to, or greater than 18. Write each expression in the correct category in the chart.

$\frac{1}{5} \times (9 \times 2)$ $(9 \times 2) \times (4 - 3)$ $(9 \times 2) \div 3$ $22 - (9 \times 2)$

$(9 \times 2) + 7$ $4 \times \frac{1}{4} \times (9 \times 2)$ $1 \times (9 \times 2)$ $3 \times (9 \times 2)$

Less than 18	Equal to 18	Greater than 18

6 Compare the expressions $8 \times 3 + 4$ and $8 \times (3 + 4)$. Explain how to evaluate each expression. Then tell which expression has the greater value.

Show your work.

✓ **Self Check** **Go back and see what you can check off on the Self Check on page 179.**

Analyze Patterns and Relationships

🅖 Use What You Know

Previously you learned to identify and continue numerical patterns. Now you will describe the relationship between two patterns. Take a look at this problem.

> Maria is working at the snack stand at a basketball game. Each frozen yogurt costs $3, and each sandwich costs $6. Create a table to show the costs for buying 0, 1, 2, 3, 4, 5, or 6 frozen yogurts. Create another table to show the costs for the same number of sandwiches. How does the cost of a given number of frozen yogurts compare to the cost of the same number of sandwiches?

a. What is the cost for buying 1 frozen yogurt? _____

b. What do you add to the cost of 1 frozen yogurt to get the cost of 2 frozen yogurts?

_____

c. Complete the table to show the cost for each number of frozen yogurts.

Number of Yogurts	0	1	2	3	4	5	6
Cost ($)							

d. What do you add to the cost of 1 sandwich to get the cost of 2 sandwiches?

_____

e. Complete the table to show the cost for each number of sandwiches.

Number of Sandwiches	0	1	2	3	4	5	6
Cost ($)							

f. How does the cost of sandwiches compare to the cost of the same number of yogurts?

_____

_____

▶▶ Find Out More

The costs of frozen yogurts and the costs of sandwiches form numerical patterns.

Cost of Frozen Yogurts ($)

+3 +3 +3 +3 +3 +3

0   3   6   9   12 15 18

Cost of Sandwiches ($)

+6 +6 +6 +6 +6 +6

0   6   12 18 24 30 36

You can use a table to write ordered pairs. An **ordered pair** is a pair of numbers. Ordered pairs could help you see relationships between **corresponding terms** in two patterns. For these ordered pairs, the first number is the cost of a certain number of frozen yogurts. The second number is the cost of the same number of sandwiches.

Cost of Yogurts ($)	Cost of Sandwiches ($)	Ordered Pairs
0	0	(0, 0)
3	6	(3, 6)
6	12	(6, 12)
9	18	(9, 18)
12	24	(12, 24)
15	30	(15, 30)
18	36	(18, 36)

There is a relationship between the two numbers of these ordered pairs. Here, the second number is always twice the first number.

▶ Reflect

1 What if the ordered pairs where written as (0, 0), (6, 3), (12, 6), (18, 9), (24, 12), (30, 15), (36, 18). Would this change the relationship between the first number and the second number? Explain.

_____

_____

_____

Learn About ▶ **Comparing Two Numerical Patterns**

Read the problem below. Then explore how to identify relationships between two numerical patterns.

In Level 1 of a game, you earn 2 points for each correct answer. In Level 2, you earn 6 points for each correct answer. Compare the number of points in Level 2 to the number of points in Level 1 if you correctly answer 0, 1, 2, 3, 4, 5, or 6 questions.

▶ **Picture It** **You can use a picture to help find each pattern.**

Level 1	Level 2
Each correct answer earns **2 points**.	Each correct answer earns **6 points**.

▶ **Model It** **Use a table to show the number of points you get for correct answers in each level of the game.**

Write ordered pairs. Have the first number be from the first pattern. Then have the second number be the corresponding number from the second pattern.

Points in Level 1	Points in Level 2	Ordered Pairs
0	0	(0, 0)
2	6	(2, 6)
4	12	
6	18	
8	24	
10	30	
12	36	

The total number of points in Level 1 increases by 2 for each correct answer. The total number of points in Level 2 increases by 6 for each correct answer.

Connect It Now you will solve the problem from the previous page by looking at the ordered pairs.

2 Look at *Picture It* on the previous page. Describe how the total number of points changes with each correct answer in Level 1 and Level 2.

Level 1 rule: _____

Level 2 rule: _____

3 Complete the table on the previous page.

4 For each ordered pair, how does the second number compare to the first number?

_____

5 Suppose the game has a third level. You get 9 points for each correct answer in Level 3. Explain how you could figure out how the points in Level 3 compare with the corresponding points in Level 2.

_____

_____

_____

_____

_____

Try It Use what you just learned about comparing two number patterns to solve this problem. Show your work on a separate sheet of paper.

6 School magnets cost $4, and shirts cost $24. Write a pattern for the costs of 0, 1, 2, 3, 4, and 5 magnets and a second pattern for the costs of 0, 1, 2, 3, 4, and 5 shirts. How do the corresponding terms of the two patterns compare?

_____

_____

_____

Learn About Graphing Ordered Pairs

Read the problem below. Then explore plotting corresponding terms of number patterns on a graph.

The scouts are making model vehicles. They have a choice of making a model plane or a model boat.

- The materials for the plane cost $2.
- The materials for the boat cost $4.

Write and graph ordered pairs to compare the cost of making one or more boats to the cost of making the same number of planes.

▶ **Picture It** **You can use a picture to find the costs of making various numbers of each model.**

Each pattern of numbers below shows the cost of making 0, 1, 2, 3, and 4 models.

Planes

+2   +2   +2   +2

0   2   4   6   8

Boats

+4   +4   +4   +4

0   4   8   12   16

▶ **Model It** **You can use a table to help understand the problem.**

List the cost of materials for the planes and boats in a table. Then write the corresponding costs as ordered pairs.

Cost of Planes ($), x	Cost of Boats ($), y	Ordered Pairs (x, y)
0	0	(0, 0)
2	4	(2, 4)
4	8	(4, 8)
6	12	(6, 12)
8	16	(8, 16)

Connect It Now you will solve the problem from the previous page by graphing ordered pairs.

7 Explain how to write ordered pairs using the numbers in each pattern.

_____

_____

8 Plot the ordered pairs on the graph to the right.
The first number tells the location along the horizontal axis.
The second number tells the location along the vertical axis.

The point (2, 4) is plotted for you.

9 How do the corresponding terms of the patterns compare?

_____

_____

10 Suppose you connect the points. How would this look?

_____

11 What directions would you give to someone to get from one point to the next point to the right on the graph? How do your directions relate to the rules for the patterns?

_____

_____

_____

Try It Use what you just learned about using graphs to compare two patterns to solve this problem. Show your work on a separate sheet of paper.

12 Consider the two patterns below. Start each pattern with 0.

Pattern A: add 1   **Pattern B:** add 3

Write five ordered pairs made up of corresponding terms from the two patterns. Plot the points on the graph to the right. Describe the relationship between the two patterns.

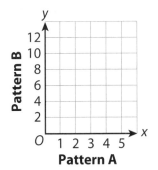

_____

_____

Practice ▶ **Analyzing Patterns and Relationships**

Study the example below. Then solve problems 13–15.

Example

Look at the following two number patterns.

Pattern A: 6, 5, 4, 3, 2, 1, 0

Pattern B: 24, 20, 16, 12, 8, 4, 0

What is the relationship between corresponding terms in the two patterns?

Look at how you could show your work using ordered pairs.

The first number is a term from Pattern A. The second number is the corresponding term from Pattern B.

Ordered pairs: (6, 24), (5, 20), (4, 16), (3, 12), (2, 8), (1, 4), (0, 0)

Solution _Each term in Pattern B is four times the corresponding_

term in Pattern A.

The student wrote ordered pairs to identify a relationship between corresponding terms.

Pair/Share
How are these patterns different from other patterns in this lesson?

---

13 One pattern starts at 0 and has the rule "add 8." Another pattern starts at 0 and has the rule "add 4." Write each pattern of numbers. How do the corresponding terms in the patterns compare?

Show your work.

How do I generate the patterns?

Solution _____

_____

Pair/Share
Does it matter how many terms you write for each pattern?

14 Identify the pattern in each column of the table. Complete the *x* and *y* columns of the table. Use those columns to write ordered pairs in the last column. Describe the relationship between corresponding terms in the patterns.

What is the rule for each pattern?

Show your work.

x	y	Ordered Pairs (x, y)
4	1	
8	2	
12	3	

Solution _____

_____

Pair/Share
Find the difference between the numbers in each ordered pair. Do you see another pattern?

15 The ordered pairs (2, 12), (3, 18), and (4, 24) are formed by corresponding terms in two patterns. How do the values of the second numbers compare to the values of the first numbers? Circle the letter of the correct answer.

What rule works for all the ordered pairs?

A 10 more

B 2 times as much

C $\frac{1}{6}$ times as much

D 6 times as much

Mike chose **C** as the correct answer. How did he get that answer?

_____

_____

_____

 Pair/Share
Does Mike's answer make sense?

Practice ▶ **Analyzing Patterns and Relationships**

Solve the problems.

1 What rule could be used to create the pattern 9, 18, 27, 36, 45, 54, . . . ?

A multiply each term by 2 to get the next term

B multiply each term by 9 to get the next term

C add 9 to get the next term

D add 3 to get the next term

2 Look at the patterns below. Choose *True* or *False* for each statement.

Pattern A: 3, 6, 9, 12, 15, 18, . . .

Pattern B: 18, 36, 54, 72, 90, 108, . . .

a. The rule for Pattern A is "multiply by 2." ☐ True ☐ False

b. The rule for Pattern B is "add 18." ☐ True ☐ False

c. Each term in Pattern A is 6 times the corresponding term in Pattern B. ☐ True ☐ False

d. Each term in Pattern B is 3 times the corresponding term in Pattern A. ☐ True ☐ False

3 Tickets at a play cost $2 for students and $8 for adults. Jason creates two patterns to compare the costs. He writes ordered pairs in the form (student cost, adult cost) for the corresponding numbers of tickets. Which ordered pair could be on Jason's list of ordered pairs? Circle the letter for all that apply.

A (8, 2)

B (10, 40)

C (4, 10)

D (10, 16)

E (6, 24)

4 Use the rules below to create two patterns each starting with 0. Then describe the relationship between corresponding terms of the two patterns.

Pattern A: add 3   **Pattern B:** add 12

Show your work.

_____

_____

5 Use the rules "add 2" and "add 5" to create two patterns each beginning with 0. Use the patterns to complete the table in Part A.

Part A

Add 2, x	Add 5, y	Ordered Pairs (x, y)

Part B Graph the ordered pairs and connect the points. How does this look?

_____

_____

Part C Describe the relationship between the corresponding terms of the patterns.

_____

_____

✔ **Self Check** **Go back and see what you can check off on the Self Check on page 179.**

Unit 3
MATH IN ACTION

👥 **Introduction**

Expressions, Patterns, and Relationships

SMP1 Make sense of problems and persevere in solving them.

Study an Example Problem and Solution

In this lesson, you will look at expressions, patterns, and relationships between numbers to solve real-world problems. Look at this problem and one solution.

Intermission Snacks

Brandi is working with a theater group to plan their next show. She needs to decide what snacks to sell during intermission. Brandi lists the costs to buy or make each item. The selling price will be about 2 or 3 times the cost.

Our Costs	
Popcorn	$0.75
Trail Mix	$1.25
Hot Dog	$1.50
Sandwich	$2.00
Small Pizza	$2.50

Choose 2 food items. Decide on a selling price for each. Use ordered pairs to compare the amount of money they will take in by selling 0, 1, 2, 3, 4, and 5 of each item. Describe how the numbers in each ordered pair are related.

Read the sample solution on the next page. Then look at the checklist below. Find and mark parts of the solution that match the checklist.

✏️ Problem-Solving Checklist

- ☐ Tell what is known.
- ☐ Tell what the problem is asking.
- ☐ Show all your work.
- ☐ Show that the solution works.

a. **Circle** something that is known.

b. **Underline** something that you need to find.

c. **Draw a box around** what you do to solve the problem.

d. **Put a checkmark** next to the part that shows the solution works.

Brandi's Solution

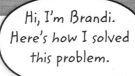

Hi, I'm Brandi. Here's how I solved this problem.

▷ **I know** what each food item costs. I'll choose popcorn and trail mix because they seem like good snacks.

▷ **I also know** that the selling price should be about 2 or 3 times the cost. I can multiply each cost by both 2 and 3. I can use either of those products. Or I can find a number somewhere between the two products.

Item	Cost	Cost x 2	Cost x 3	My Selling Price
Popcorn	$0.75	$1.50	$2.25	$2.00
Trail Mix	$1.25	$2.50	$3.75	$3.00

I used a table so the money amounts are clearly labeled and easy to see.

▷ **I'll check** that the selling price is between 2 and 3 times the cost.

$2.00 > $1.50   and $2.00 < $2.25

$3.00 > $2.50   and $3.00 < $3.75

▷ **I can make a** table to find the price to buy 0, 1, 2, 3, 4, and 5 of each item.

I decided to use whole-dollar amounts so it will be easier to compare numbers.

Number of items	0	1	2	3	4	5
Price of Popcorn	0	2	4	6	8	10
Price of Trail Mix	0	3	6	9	12	15
Ordered Pair	(0, 0)	(2, 3)	(4, 6)	(6, 9)	(8, 12)	(10, 15)

$1\frac{1}{2}$ is the same as $\frac{3}{2}$.

▷ **I'll look at the ordered pairs** to see how the numbers are related. It looks like each second number is $1\frac{1}{2}$ times the first number.

$2 \times \frac{3}{2} = 3$ $4 \times \frac{3}{2} = 6$ $6 \times \frac{3}{2} = 9$ $8 \times \frac{3}{2} = 12$ $10 \times \frac{3}{2} = 15$

I'm right. The price of trail mix in each ordered pair is $1\frac{1}{2}$ times the price of popcorn.

Try> **Another Approach**

There are many ways to solve problems. Think about how you might solve the Intermission Snacks problem in a different way.

Intermission Snacks

Brandi is working with a theater group to plan their next production. She needs to decide what snacks to sell during intermission. Brandi lists the costs to buy or make each item. The selling price will be about 2 or 3 times the cost.

Our Costs	
Popcorn	$0.75
Trail Mix	$1.25
Hot Dog	$1.50
Sandwich	$2.00
Small Pizza	$2.50

Choose 2 food items. Decide on a selling price for each. Use ordered pairs to compare the amount of money they will take in by selling 0, 1, 2, 3, 4, and 5 of each item. Describe how the numbers in each ordered pair are related.

▶ **Plan It** **Answer these questions to help you start thinking about a plan.**

A. Look at the list of items. What would be a reasonable price to charge for each of them?

_____

_____

B. Will you use whole-dollar amounts as your selling prices? Why or why not?

_____

_____

▶ **Solve It** **Find a different solution for the Intermission Snacks problem. Show all your work on a separate sheet of paper.**

You may want to use the problem-solving tips to get started.

Problem-Solving Tips

- **Tools** You may want to use . . .
  - a table.
  - a graph.

- **Word Bank**

ordered pair	times	pattern
corresponding	rule	relationship
terms		

- **Sentence Starters**

  - In each ordered pair _____

  - I can compare _____

▶ **Reflect**

Use Mathematical Practices As you work through the problem, discuss these questions with a partner.

- **Reason Mathematically** How can you decide what is a reasonable selling price for an item?

- **Repeated Reasoning** What is the pattern in the prices for 0, 1, 2, 3, 4, and 5 items?

Read the problem. Write a solution on a separate sheet of paper. Remember, there can be lots of ways to solve a problem!

Printing Costs

Brandi is checking prices for printing programs for the play. The program will be printed as a booklet. Here is information from a printer's website.

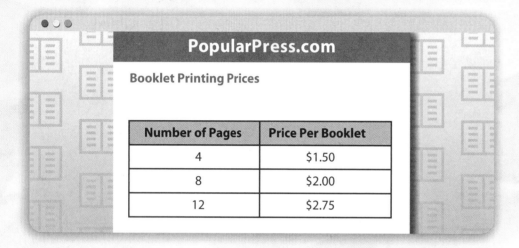

PopularPress.com

Booklet Printing Prices

Number of Pages	Price Per Booklet
4	$1.50
8	$2.00
12	$2.75

Brandi is not sure how many pages to have in the program. She also needs to know how many programs to print. Her decision will be partly based on price.

What will it cost to print different numbers of booklets with different numbers of pages?

▶ Plan It and Solve It Find a solution to the Printing Costs problem.

Compare the costs to print booklets with different numbers of pages.

- Choose two different size booklets.
- Find the cost of printing 1, 2, 3, 4, and 5 booklets with these number of pages.
- Make a graph to compare the costs.
- What is the relationship between the two numbers in each ordered pair? Write a statement to describe this relationship.

Problem-Solving Tips

- **Questions**
  - What will you use as a scale on your graph?
  - Look at the numbers in each ordered pair. What operation can you use to describe the relationship between these numbers?

- **Word Bank**

ordered pair	patterns	table
corresponding	graph	coordinates
terms		

Problem-Solving Checklist

Make sure that you . . .
- ☐ tell what you know.
- ☐ tell what you need to do.
- ☐ show all your work.
- ☐ show that the solution works.

▶ Reflect

Use Mathematical Practices As you work through the problem, discuss these questions with a partner.

- **Reason Mathematically** When you describe the relationship between corresponding terms, how do you know what operation to use?

- **Make Sense of Problems** How can the information in the problem help you choose the number of pages to use?

Persevere ⟩ **On Your Own**

Read the problems. Write a solution on a separate sheet of paper.
Remember, there are many different ways to solve a problem.

Snack Discounts

Brandi does not want to have much leftover food when the play is over.
She will check what is left about halfway through the intermission. If there
is a lot of food left, Brandi will offer a discount.

Here are two discounts Brandi is considering.

- Pay $\frac{1}{2}$ of the total price if you buy two items.

- Pay $\frac{1}{4}$ of the total price if you buy four items.

Here is Brandi's regular price list.

Price List	
Popcorn	$2
Trail Mix	$3
Hot Dog	$4
Sandwich	$6
Small Pizza	$8

How much will it cost to buy different food items with the discounts?

▶ **Solve It** Help Brandi get an idea of what customers will pay for food
with the discounts.

- Choose two different combinations of items for each discount.
- Write an expression that can be used to find the total costs.
- Evaluate the expressions and show the total cost for each combination.

▶ **Reflect**

Use Mathematical Practices After you complete the task, choose one
of these questions to discuss with a partner.

- **Reason with Numbers** What do the numbers in your expressions mean
  in the context of the problem?

- **Repeated Reasoning** How did you calculate the fraction of a price? Explain.

Play Programs

Now Brandi is considering the size of the program.

> **Printing Costs**
> - $1.50 for each 4-page booklet
> - $2.00 for each 8-page booklet

Brandi will double the printing cost to find the *selling price* of a program. The money she makes selling programs will be used to pay the printing costs. The money she has left is her *profit*.

Brandi needs to decide whether to make 4-page or 8-page programs. She thinks that she can sell more programs at a lower price. But she thinks she might make more profit with higher-price programs. Here are Brandi's sales estimates.

> - I can sell 280 to 300 of the 4-page programs.
> - I can sell 250 to 280 of the 8-page programs.

About how much profit might Brandi make selling programs? How many pages should the programs be?

▶ **Solve It** Help Brandi decide whether to make 4-page or 8-page programs.

- Choose a number of 4-page programs and a number of 8-page programs from Brandi's sales estimates.
- Use these numbers to write and evaluate expressions that show how much profit Brandi will make after paying for the programs to be printed.
- Tell which page length Brandi should use and support your recommendation.

▶ **Reflect**

Use Mathematical Practices After you complete the task, choose one of these questions to discuss with a partner.

- **Make an Argument** How did you support your recommendation?
- **Reason Mathematically** How did you choose the number of 4-page and the number of 8-page programs?

Solve the problems.

1 Bodi and 4 friends each bought a $15 ticket to the Pro Football Hall of Fame. Bodi had a coupon for $10 off the total cost of the tickets. Which expression can be used to find the total amount paid by Bodi and his friends?

A $(5 \times 15) - 10$

B $5 \times (15 - 10)$

C $(15 - 10) \times 5$

D $(15 + 10) \times 5$

2 Zhen and Justin made two different number patterns that each started at 0. Zhen wrote terms using the rule "add 18." Justin wrote terms using the rule "add 6." What is the relationship between the two patterns?

A The terms in Zhen's pattern are 3 greater than the corresponding terms in Justin's pattern.

B The terms in Zhen's pattern are 3 less than the corresponding terms in Justin's pattern.

C The terms in Zhen's pattern are 3 times the corresponding terms in Justin's pattern.

D The terms in Zhen's pattern are $\frac{1}{3}$ times the corresponding terms in Justin's pattern.

3 Look at the equations below. Choose *True* or *False* for each equation.

a. $15 \div (1 + 4) = 19$

☐ True   ☐ False

b. $20 - (10 \times 2) = 20$

☐ True   ☐ False

c. $(5 + 1) \times (5 - 1) = 24$

☐ True   ☐ False

d. $(12 + 3) \div (10 \div 2) = 3$

☐ True   ☐ False

4 Phil created two patterns. For Pattern A, he started at 0 and used the rule "add 2." The first four terms are 0, 2, 4, and 6. For Pattern B, he started at 0 and used a rule that added the same number to each term. Each term in Pattern B is 10 times the corresponding term in Pattern A. Complete the table below.

Pattern A	Pattern B
0	0
2	_____
4	_____
6	_____

What is the rule for Pattern B?

The rule for Pattern B is _____.

5 Nydia is learning how to evaluate expressions in math class.

Part A If Nydia correctly evaluates $4 \times (6 + 8)$, what value will she get?

Show your work.

Solution _____

Part B If the expression is written as $4 \times 6 + 8$, is the value the same? If not, what is this value?

Show your work.

6 Asim is writing expressions for math class.

Part A What mathematical expression could Asim write for "subtract 13 from the product of 4 and 7"?

Part B Compare the expression you wrote in Part A with the expression $5 \times (4 \times 7 - 13)$.

Performance Task

Answer the questions and show all your work on separate paper.

Your friend Sophie has asked you to check her math homework. She sends you a text message with the expressions she evaluated and the values she found. Unfortunately, she didn't include any parentheses in her message.

Copy each equation below. If the equation is true as written, write a check mark (✓) next to it. If the equation is not true, insert parentheses to make the equation true.

<table>
<tr><td>$6 + 5 \times 3 - 1 = 32$</td><td>$12 \div 2 + 4 \times 5 = 10$</td><td>$15 - 3 + 4 \times 2 = 20$</td></tr>
<tr><td>$6 + 5 \times 3 - 1 = 16$</td><td>$12 \div 2 + 4 \times 5 = 26$</td><td>$15 - 3 + 4 \times 2 = 1$</td></tr>
</table>

Then write a message to Sophie explaining why she needed to include the parentheses in order for you to check her homework.

Checklist

Did you . . .

☐ check your calculations?

☐ use order of operations?

☐ use complete sentences?

▶ Reflect

Use Mathematical Practices After you complete the task, choose one of the following questions to answer.

- **Be Precise** How did you decide where to insert the parentheses in each equation?

- **Use Structure** Consider the expression $6 + 7 \times 5 - 2$. Would you rewrite it as $6 + (7 \times 5) - 2$? Why or why not?

Unit 4
Measurement and Data

Let's learn about finding volume using different units of measurement.

Real-World Connection You can talk about the same measurement in different ways. You might say that 52 buckets of sand will fill your backyard sandbox. The clerk at the hardware store where you bought the sand might say the sandbox needs 24 cubic feet of sand. If it's summertime, you could fill your sandbox with water instead of sand. Then you might say that it will hold about 180 gallons of water. All of these different measurements are ways to talk about the volume of the sandbox.

In This Unit You will find the volume of different kinds of figures using different units of measurement. You will use what you know about multiplication to find the volume of figures using a formula. You will also solve word problems involving different units of measurement and create line plots using measurement data and then interpret the data.

✔ Self Check

Before starting this unit, check off the skills you know below. As you complete each lesson, see how many more skills you can check off!

I can:	Before this unit	After this unit
convert from one measurement unit to another, for example: 4 feet = 48 inches.	☐	☐
make a line plot of data represented as fractions of measurements.	☐	☐
find volume of a solid figure by counting unit cubes.	☐	☐
find volume by using a formula.	☐	☐
find volume of composite figures.	☐	☐

Lesson 21 👥 Introduction
Convert Measurement Units

ⓒ Use What You Know

You have worked with measurement units in earlier grades. Now you will convert between different units in the same measurement system.

Is the number of cups in 5 gallons greater than or less than the number of gallons?

1 gallon

1 cup

a. Circle the greater amount in each row:

1 gallon   or   1 cup

2 gallons   or   2 cups

5 gallons   or   5 cups

b. If you pour 5 gallons of water into 1-cup containers, would you need more than or fewer than 5 containers?

_____

c. Is the number of cups in 5 gallons greater than or less than the number of gallons?

_____

You measure for many different reasons. You might measure to find how long or tall something is, how much liquid something holds, or how much something weighs.

You can choose different units when you measure. Think about your height. You could measure your height in inches or feet. Your height does not change if you are measured in inches instead of feet. It is just recorded using different units.

Look at the picture at the right. **1 gallon = 16 cups**

The same amount of liquid could also be measured in quarts. Quarts are smaller than gallons.

   1 gallon = 4 quarts

Quarts are larger than cups. **1 quart = 4 cups**

1 gallon

4 quarts	16 cups
3 quarts	12 cups
2 quarts	8 cups
1 quart	4 cups

1 gallon   1 quart

1 cup

Imagine filling the 1-gallon container using cups or quarts. You would need to fill the quart container 4 times to have enough liquid to fill the gallon container. You would need to fill the cup container 16 times to have enough liquid to fill the gallon container.

▶ Reflect

1 Describe a real-world object that can be measured using two different units. Which unit would you need more of to measure the object?

_____

_____

_____

Learn About ▷ Converting Measurements Using Multiplication

Read the problem below. Then explore different ways to convert measurement units.

> How many meters are in 3.5 kilometers?

▶ **Model It** **You can use a table to help understand the problem.**

The table below shows the relationship between meters and kilometers.

kilometers	1	2	3	4	5	6
meters	1,000	2,000	3,000	4,000	5,000	6,000

▶ **Solve It** **Use the information from the table to understand how to solve the problem.**

The pattern in the table shows that the number of meters is always 1,000 times the number of kilometers.

kilometers	1	2	3	3.5	4	5	6
meters	1,000	2,000	3,000		4,000	5,000	6,000

To find the number of meters in 3.5 kilometers, multiply 3.5 by 1,000.

Connect It Now you will solve the problem from the previous page using unit conversions.

2 Which is the smaller unit, meters or kilometers? _____

How do you know? _____

_____

3 What operation do you use to convert from a larger measurement unit to a smaller measurement unit? _____

4 3.5 kilometers = _____ meters

Write your answer in the table on the previous page.

5 Use what you learned about the relationship between meters and kilometers to complete the table below.

kilometers	0.8	1	1.85	2	2.03	3
meters		1,000		2,000		3,000

6 How many meters are in *k* kilometers? _____

7 There are 3 feet in 1 yard. Explain how you decide whether to multiply or divide by 3 if you need to convert yards to feet. _____

_____

_____

_____

Try It Use what you just learned about converting measurement units to solve these problems. Show your work on a separate sheet of paper.

8 There are 16 ounces in 1 pound. How many ounces are in $10\frac{1}{2}$ pounds? _____

9 There are 10 millimeters in 1 centimeter. How many millimeters are in 9.25 centimeters? _____

Learn About ▸ **Converting Measurements Using Division**

Read the problem below. Then explore ways to understand how to convert measurement units.

> How many quarts are equivalent to 6 cups?

▶ **Model It** **You can use a table to help understand the problem.**

The table below shows the relationship between cups and quarts.

quarts	1	2	3	4	5	6
cups	4	8	12	16	20	24

▶ **Solve It** **Use the information from the table to understand how to solve the problem.**

The pattern in the table shows that there are 4 cups in every quart.

quarts	1		2	3	4	5	6
cups	4	6	8	12	16	20	24

To find the number of quarts equivalent to 6 cups, divide by 4.

Connect It Now you will solve the problem from the previous page using unit conversions.

10 Which is a smaller unit, quarts or cups? _____

How do you know? _____

_____

11 What operation do you use to convert from a smaller measurement unit to a larger measurement unit? _____

12 6 cups = _____ quarts

Write your answer in the table on the previous page. Explain your reasoning.

_____

_____

13 Use what you learned about the relationship between cups and quarts to complete the table below.

quarts		1		2		3		4
cups	2	4	5	8	9	12	15	16

14 One gallon is equivalent to 8 pints. Describe how to convert from pints to gallons. Explain your reasoning. _____

_____

_____

Try It Use what you just learned about converting measurement units to solve these problems. Show your work on a separate sheet of paper.

15 There are 1,000 milliliters in 1 liter. How many liters are in 100 milliliters? _____

16 One yard is equivalent to 3 feet. How many yards are equivalent to 25 feet? _____

Practice ▶ Converting Measurement Units

Study the example below. Then solve problems 17–19.

Example

There are 12 inches in 1 foot. Write 75 inches in feet and inches.

Look at how you could explain your work using conversions.

Feet are larger than inches, so the number of feet will be less than the number of inches. Divide.

There are 12 inches in 1 foot: $75 \div 12 = \frac{75}{12} = 6\frac{3}{12}$.

The whole number, 6, is the number of feet and the fraction, $\frac{3}{12}$, is $\frac{3}{12}$ foot. $\frac{1}{12}$ foot is 1 inch, so $\frac{3}{12}$ foot is 3 inches.

75 inches = 6 feet, 3 inches

Solution _6 feet, 3 inches_

The student used division because inches are a smaller unit than feet!

 Pair/Share
How can you check your answer?

---

17 How many quarts are there in $10\frac{1}{2}$ gallons? (4 quarts = 1 gallon)

Show your work.

How many quarts are in $\frac{1}{2}$ gallon?

Pair/Share
Draw a picture or make a table to support your answer.

Solution _____

18 One kilogram is equivalent to 1,000 grams. How many kilograms are equivalent to 450 grams?

Show your work.

Will the number of kilograms be greater or less than 450?

Pair/Share

Did you and your partner solve the problem the same way?

Solution _____

---

19 There are 1,000 millimeters in 1 meter. How many millimeters are in 118 meters? Circle the letter of the correct answer.

A 0.0118 millimeter

B 0.118 millimeter

C 118,000 millimeters

D 1,180,000 millimeters

Emily chose **B** as the correct answer. How did she get that answer?

Which is a larger unit, millimeters or meters?

_____

_____

_____

Pair/Share

Does Emily's answer make sense?

Practice ▶ **Converting Measurement Units**

Solve the problems.

1 How many grams are equivalent to 75 kilograms?

   A 0.0075 gram

   B 0.075 gram

   C 75,000 grams

   D 750,000 grams

2 How many yards and feet are equivalent to 10,000 feet?

   A 3,333 yards, 0 feet

   B 3,333 yards, 1 foot

   C 277 yards, 28 feet

   D 30,000 yards, 0 feet

3 Write each measurement below in the table under an equivalent measure. Some of the measurements may not have an equivalent measure.

$\frac{1}{2}$ quart   4 pints   16 cups $\frac{1}{4}$ gallon   8 pints

1 gallon	1 quart	1 pint

4 Five measurements are shown below. Write one of the measurements on each of the lines to create two true equations.

300 millimeters   30 meters   3,000 meters   3 kilometers   3,000 centimeters

_____ = _____

_____ = _____

5 How many pints are equivalent to 3 gallons?

Show your work.

Answer _____ pints

6 Complete each conversion below.

Show your work.

a. 3 feet + 7 inches = _____ inches

b. 2 gallons − 5 quarts = _____ quarts

c. 5 pounds − 38 ounces = _____ ounces

d. 60 centimeters + 4 meters = _____ centimeters

e. 2,000 meters + 5,000 meters = _____ kilometers

f. 1 liter − 150 milliliters = _____ milliliters

Units of Length
1 foot = 12 inches
1 yard = 3 feet
1 mile = 5,280 feet
1 meter = 100 centimeters
1 meter = 1,000 millimeters
1 kilometer = 1,000 meters

Units of Capacity
1 quart = 2 pints
1 quart = 4 cups
1 gallon = 4 quarts
1 liter = 1,000 milliliters

Units of Mass
1 kilogram = 1,000 grams

Units of Weight
1 pound = 16 ounces

✓ **Self Check** **Go back and see what you can check off on the Self Check on page 211.**

↻ Use What You Know

In Lesson 21, you converted between different units of measure. In this lesson, you will convert measurement units to solve real-world problems.

Ray finds a log that is 90 inches long. How long is the log in yards and inches?

(1 yard = 3 feet = 36 inches)

⊢———————————— 90 inches ————————————⊣

a. The length of the log is given in what unit? _____

b. The problem asks to find the length of the log in what units? _____

c. Circle the larger unit below.

      yard   inch

d. To convert yards to inches, what operation do you use? _____

    To convert inches to yards, what operation do you use? _____

e. 1 yard is equivalent to 3 feet or _____ inches.

f. Explain how to express 90 inches in yards and inches.

_____

_____

_____

_____

▷▷ Find Out More

When you convert from one unit of measure to another, you need to know the relationship between the two units.

90 inches

2 yards 18 inches

Think about the log. Instead of giving the length in yards, you could give the length in feet.

- To change yards to feet, you need to know that there are 3 feet in 1 yard. Because feet are smaller than yards, you will have more feet than yards.

- To change feet to inches, you need to know that there are 12 inches in 1 foot. Because feet are larger than inches, you will have fewer feet than inches.

A yardstick is shown below. Look at the relative sizes of 1 yard, 1 foot, and 1 inch.

Yardstick on this page is not life-sized.

▶ Reflect

1 Describe how you know whether to multiply or divide when converting one unit of measure to another.

_____

_____

_____

_____

_____

Learn About ▶ **Converting Units Using Equations**

Read the problem below. Then explore different ways to understand how to convert the units to solve the problem.

> Corrina is making punch for a family reunion. Her recipe calls for $2\frac{1}{2}$ cups of lemonade per batch. She plans to make 20 batches of punch for the reunion. How many gallons of lemonade does she need?

▶ **Picture It** **You can use a picture to understand the relationship between cups and gallons.**

1 gallon

1 cup

1 gallon = 16 cups

▶ **Model It** **You can write an equation to find how many cups of lemonade Corrina needs.**

Corrina needs to make 20 batches of punch. You need to multiply 20 by the number of cups Corrina needs for 1 batch.

$$20 \times 2\frac{1}{2} = 20 \times \left(2 + \frac{1}{2}\right)$$
$$= 20 \times 2 + 20 \times \frac{1}{2}$$
$$= 40 + 10$$
$$= 50$$

Corrina needs 50 cups of lemonade.

Connect It Now you will solve the problem from the previous page by converting units.

2 Why do you need to convert units of measure to solve the problem?

_____

_____

_____

3 What operation do you use to convert 50 cups to gallons? Explain.

_____

_____

4 Find how many full gallons of lemonade Corrina needs. Will there be any cups left over?

_____

5 If Corrina could only buy whole gallons of lemonade at the store, how many gallons would she need to buy? _____

Explain your reasoning. _____

_____

_____

6 What if lemonade is only sold in quarts? How could you find the number of quarts Corrina would need? (1 quart = 4 cups) _____

_____

_____

Try It Use what you just learned about converting units of measure to solve this problem. Show your work on a separate sheet of paper.

7 The pet store salesman told Evan to feed his dog 8 ounces of food per day. At that store, dog food is sold by the pound. How many pounds of food does Evan need to buy to feed his dog for 2 weeks? (16 ounces = 1 pound) _____

Learn About ▸ **Solving Word Problems Involving Conversions**

Read the problem below. Then explore different ways to understand how to convert the units to solve the problem.

> Heather and Diego measured worms in their class compost bin. Heather measured a 3.5-centimeter worm and Diego measured a 28-millimeter worm. Who measured the longer worm?

▸ **Picture It** **You can use a picture to help understand the relationship between centimeters and millimeters.**

There are 10 millimeters in each centimeter.

▸ **Model It** **You can write equations to convert centimeters to millimeters or millimeters to centimeters.**

To compare the lengths, both measurements need to be in the same unit.

Convert centimeters to millimeters:

There are 10 millimeters in each centimeter.

$$3.5 \times 10 = 35$$

3.5 centimeters is 35 millimeters.

Convert millimeters to centimeters:

There are 10 millimeters in each centimeter.

$$28 \div 10 = 2.8$$

28 millimeters is 2.8 centimeters.

Connect It Now you will solve the problem from the previous page by converting units.

8 Why do you need to convert one of the units of measure to solve the problem?

_____

_____

_____

9 Why do you multiply to convert centimeters to millimeters? _____

_____

_____

Why do you divide to convert millimeters to centimeters? _____

_____

_____

10 Who measured the longer worm? How do you know? _____

_____

_____

11 If a third student measured a worm in centimeters, how could you figure out which of the three students measured the longest worm? _____

_____

_____

_____

Try It Use what you just learned about converting units of measure to solve this problem. Show your work on a separate sheet of paper.

12 A lemur at an animal park weighs 8 pounds, 3 ounces. The zookeeper records the weight of the lemur in ounces. What will the zookeeper write for the weight of the lemur? (1 pound = 16 ounces) _____

Practice ▶ **Solving Word Problems Involving Conversions**

Study the example below. Then solve problems 13–15.

Example

Pierre is 53 inches tall. What is his height in feet and inches?

Look at how you could explain your work.

Feet are longer than inches, so there are fewer feet than inches. You need to divide.

There are 12 inches in 1 foot, so divide 53 by 12.

$53 \div 12$ is 4 with a remainder of 5.

53 inches = 4 feet, 5 inches

Solution _4 feet, 5 inches_____

The student used the relationship between feet and inches to solve the problem.

Pair/Share
What is 53 inches in yards, feet, and inches?

---

13 Venell put together a model train with 25 train cars. Each train car is 80 millimeters long. How many meters long is Venell's model train if there are no gaps between the cars? (1 meter = 1,000 millimeters)

Show your work.

Which is the larger unit, meters or millimeters?

Pair/Share
There are 100 centimeters in 1 meter. How long is the train in centimeters?

Solution _____

14 Orla bought a 1-quart container of buttermilk to make pancakes. Her recipe uses $\frac{1}{2}$ cup of buttermilk for 3 pancakes. How many pancakes can Orla make? (1 quart = 4 cups)

Show your work.

Solution _____

15 Bennett is getting in shape for football season. He runs 400 yards 3 times each day for 5 days. Which shows the correct way to find the number of miles Bennett will run in 5 days? Circle the letter of the correct answer. (1 mile = 1,760 yards)

A $400 \times 3 \times 5 \times 1{,}760$

B $400 \div (3 \times 5) \div 1{,}760$

C $400 \times (3 + 5) \div 1{,}760$

D $400 \times 3 \times 5 \div 1{,}760$

Jory chose **A** as the correct answer. How did he get that answer?

_____

_____

_____

Practice ▶ **Solving Word Problems Involving Conversions**

Solve the problems.

1 A football field is marked every 5 yards. Garrett ran from the first mark to the eleventh mark. Which shows a correct expression to find the number of feet Garrett ran?

> 1 yard = 3 feet

A 10 × 5 ÷ 3

B 10 ÷ 5 ÷ 3

C 10 × 5 × 3

D 5 × 3

2 Mr. Wayne's class collected empty soda cans for a recycling project. Each of the 20 students had to collect 40 cans. Each can has a mass of 15 grams. How many kilograms of cans did the class collect to recycle?

> 1 kilogram = 1,000 grams

A 0.6 kilogram

B 12 kilograms

C 12,000 kilograms

D 12,000,000 kilograms

3 Susan is stacking boxes on a shelf. Each box is shaped like a rectangular prism and has a length of 2 feet, a width of 15 inches, and a height of 3 inches, as shown below.

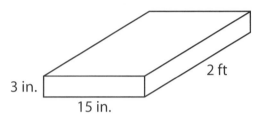

Susan will stack the boxes on top of each other, as shown in the diagram below. The space above the shelf is $1\frac{1}{2}$ yards high.

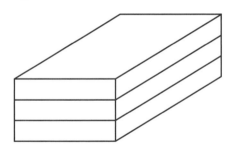

What is the greatest number of boxes that Susan can stack on the shelf?

_____ boxes

4 The Russell family is keeping track of the milk they drink each week.

- The first week they drank 2 gallons, 1 quart, and 1 cup of milk.

- The second week they drank 3 gallons of milk.

How many more cups of milk did they drink the second week than the first? _____ cups

1 gallon = 4 quarts = 16 cups

5 Lana's family entered a 5-kilometer race.

1 kilometer = 1,000 meters

Part A Lana's dad said his average step length is about 1 meter. About how many steps will he need to take to finish the race?

Show your work.

Answer About _____ steps

Part B Lana's average step length is about 0.5 meter. How many steps will she need to take to finish the race?

Show your work.

Answer About _____ steps

 Self Check **Go back and see what you can check off on the Self Check on page 211.**

⌾ Use What You Know

You have created and used line plots before. Now you will create line plots and use them to answer more complex questions about data. Take a look at this problem.

Tomatoes come in different sizes and types. Mrs. May's class weighed several different tomatoes to the nearest $\frac{1}{8}$ pound. The results are shown in the line plot below. Use the line plot to describe how the weights varied.

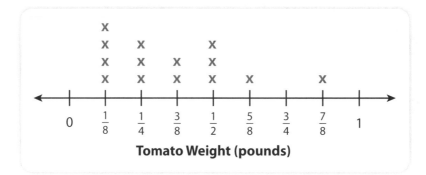

Tomato Weight (pounds)

a. The greatest number of tomatoes weigh _____ .

b. Which best describes how the weights are spread out? Circle the best description.

    clustered between   clustered between   spread out
       0 lb and $\frac{1}{2}$ lb $\frac{1}{2}$ lb and 1 lb   between 0 lb and 1 1b

c. Are most of the tomatoes on the heavier or lighter end of the scale? _____

d. Are there any tomatoes whose weight is very different from the rest?

    If so, what does it weigh? _____

e. What is the difference between the weights of the heaviest and lightest tomato?

    _____

f. How many times the weight of the lightest tomato is the heaviest tomato?

    _____

▶▶ Find Out More

Plotting data on a line plot helps you get a "picture" of what the data look like and how the data are spread out. Each X represents one piece of data. So the taller stacks of Xs mean more data with the same value.

You can use the *Tomato Weight* line plot to talk about the distribution of tomato weights. **Distribution** is how spread out or how clustered the data are.

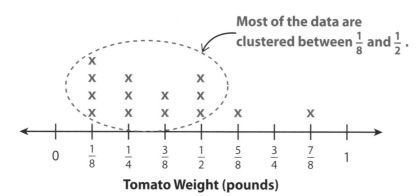

Most of the data are clustered between $\frac{1}{8}$ and $\frac{1}{2}$.

Tomato Weight (pounds)

You can also use operations with data values to come up with ways to describe the data. For example:

- Subtract $\frac{7}{8} - \frac{1}{8}$ to find the difference between the weights of the heaviest and lightest tomato. The difference tells how much the weights vary.

- Divide $\frac{7}{8} \div \frac{1}{8}$ to find that the heaviest tomato is 7 times heavier than the lightest tomato. This gives a comparison between the least and greatest data value.

▶ Reflect

1 Suppose you have one more tomato with a weight of $\frac{3}{4}$ pound. Would that change how much the weights vary? Explain.

_____

_____

_____

_____

Learn About ▷ **Making a Line Plot**

Read the problem below. Then explore different ways to understand how to make a line plot.

> Kiera bought a bag of stickers to decorate her scrapbook pages. She sorted the stickers by width. She counted the stickers and found 18 stickers that are $\frac{1}{4}$ inch wide, 11 stickers that are $\frac{1}{2}$ inch wide, and 14 stickers that are $\frac{1}{8}$ inch wide. Kiera wants to see the distribution of the widths so she can plan how to use the stickers. Make a line plot of the data.

▶ **Model It** **You can use a table to understand the data given in the problem.**

List the number of stickers in a table from least width to greatest width.

Sticker Width (in inches)	Number of Stickers
$\frac{1}{8}$	14
$\frac{1}{4}$	18
$\frac{1}{2}$	11

▶ **Model It** **Use the table to list what you know and to plan how to make the line plot.**

- The fractions are in eighths, fourths, and halves.

- The least fraction is $\frac{1}{8}$. The greatest fraction is $\frac{1}{2}$.

- Label the line plot in eighths: $0, \frac{1}{8}, \frac{1}{4}, \frac{3}{8}, \frac{1}{2}$.

- The least number of stickers is 11.

- The greatest number of stickers is 18.

Connect It Now you will make the line plot for the problem on the previous page.

2 What scale is used for the line plot? Explain.

_____

_____

3 How many Xs will you draw above each width?

$\frac{1}{8}$ in. _____ $\frac{1}{4}$ in. _____ $\frac{3}{8}$ in. _____ $\frac{1}{2}$ in. _____

4 Use the number line at the right to make a line plot of the sticker widths.

5 Based on how the data are distributed, what is one conclusion you can make about Kiera's stickers?

_____

_____

6 How do you use a line plot to show the distribution of measurement data? _____

_____

_____

Sticker Width (inches)

_____

Try It Use what you just learned about creating line plots to solve this problem. Show your work on a separate sheet of paper.

7 At a health fair, Shawn recorded the number of cups of sugar per gallon for several different sports drinks and sodas. Make a line plot of the data.

$1\frac{5}{8}, 3\frac{1}{4}, 1\frac{3}{4}, 2\frac{7}{8}, 1\frac{3}{4}, 3\frac{1}{4}, 1\frac{5}{8}, 2\frac{3}{8}, 1, 1\frac{3}{4}$

Learn About Solving Problems Using Data in a Line Plot

Read the problem below. Then explore different ways to understand how to solve the problem using the data from a line plot.

Look at the line plot of sticker widths that you made on the previous page. Kiera wants to make a 5-inch wide row of stickers under a photo. She wants to use the same stickers for the whole row. How many of which sticker width can she use?

▶ **Picture It** You can use a picture to help understand the data in the problem.

Kiera has 14 stickers that are $\frac{1}{8}$-inch wide:

1 in. $1\frac{6}{8}$ in.

Kiera has 18 stickers that are $\frac{1}{4}$-inch wide:

1 in.   2 in.   3 in.   4 in. $4\frac{2}{4}$ in.

Kiera has 11 stickers that are $\frac{1}{2}$-inch wide:

1 in.   2 in.   3 in.   4 in.   5 in. $5\frac{1}{2}$ in.

▶ **Model It** You can use a model to help understand the data in the problem.

Line up all the stickers of each width above a ruler.

$\frac{1}{8}$ inch

$\frac{1}{4}$ inch

$\frac{1}{2}$ inch

Connect It Now you will solve the problem from the previous page using the line plot.

8 How wide is the row Kiera can make with the $\frac{1}{8}$-inch stickers? _____

9 Can she make a 5-inch row with the $\frac{1}{4}$-inch stickers? Explain. _____

10 Can she make a 5-inch row with the $\frac{1}{2}$-inch stickers? Explain. _____

11 Which sticker width does Kiera need to use to make a 5-inch row? _____
How many of these stickers does she need? Explain.

_____

_____

12 How did the line plot help you to answer problem 11? _____

_____

_____

_____

_____

13 Give an example of another question that can be answered using the line plot.
Include the answer. _____

_____

_____

Try It Use what you just learned about using data in line plots to solve these problems. Show your work on a separate sheet of paper.

Look at the line plot you made about the amount of sugar in different drinks in problem 7.

14 How many times the amount of sugar in one gallon of the least sugary drink is in one gallon of the most sugary drink? _____

15 Suppose you take all of the sugar in one gallon of each of the three most sugary drinks and split it equally among them. How many cups of sugar will be in each gallon? _____

Practice ▶ **Making Line Plots and Interpreting Data**

Study the example below. Then solve problems 16–18.

Example

For a cookout, Mel made burgers of different weights. She recorded how many burgers of each weight she made. The line plot shows her data. How many pounds of meat did she use to make all the burgers?

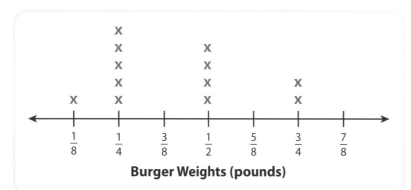

Burger Weights (pounds)

The student multiplied the number of burgers of each weight by the weight, then added the amounts to get the total.

Look at how you could use the data in the line plot.

One $\frac{1}{8}$-lb burger: $\frac{1}{8}$ Five $\frac{1}{4}$-lb burgers: $5 \times \frac{1}{4} = 1\frac{1}{4}$

Four $\frac{1}{2}$-lb burgers: $4 \times \frac{1}{2} = 2$ Two $\frac{3}{4}$-lb burgers: $2 \times \frac{3}{4} = 1\frac{1}{2}$

Total: $\frac{1}{8} + 1\frac{1}{4} + 2 + 1\frac{1}{2} = 4\frac{7}{8}$

Solution ___$4\frac{7}{8}$ pounds___

💬 **Pair/Share**
Check the student's answer using addition instead of multiplication.

---

16 Look at the *Burger Weight* line plot above.

One friend at the cookout asked for a triple quarter-pound burger. Where on the number line could that burger be represented?

Show your work.

What would two $\frac{1}{4}$-pound burgers put together be?

💬 **Pair/Share**
Draw a picture to show a triple quarter-pound burger.

Solution _____

17 A veterinarian's scale weighs animals to the nearest one eighth pound. The list below shows the weights, in pounds, of the last 14 dogs that the veterinarian saw.

$15\frac{1}{8}$, 19, $17\frac{1}{2}$, $15\frac{1}{8}$, $16\frac{1}{4}$, $17\frac{1}{2}$, $17\frac{1}{2}$, $18\frac{1}{4}$, $16\frac{5}{8}$, $14\frac{1}{4}$, 19, $17\frac{3}{8}$, $17\frac{1}{8}$, 18

Create a line plot to show the data.

How should the line plot's scale be labeled to show these data?

Pair/Share

How is your line plot the same as your partner's? How is it different?

18 Look at your line plot for problem 17. Which statement about the data is true? Circle the letter of the correct answer.

A The heaviest dog weighed about 5 times as much as the lightest dog.

B Most of the dogs weighed more than 17 pounds.

C All of the dogs weighed between 15 and 19 pounds.

D At most, only 2 dogs weighed the same amount.

Michelle chose **A** as the correct answer. How did she get that answer?

_____

_____

_____

_____

Read each statement carefully and check it against the data to see if it is true.

Pair/Share

Does Michelle's answer make sense?

Practice ▶ **Making Line Plots and Interpreting Data**

Solve the problems.

1 Juan drives a race car. The race tracks vary in length. To prepare for the racing season, he recorded the lengths, in miles, of the tracks in the list shown below. Juan would like to see the distribution of the track lengths. Which line plot correctly shows the track data?

$$\frac{1}{4}, \frac{1}{2}, \frac{3}{8}, \frac{1}{2}, \frac{1}{4}, \frac{1}{2}, 1, 1\frac{1}{4}, \frac{3}{4}, \frac{1}{2}, \frac{7}{8}, \frac{1}{2}, \frac{3}{4}$$

A

C

B

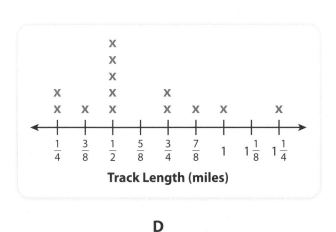

D

2 Look at the data in problem 1. Choose *True* or *False* for each statement.

a. Most of the tracks are more than 1 mile long.   ☐ True   ☐ False

b. The most common track length is $\frac{1}{4}$ mile.   ☐ True   ☐ False

c. None of the tracks are $\frac{5}{8}$ mile long.   ☐ True   ☐ False

d. The longest track is 5 times as long as the shortest track.   ☐ True   ☐ False

3 Look at the data in problem 1. What is the total length of all the tracks that are longer than $\frac{5}{8}$ mile? _____ miles

4 Sara owns Sara's Hardware. She made the line plot below to compare the fuel capacity of several types of yard trimmers.

Tank Capacity of Yard Trimmers

Fuel Capacity (cups)

Part A What is the most common fuel capacity of the trimmers Sara sells?

Answer _____ cups

Part B The tanks of all of Sara's yard trimmers are empty. How much fuel does Sara need to fill the tanks of all the trimmers?

Show your work.

Answer _____ cups

✔ Self Check Go back and see what you can check off on the Self Check on page 211.

Think It Through

What does volume measure?

The **volume** of a three-dimensional figure is the amount of space contained inside the figure. Volume is measured by the number of cubic units that can be packed into a figure.

A cube with edge lengths of 1 unit is called a unit cube. A unit cube has 1 **cubic unit** of volume.

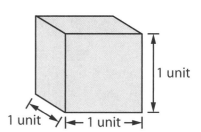

Think How is volume different from area?

Area is the number of *square units* needed to *cover* a *plane figure*. Volume is the number of *cubic units* needed to *fill* a *solid figure*.

A **plane figure** is a two-dimensional figure. To find the area of a plane figure, you need measurements in two dimensions: length and width. One way you can find the area of a plane figure is by covering it in unit squares, without gaps or overlap. A unit square has an area of 1 square unit.

A **solid figure** is a three-dimensional figure. To find the volume of a solid figure, you need measurements in three dimensions: length, width, and height. One way you can find the volume of a solid figure is by packing it with unit cubes, without gaps or overlaps.

✏️ **Circle** the figures below that have volume.

Unit Square

Area = 4 square units

Unit Cube

Volume = 4 cubic units

Think When might you need to measure volume?

Suppose you need to buy a storage box to hold all of your number cubes. All of the cubes are the same size, with edges that are 1 unit long. How would you decide which storage box to buy?

One way to make sure you are buying a big enough box is to use volume. You need a storage box with a volume that will hold all of your cubes.

You know you have 24 number cubes. You can use that number and the volume of each cube to find the volume of the box you need. Then you could make sure that you buy a box big enough to hold all of the cubes.

> I need to count how many cubes are in the whole box, but I can't see all of the cubes. I can see that there are 8 cubes in 1 layer and that there are 3 of the same-size layers.
> **8 + 8 + 8** = 24

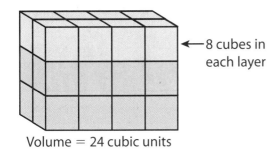

← 8 cubes in each layer

Volume = 24 cubic units

▶ Reflect

1 Explain how 9 square units and 9 cubic units are different.

_____

_____

_____

_____

_____

_____

Think About ▸ **Finding Volume with Unit Cubes**

🔍 **Let's Explore the Idea** **You can use unit cubes to build or fill a solid figure. The volume of the figure is the number of unit cubes needed to build or fill the solid figure.**

2 The measure of each edge length of a unit cube is _____ .

3 The volume of each unit cube is _____ .

Alexander stacked unit cubes to build the rectangular prism below. Use the rectangular prism to answer problems 4 and 5.

4 There are _____ unit cubes in the bottom layer and there are _____ layers. The figure has _____ unit cubes.

5 The volume of the figure is _____ cubic units.

Now try these two problems. Use the figures below to answer problems 6 and 7. Each figure was built using unit cubes.

A   B

6 What is the volume of Figure *A*? _____

7 How many of Figure *A* does it take to fill or build Figure *B*? _____
What is the volume of Figure *B*? _____

Let's Talk About It
Solve the problems below as a group.

8 Why do you use cubic units instead of square units to find the volumes of solid figures?

_____

_____

9 Candace places blocks with a volume of 1 cubic unit each into her jewelry box, as shown at the right.

How many blocks does it take to fill the jewelry box? _____

What is the volume of Candace's jewelry box? _____

1 cubic unit

10 Candace has another jewelry box that is like the box in problem 9, but taller. It holds 1 more layer of blocks. What is the volume of this second box?

_____

_____

▶ Try It Another Way
Work with your group to show the connection between the volume of the solid figure below, the number of layers in the figure, and the number of unit cubes in each layer.

11 How many unit cubes are in each layer? _____

How many layers are in the figure? _____

12 Explain how you can use multiplication to find the volume of the figure. Then find the volume.

_____

_____

Connect▶ Ideas About Volume with Unit Cubes

Talk through these problems as a class. Then write your answers below.

13 Infer Eli is stacking unit cubes in a box. He partially fills the box, pauses, and says, "The volume of this box is 18 cubic units."

Explain how Eli found the volume of the box. _____

_____

_____

14 Explain Zoe says that a box that is 1 unit wide, 2 units long, and 3 units tall has a greater volume than a box that is 2 units wide, 3 units long, and 1 unit tall. Is she correct? Explain your answer.

_____

_____

_____

_____

15 Compare Each cube in Figures *A* and *B* has a volume of 1 cubic unit. Which figure has less volume, Figure *A* or Figure *B*? Explain your answer.

_____

_____

_____

Apply > **Ideas About Volume with Unit Cubes**

16 Put It Together Use what you have learned to complete this task.

> Niles used 16 blocks, each having a volume of 1 cubic unit, to build a rectangular prism.

Part A Draw or build a model to represent the situation.

Part B Look at your model. Describe the number of layers and the number of blocks in each layer. Then describe a different rectangular prism that also has a volume of 16 cubic units.

_____

_____

_____

_____

_____

_____

⟳ Use What You Know

In Lesson 24, you learned that you can fill a solid figure with unit cubes to find its volume. Now take a look at this problem.

Carl filled the clear box shown below with unit cubes to find its volume.

2 ft   1 ft   3 ft

What is the volume of the box?

a. How many cubes are in the bottom layer of the box? _____

b. How many cubes are in each layer? _____

c. How many layers of cubes are in the box? _____

d. Should Carl use square units or cubic units to find the volume of the box? Explain.

_____

_____

_____

e. Describe how Carl can find the volume, including what unit he should use.

_____

_____

_____

_____

_____

Volume is measured in cubic units.

The size of the cubic units used to measure volume can be based on the units used to measure edge lengths. For example, the box on the previous page has edge lengths measured in feet, so its volume is most easily measured in cubic feet.

Each unit cube used to pack the box is 1 foot long, 1 foot wide, and 1 foot high.

1 ft
1 ft   1 ft   ←—— Volume = 1 cubic foot

One way to find the volume of the box is to count how many cubes fill the box. There are a total of 6 cubes in the box. Each cube has a volume of 1 cubic foot. So, the volume of the box is 6 cubic feet.

Here are two other units you might use to measure volume.

Units of Volume	cubic inch	cubic centimeter
Unit Cube	1 in. 1 in. 1 in.	1 cm 1 cm 1 cm

▶ Reflect

1 Suppose Carl's box was 4 feet high instead of 2 feet. What would be its volume? Explain your reasoning.

_____

_____

_____

_____

_____

Learn About > **Finding the Volume of a Rectangular Prism**

Read the problem below. Then explore different ways to find the volume of a rectangular prism.

Abigail used cardboard to build a rectangular prism like the one shown below.

What is the volume of the prism?

▶ **Picture It** **You can find the volume of the prism by filling it with unit cubes and counting the number of cubes.**

Use cubes that are each 1 cubic centimeter. 24 cubes fill the rectangular prism.

▶ **Model It** **You can also find the volume by counting the number of cubes in one layer and multiplying by the number of layers.**

one layer   3 layers

Use cubes that are each 1 cubic centimeter. There are 8 cubes in each layer and 3 layers.

8 cubes × 3 layers = 24 cubes

Connect It   Now you will solve the problem from the previous page by multiplying.

2 Look at the models on the previous page. How could you find the number of cubes in one layer without counting the cubes? _____

_____

3 Once you know how many cubes are in one layer, what else do you need to know to find the volume? _____

4 Since there are 8 cubes in each layer, and you know there are 3 layers, what multiplication expression can you write to find the volume of the prism? _____

5 What is the volume of Abigail's rectangular prism? _____

6 Explain how you can use multiplication to find the volume of any rectangular prism.

_____

_____

_____

Try It   Use what you just learned about ways to find the volume of a rectangular prism to solve these problems. Show your work on a separate sheet of paper.

7 What is the volume of the rectangular prism below? _____

3 in.
3 in.
3 in.

8 Mr. Wong filled the figure below with 1-foot unit cubes to find its volume.

2 ft
1 ft
2 ft

What is the volume of Mr. Wong's figure? _____

Practice ▶ Finding Volume Using Unit Cubes

Study the example below. Then solve problems 9–11.

Example

Pedro has a storage box with a volume of 36 cubic feet. He knows that the box is 4 feet long and 3 feet wide. How high is the box?

Look at how you could show your work using a drawing and multiplication facts.

3 ft

4 ft

$3 \times 4 = 12$

$12 \times \square = 36$

$\square = 36 \div 12$

$\square = 3$

Solution _3 feet_

The student started by finding the number of cubes in the bottom layer.

💬 **Pair/Share**
Could you solve this problem another way?

9 A box measures 6 centimeters long, 2 centimeters wide, and 4 centimeters high. What is the volume of the box?

4 cm

2 cm

6 cm

Show your work.

How many layers of cubes will there be in the box?

💬 **Pair/Share**
Can you use multiplication to solve this problem?

Solution _____

10 Kamala made the figure below using cubes.

3 in.

2 in.

5 in.

What is the volume of Kamala's figure?

Show your work.

Solution _____

11 What is the volume of the rectangular prism below?

6 ft   1 ft

1 ft

A   6 square feet

B   6 cubic feet

C   8 square feet

D   8 cubic feet

Nam chose **D** as the correct answer. How did he get that answer?

_____

_____

_____

_____

Practice ▶ Finding Volume Using Unit Cubes

Solve the problems.

1 How many cubes are in the bottom layer of the rectangular prism below?

A 3

B 6

C 12

D 24

2 Which expressions can be used to find the volume of the rectangular prism below? Circle the letter for all that apply.

4 ft
6 ft
5 ft

A 30 × 4

B (5 + 6) × 4

C 30 + 30 + 30 + 30

D 5 + 6 + 4

E 30 + 4

3 Flora has a rectangular gift box that has a volume of 24 cubic inches. The box is 2 inches tall. What could be the length and width of the box? Select *Yes* or *No* for each length and width.

a. 11 inches long, 11 inches wide

☐ Yes   ☐ No

b. 4 inches long, 3 inches wide

☐ Yes   ☐ No

c. 2 inches long, 10 inches wide

☐ Yes   ☐ No

d. 6 inches long, 2 inches wide

☐ Yes   ☐ No

e. 1 inch long, 12 inches wide

☐ Yes   ☐ No

4 Both figures are filled with unit cubes of the same size. Which rectangular prism has the larger volume, figure *A* or figure *B*?

Show your work.

 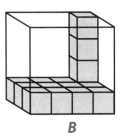

A   *B*

Answer _____ has the larger volume.

5 Mato drew the rectangular prism shown below.

4 cm

2 cm   5 cm

Part A Draw and label a different rectangular prism with the same volume as Mato's prism.

Part B Explain how you know that the volume of your prism is the same as the volume of Mato's prism.

_____

_____

_____

_____

 Self Check **Go back and see what you can check off on the Self Check on page 211.**

Use What You Know

In previous lessons, you learned how to find volume by counting unit cubes. In this lesson, you will learn how to find volume using a formula. Take a look at this problem.

Becky uses 1-inch cubes to create a model for a small paper gift bag she is making. Her model is a rectangular prism. What is the volume of Becky's model?

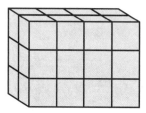

a. The model has a length of _____ inches and a width of _____ inches.

b. How many cubes are in the top layer of the model? _____

c. How can you find the number of cubes in the top layer without counting the cubes?

_____

d. How many layers of cubes does the model have? _____

e. How many cubes are in Becky's model? _____

f. Explain how you can find the volume of Becky's model without counting each cube.

_____

_____

_____

_____

Below is a picture of Becky's gift bag next to her model.

3 in.

2 in.

4 in.

Notice that the base of the bag is a rectangle **4 inches long** and **2 inches wide**. The area of the base is **8 square inches**. The height of the bag is **3 inches**.

Look at the model. There are **8 cubes** in each layer. There are **3 layers** of cubes.

$$\text{Volume} = \frac{\text{number of cubes}}{\text{in each layer}} \times \frac{\text{number}}{\text{of layers}}$$

$$8 \quad \times \quad 3$$

$$4 \times 2 \quad \times \quad 3$$

length   width   height

$$\text{Volume} = \text{length} \times \text{width} \times \text{height}$$
$$V = \ell \times w \times h$$

▶ Reflect

1 The area of the base of the gift bag is the product of the length and width of the bag. What is the volume of the bag? Explain how you can use the area of the base of the gift bag to find the volume of the bag.

_____

_____

_____

Learn About ▶ **Using a Formula to Find Volume**

Read the problem below. Then explore different ways to find the volume of a rectangular prism.

> Gareth has a rectangular pencil cup on his desk. The cup is 3 inches long, 2 inches wide, and 5 inches high. What is the volume of the pencil cup?

▶ **Picture It** **You can picture the pencil cup as a rectangular prism made up of 1-inch cubes.**

▶ **Model It** **You can draw a model of the pencil cup and label its dimensions.**

5 in.

2 in.

3 in.

Connect It Now you will solve the problem from the previous page using the picture and model of the pencil cup.

2 Explain how you can find the volume of the pencil cup using the picture. Find the volume.

_____

_____

_____

3 Explain how the area of the base of the model of the pencil cup in *Model It* relates to the prism in *Picture It*. _____

_____

_____

4 Explain how you can find the volume of the pencil cup using the model.

_____

_____

_____

5 Write two different multiplication equations you can use to find the volume of the pencil cup.

_____

6 Explain how you can use the dimensions of a rectangular prism to find its volume.

_____

_____

Try It Use what you just learned about finding volume to solve these problems. Show your work on a separate sheet of paper.

7 What is the volume of a rectangular jewelry box with a length of 8 centimeters, a width of 5 centimeters, and a height of 4 centimeters? _____

8 How much space is taken up by a book that is 12 inches long, 10 inches wide, and 1 inch tall? _____

Practice **Using the Formula for Volume**

Study the example below. Then solve problems 9–11.

Example

Coen is making a clay vase. He wants the interior of the vase to be a rectangular prism with base 3 inches long and 3 inches wide. He wants the vase to hold 45 cubic inches of water. How tall should Coen make the vase?

Look at how you could use a formula to solve the problem.

$$\text{Volume} = \ell \times w \times h$$
$$45 = 3 \times 3 \times h$$
$$45 = 9 \times h$$
$$45 \div 9 = h$$
$$5 = h$$

Solution <u>5 inches</u>

The student wrote an equation using the formula for volume. The height is the unknown.

Pair/Share
Did you and your partner solve the problem the same way?

9 Evie uses 20 square inches of cardboard for the base of a box. The box has a height of 6 inches. What is the volume of the box?

Show your work.

What does 20 square inches represent?

Pair/Share
What are some possible dimensions of the base of the box?

Solution

10 The rectangular prism shown below has a volume of 42 cubic meters. What is the length of the prism?

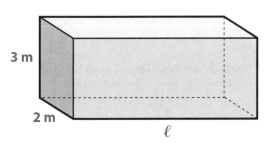

3 m

2 m

ℓ

Show your work.

Solution _____

---

11 A cube is a rectangular prism whose edge lengths are all the same. What is the volume of a cube with an edge length of 2 feet? Circle the letter of the correct answer.

A 4 cubic feet

B 6 cubic feet

C 8 cubic feet

D 12 cubic feet

Danny chose **B** as the correct answer. How did he get that answer?

_____

_____

_____

_____

Practice ▶ Using the Formula for Volume

Solve the problems.

1 A rectangular prism has a square base with side lengths of 5 centimeters and a height of 7 centimeters. What is the volume of the prism?

   A 35 cubic centimeters

   B 140 cubic centimeters

   C 175 cubic centimeters

   D 245 cubic centimeters

2 A rectangular prism has a volume of 100 cubic meters. One of the dimensions is 5 meters. Which could be the other two dimensions of the prism? Circle the letter for all that apply.

   A 1 meter, 20 meters

   B 5 meters, 10 meters

   C 10 meters, 10 meters

   D 4 meters, 5 meters

   E 20 meters, 20 meters

3 Henry evenly pours 960 cubic inches of sand into the fish tank shown below. Using the guide on the left side of the tank, shade the front of the tank to show how deep the sand is.

4 A cardboard box has a volume of 60 cubic feet. Give four different sets of measurements that could be the dimensions of the box.

Show your work.

_____ feet × _____ feet × _____ feet

_____ feet × _____ feet × _____ feet

_____ feet × _____ feet × _____ feet

_____ feet × _____ feet × _____ feet

5 The number of guppies that a fish tank can safely hold depends on its volume. A fish tank should have a volume of 576 cubic inches to safely hold 3 guppies. How many guppies can a fish tank that is 24 inches long, 12 inches wide, and 16 inches high safely hold?

Show your work.

Answer _____ guppies

 Self Check **Go back and see what you can check off on the Self Check on page 211.**

Use What You Know

You learned how to use a formula to find the volume of a rectangular prism. In this lesson, you will find the volume of a solid figure made up of more than one rectangular prism. Take a look at this problem.

What is the volume of the L-shaped solid figure below?

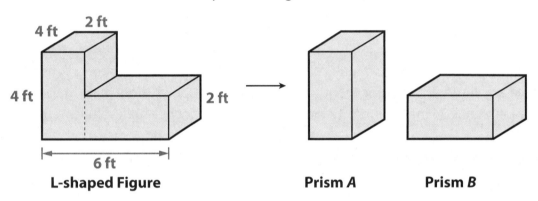

L-shaped Figure   **Prism A**   **Prism B**

a. Look at the dashed segment in the L-shaped figure. Imagine slicing the solid figure along the dashed line to make two rectangular prisms.

What would be the dimensions of Prism A? _____

What would be the dimensions of Prism B? _____

b. How could you find the volume of each rectangular prism? _____

_____

c. What is the volume of Prism A? _____

What is the volume of Prism B? _____

d. How could you find the volume of the L-shaped figure using the two prisms?

_____

e. What is the volume of the L-shaped solid figure? _____

Rectangles can be combined in different ways to create different two-dimensional shapes. You can find the areas of these shapes by breaking them apart into the rectangles that make them up. There may be more than one way to break apart these shapes.

Rectangular prisms can be combined in different ways to make solid figures. You can find the volume of these solid figures by breaking them apart into the prisms that make them up. There may be more than one way to break apart these solid figures.

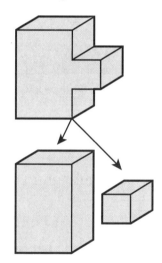

▶ Reflect

1 Circle one of the solid figures above. Explain how you could find its volume.

_____

_____

_____

_____

Learn About ▸ Breaking Apart Figures to Find Volume

Read the problem. Then explore how to find the volume of a solid figure by breaking it apart into rectangular prisms in different ways.

Bethany has a raised garden bed. The diagram shows its measurements. All of the corners are right angles. If she fills the bed to the top with soil, how many cubic feet of soil will Bethany need?

▶ **Model It** **You can break the garden bed into two rectangular prisms this way.**

One rectangular prism measures 6 feet × 4 feet × 2 feet.

The other rectangular prism measures 12 feet × 6 feet × 2 feet.

▶ **Model It** **You can also break the garden bed into two rectangular prisms in a different way.**

One rectangular prism measures 6 feet × 10 feet × 2 feet.

The other rectangular prism measures 6 feet × 6 feet × 2 feet.

Connect It Now you will solve the problem from the previous page using the formula for volume of a rectangular prism.

2 Look at the first model. How can you find the volume of each rectangular prism?

_____

3 How can you find the volume of the entire garden bed?

_____

4 What is the volume of the entire garden bed? Show your work. _____

5 Now look at the second model. Show how to find the volume of the garden bed if you break it apart this way.

6 Do you need to break apart a solid figure in a certain way to find its volume? Use the problem from the previous page to explain your reasoning.

_____

_____

Try It Use what you just learned about breaking apart solid figures to solve these problems. Show your work on a separate sheet of paper.

7 The Recreation Center has an L-shaped pool. One part of the pool is 8 meters by 6 meters. The other part is 12 meters by 6 meters. The whole pool is 4 meters deep. What is the volume of the entire pool? _____

8 What is the volume of the solid figure below? _____

2 ft
4 ft
6 ft
3 ft
8 ft

Practice ▶ **Finding the Volume of Composite Figures**

Study the example below. Then solve problems 9–11.

Example

Adam drew a model of a flowerpot. All of its edges meet at right angles. What is the volume of the flowerpot?

10 cm
30 cm
20 cm
30 cm
30 cm

The student drew a dashed segment to show how to break apart the solid figure.

Look at how you could break apart the figure into two rectangular prisms.

30 cm
30 cm
10 cm

30 cm
20 cm
20 cm

$10 \times 30 \times 30 = 9{,}000$ $20 \times 30 \times 20 = 12{,}000$

$9{,}000 + 12{,}000 = 21{,}000$

Solution <u>21,000 cubic centimeters</u>

Pair/Share
Could you break apart the solid figure in a different way?

---

9 Tia made a two-layer cake. Each layer is a rectangular prism that is 2 inches high. The base of the bottom layer is 100 square inches. The base of the top layer is 64 square inches. What is the total volume of the cake?

Show your work.

Would it help to draw a diagram to represent the problem?

Pair/Share
Can you solve the problem in a different way?

Solution _____

10 The diagram shows the dimensions of a cement walkway, where all of the sides meet at right angles. What is the total volume of cement needed to make the walkway?

After I break apart the figure, how will I find the missing measurements?

Show your work.

Pair/Share

How did you and your partner decide how to break apart the solid figure?

Solution _____

11 A candy store is building a display with two rectangular prisms. The base of each prism is a square with a edge length of 5 inches. One prism is 12 inches tall and the other is twice as tall. The two prisms are stacked so that the pieces do not overlap. What is the total volume of the display?

What is the total height of the display?

A   36 cubic inches

B   60 cubic inches

C   180 cubic inches

D   900 cubic inches

Kali chose **A** as the correct answer. How did she get that answer?

_____

_____

_____

Pair/Share

Does Kali's answer make sense?

Practice ▶ **Finding the Volume of Composite Figures**

Solve the problems.

1 A pool shaped like a rectangular prism is 40 feet long, 20 feet wide, and 4 feet deep. Attached to the side of the pool is a hot tub with $\frac{1}{4}$ the volume of the pool. What is the total volume of the pool and hot tub?

A 800 cubic feet

B 1,000 cubic feet

C 3,200 cubic feet

D 4,000 cubic feet

2 The diagram below shows the measurements of a mold used to make sandcastles. Which expression can be used to find the volume of the mold, in cubic inches? Circle the letter for all that apply.

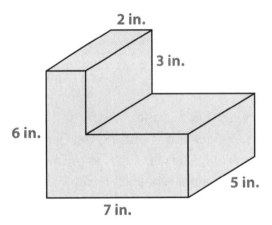

A $(2 \times 5 \times 3) + (5 \times 5 \times 3)$

B $(2 \times 5 \times 3) + (7 \times 5 \times 3)$

C $(2 \times 5 \times 6) + (5 \times 5 \times 3)$

D $(2 \times 5 \times 6) + (7 \times 5 \times 3)$

E $(2 \times 5 \times 3) + (7 \times 5 \times 6)$

3 The diagram below shows the dimensions of two identical rectangular prisms joined together.

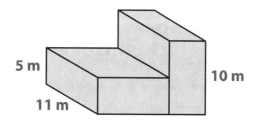

What is the combined volume of the two prisms? _____ cubic meters

4 Rami designed a small pond for a restaurant. The diagram below shows the measurements of the pond. How many cubic feet of water are needed to fill the pond?

Show your work.

Answer _____ cubic feet

 Self Check Go back and see what you can check off on the Self Check on page 211.

Unit 4
MATH IN
ACTION

👥 **Introduction**

Work with Measurement and Data

SMP1 Make
sense of problems
and persevere in
solving them.

Study an Example Problem and Solution

In this lesson, you will use what you know about measurement and data to
solve real-world problems. Look at this problem and one solution.

Salad Dressing

Sweet T needs to make salad dressing for an event. He knows that 2 gallons is
not enough and 3 gallons is too much. Sweet T finds 2 quarts of vinegar and
2 gallons of oil in the cabinet. Read the salad dressing recipe.

Salad Dressing Recipe

• Mix equal parts of water, lemon juice, and vinegar.

• Add an amount of oil equal to the other three
ingredients combined.

• Mix in your favorite herbs and spices and shake.

Sweet T wants to know how much water, lemon juice, vinegar, and oil he
needs to make the dressing. He also wants to know how much oil and
vinegar will be left over.

**Read the sample solution on the next page. Then look at the checklist
below. Find and mark parts of the solution that match the checklist.**

🖉 Problem-Solving Checklist

☐ Tell what is known.

☐ Tell what the problem
is asking.

☐ Show all your work.

☐ Show that the
solution works.

a. Circle something that is known.

b. Underline something that you need
to find.

c. Draw a box around what you do to
solve the problem.

d. Put a checkmark next to the part that
shows the solution works.

Sweet T's Solution

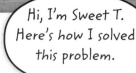

> Hi, I'm Sweet T. Here's how I solved this problem.

▷ **I know** the four different ingredients and how the amounts compare.

▷ **I have to decide** what units to use to find the amount of each ingredient and the amount left over. The information in the problem has both quarts and gallons. I think it will be easier to convert all amounts to cups.

There are 16 cups in a gallon.   There are 4 cups in a quart.
2 gallons = 2 × 16, or 32 cups   2 quarts = 2 × 4, or 8 cups
3 gallons = 3 × 16, or 48 cups

> I can also use quarts, but I might end up using cups to find leftover amounts anyway.

▷ **Now I know** that the total amount is greater than 32 cups and less than 48 cups.

▷ **One way to think about** the amounts is that half of the dressing is oil and half is a combination of water, lemon juice, and vinegar. I'll look for half of a number between 33 and 47.

▷ **I'll use 36** for the total.
$\frac{1}{2}$ × 36 = 18 so I need 18 cups of oil.

Then divide by 3 to find the other amounts.
18 ÷ 3 = 6 so I need 6 cups of each of the other ingredients.

> I multiplied 36 by $\frac{1}{2}$ but I also could have divided by 2.

▷ **I can check by adding.**
18 cups + 6 cups + 6 cups + 6 cups = 36 cups
36 > 32 and 36 < 48

▷ **Now I can write** the amount of each ingredient and find the leftovers.

Amount for dressing
18 c oil
6 c vinegar
6 c water
6 c lemon juice

Amount leftover
32 c – 18 c = 14 c leftover oil
8 c – 6 c = 2 c leftover vinegar

> I used the abbreviation for cups since I had to write it so many times!

Try ▸ Another Approach

There are many ways to solve problems. Think about how you might solve the Salad Dressing problem in a different way.

Salad Dressing

Sweet T needs to make salad dressing for an event. He knows that 2 gallons is not enough and 3 gallons is too much. Sweet T finds 2 quarts of vinegar and 2 gallons of oil in the cabinet. Read the salad dressing recipe.

> **Salad Dressing Recipe**
> - Mix equal parts of water, lemon juice, and vinegar.
> - Add an amount of oil equal to the other three ingredients combined.
> - Mix in your favorite herbs and spices and shake.

Sweet T wants to know how much water, lemon juice, vinegar, and oil he needs to make the dressing. He also wants to know how much oil and vinegar will be left over.

▶ **Plan It** **Answer these questions to help you start thinking about a plan.**

A. How could you convert the ingredients to quarts to find a solution?

_____

_____

B. What are some total amounts of dressing that you could choose? Explain.

_____

_____

Solve It Find a different solution for the Salad Dressing problem. Show all your work on a separate sheet of paper.

You may want to use the problem-solving tips to get started.

Problem-Solving Tips

- **Tools** You might want to use . . .
  - a table.
  - a bar model.

- **Word Bank**

cup	gallon	subtract
pint	convert	divide
quart	add	

- **Sentence Starters**
  - One quart is equal _____
  - The total amount _____

Problem-Solving Checklist

Make sure that you . . .

☐ tell what you know.

☐ tell what you need to do.

☐ show all your work.

☐ show that the solution works.

Reflect

Use Mathematical Practices As you work through the problem, discuss these questions with a partner.

- **Persevere** How can you use your answers to the *Plan It* questions to help choose a solution path?

- **Be Precise** Why should you label your numbers with units as you work through the solution?

Discuss ▶ **Models and Strategies**

Read the problem. Write a solution on a separate sheet of paper. Remember, there can be lots of ways to solve a problem!

Goldfish Pool

Sweet T is helping design a small goldfish pool to be built in front of his friends' bakery store.

The pool will be shaped like the diagram shown below. The two ends are the same depth. The middle section is deeper.

Pool Plans

· The total length is between 10 and 16 feet.

· The width is between 6 and 8 feet.

· The deepest part of the pool is no more than 4 feet deep.

· The total volume is 300 cubic feet or less.

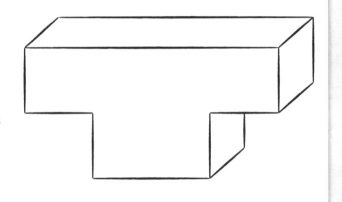

What should the dimensions of the pool be?
What will the volume of the pool be?

▶ Plan It and Solve It Find a solution to the Goldfish Pool problem.

Use the Goldfish Pool Activity Sheet.

- Fill in all the missing dimensions.
- Verify that the lengths, widths, and depths you chose meet all of the requirements in the pool plans.
- Find the volume of the pool.

Problem-Solving Tips

- **Questions**
  - How deep will the shallow section be? The deep section?
  - How can you divide the solid figure into rectangular prisms?

- **Word Bank**

rectangular prism	length	volume
solid figure	width	cubic feet

Problem-Solving Checklist

Make sure that you . . .

☐ tell what you know.

☐ tell what you need to do.

☐ show all your work.

☐ show that the solution works.

▶ Reflect

Use Mathematical Practices As you work through the problem, discuss these questions with a partner.

- **Use a Model** How can the model help you find appropriate dimensions?

- **Be Precise** What measurement units will you use when you work out the solution? Explain.

Read the problems. Write a solution on a separate sheet of paper.
Remember, there are many different ways to solve a problem.

Backyard Barbecue

Sweet T is planning a barbecue for 50 people.
There will be 2 different kinds of protein and
3 side dishes on the menu. Here are his choices,
including amounts to estimate per person.

Protein
· Choose from ground beef, chicken, steak, or salmon.
· Estimate 6 to 8 ounces per person.

Sides
· Baked beans: 2 to 3 ounces per person
· Coleslaw: 3 to 4 ounces per person
· Potato salad: 4 to 5 ounces per person
· Grilled vegetables: 3 to 4 ounces per person
· Rice: 1 to 2 ounces per person

What food and how much of each should Sweet T make?

▶ **Solve It** Suggest a menu for Sweet T.

• Choose the items for the menu.

• Tell how many pounds and ounces are needed for each dish. Explain.

▶ **Reflect**

Use Mathematical Practices After you complete the task, choose one
of these questions to discuss with a partner.

• **Make Sense of Problems** What was the first step you took to find your
solution? Why?

• **Reason Mathematically** What operations did you use to find your solution?
Explain why.

Layered Dessert

Sweet T is making his favorite layered dessert. Read his notes.

Layered Dessert Notes
- Cut brownies, marshmallows, and cake into cubes.
- First layer is brownie cubes.
- Second layer is marshmallow cubes.
- Third layer is cake cubes.
- Use more than 3 layers.
- You choose the thickness of each layer.
- Repeat layers as many times as you want to fill the bowl.

12 in. 9 in. 8 in.

The picture above shows the container Sweet T uses to make the dessert. How many layers should Sweet T use? How thick should each layer be?

▶ Solve It Help Sweet T make a plan.

- Tell which item is in each layer.
- Give the length, width, and volume of each layer.
- Find the total volume of the completed dessert.

▶ Reflect

Use Mathematical Practices After you complete the task, choose one of these questions to discuss with a partner.

- **Use a Model** What models did you use and how did they help you find a solution?

- **Persevere** What did you do to get through any difficult parts of the solution?

Solve the problems.

1 Regan wants to convert 2 kilograms to grams. What number does she need to multiply by 2 to find the number of grams?
(1 kilogram = 1,000 grams)

A 0.001

B 0.1

C 100

D 1,000

2 Mrs. Davis had 6 bowls of flour for a group project. The line plot below shows the fraction of a cup of flour that was left in each bowl after the project.

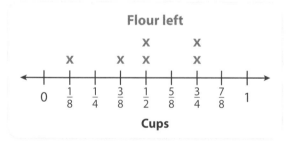

Flour left

Cups

What is the total amount of flour left in the bowls after the project?

A 4 cups

B 3 cups

C $1\frac{3}{4}$ cups

D $\frac{15}{28}$ cup

3 The solid figure below is made up of two rectangular prisms.

[not drawn to scale]

What is the volume of the solid figure?

A 5,170 cubic inches

B 2,970 cubic inches

C 2,860 cubic inches

D 1,980 cubic inches

4 Kyle has an aquarium in the shape of a rectangular prism. The aquarium is 24 inches long and 10 inches wide. The volume of the aquarium is 2,880 cubic inches. How high is the aquarium?

_____ inches

5 Which measurement is equivalent to 84 inches? Circle the letter for all that apply.

A 8 feet

B 1 yard, 2 feet, 24 inches

C 7 feet

D $2\frac{1}{3}$ yards

E 4 feet, 40 inches

6 Taner and Jaylen are practicing for a track meet. Last week, Taner ran 900 meters on each of 3 days. Jaylen ran 1.2 kilometers on each of 2 days. (1 kilometer = 1,000 meters)

Part A Which boy ran farther last week and by how much?

Show your work.

Solution _____

Part B Taner wants to run a total of 6 kilometers between last week and this week. How far does Taner need to run this week to reach his goal?

Show your work.

Answer _____ kilometers

7 The figure below is a rectangular prism.

Explain how you can use the area of the base to find the volume of a rectangular prism.

_____

_____

_____

_____

Performance Task

Answer the questions and show all your work on separate paper.

Jack wants to make a terrarium for the science fair. The first steps of the instructions are shown below.

How To Make a Terrarium

Step 1 Fill the bottom of the tank with a 2-inch layer of small rocks.

Step 2 Add a layer of soil. There should be 5 inches from the top of the soil to the top of the tank.

soil

small rocks

Jack already has one cubic foot (1,728 cubic inches) of soil and $\frac{1}{3}$ cubic foot (576 cubic inches) of small rocks to use. Now he has to choose a tank. Which of the tanks below can he use without having to buy more rocks and soil?

Tank A: $1\frac{1}{2}$ feet long, 15 inches wide, 15 inches tall

Tank B: 2 feet long, 1 foot wide, 1 foot tall

Tank C: 21 inches long, 18 inches wide, 10 inches tall

Reflect

Use Mathematical Practices   After you complete the task, choose one of the following questions to answer.

- **Be Precise** How did you decide which units to use to calculate the amount of rocks and soil needed for each tank?

- **Model** How does drawing and labeling a diagram help you solve the problem?

Unit 5
Geometry

Let's learn about the coordinate plane.

Real-World Connection Knowing how to tell where a place is located is important. You might make arrangements to meet someone at a certain location or you might need to give someone directions to a location.

For example, you might need to find the subway station at the corner of 23rd Street and Broadway in New York City. Describing locations is even important in games! In chess, you can move your pawn from c2 to c4 on the chess board. Other players know the direction you moved based on the description. Both these situations use coordinates.

In This Unit You will learn to locate points on a coordinate plane and use what you know about coordinates to solve problems. You will also study some two-dimensional figures and sort them into different categories according to their side lengths, angles, and other properties.

✓ Self Check

Before starting this unit, check off the skills you know below. As you complete each lesson, see how many more skills you can check off!

I can:	Before this unit	After this unit
graph points on a coordinate plane.	☐	☐
find the distance between two points on a coordinate plane.	☐	☐
graph quantities that represent real-world situations on a coordinate plane and use the graph to solve a problem.	☐	☐
classify two-dimensional figures based on their properties, for example: a square is also a rhombus or rectangle, but not all rhombuses and rectangles are squares.	☐	☐

Think It Through

What is the coordinate plane?

In the past, you have used a number line to represent a single quantity. A number line can be vertical or horizontal.

When a horizontal number line and a vertical number line are lined up so that the 0s meet, a **coordinate plane** is formed.

Vertical Number Line

Horizontal Number Line

Coordinate Plane

Think How do we distinguish between the two number lines?

A coordinate plane is made up of two perpendicular number lines. The number lines meet at the zeros. That point is labeled with the letter *O* for origin.

Coordinate Plane

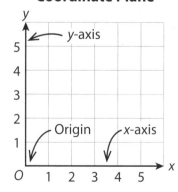

The horizontal number line is called the **x-axis**. The vertical number line is called the **y-axis**. The point where the *x*- and *y*-axes meet is the **origin**.

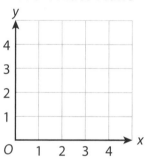

✏ **Circle** all of the numbers on the *x*-axis. **Box** all of the numbers on the *y*-axis.

 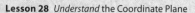

Think How can you locate points on the coordinate plane?

An **ordered pair** is a pair of numbers that describes the location of a point in the coordinate plane. The first number is called the **x-coordinate**. The second number is called the **y-coordinate**.

An ordered pair is a pair of coordinates that always appear in the same order: first x, then y.

Ordered Pair

(x, y)

x-coordinate   y-coordinate

The x-coordinate tells the distance from the origin along the x-axis. The y-coordinate tells the distance from the origin along the y-axis.

The origin is the point where the x-axis and the y-axis meet. Since the origin is 0 units along the x-axis and 0 units along the y-axis, the location is (0, 0).

Term	Definition
coordinate plane	a space formed by two perpendicular number lines called axes
x-axis	the horizontal number line in the coordinate plane
y-axis	the vertical number line in the coordinate plane
origin	the point, (0, 0), where the x-axis and y-axis intersect
ordered pair	a pair of numbers that describes the location of a point in the coordinate plane
x-coordinate	the first number in an ordered pair
y-coordinate	the second number in an ordered pair

▶ Reflect

1 Think about how you have heard the word *origin* used outside of math. Why do you think the point (0, 0) is called the *origin*?

_____

_____

_____

Think About ⟩ **Points on a Coordinate Plane**

🔍 **Let's Explore the Idea** Ordered pairs represent the location of points on the coordinate plane. The ordered pair for the origin is (0, 0).

2 Locate point *D* in the coordinate plane above. Start at the origin. How many units do you move along the *x*-axis to be lined up under point *D*? _____ Write this as the first number in the ordered pair at the right.

Ordered Pair for Point *D*
(*x, y*) ⟶ (_____ , _____)

3 The second number in an ordered pair is the *y*-coordinate. Start at the origin. How many units do you move along the *y*-axis to be lined up across from point *D*? _____ Write this as the second number in the ordered pair above.

4 Locate point *A* in the coordinate plane above. Start at the origin. How many units do you move along the *x*-axis to be on point *A*? _____
Start at the origin. How many units do you move along the *y*-axis to be lined up across from point *A*? _____

The ordered pair for point *A* is (_____ , _____).

5 Locate point *B* in the coordinate plane above. Identify the ordered pair for point *B*.
(_____ , _____)

6 Locate point *C* in the coordinate plane above. Identify the ordered pair for point *C*.
(_____ , _____)

7 How did you determine the coordinates for points *C* and *D*? _____

_____

_____

Let's Talk About It
Solve the problems below as a group.

Use the coordinate plane from the previous page. Now you will describe the points as movements from the origin.

8 Place your finger on the origin. Move right and then move up to point *D*. Use words to describe how far to the right and how far up point *D* is from (0, 0). _____

_____

How is the location of point *D* related to the ordered pair (2, 3)? _____

_____

9 Start at (0, 0). Move to point *A*. How is your move related to the ordered pair (1, 0)?

_____

_____

10 Describe how you move from the origin to the point (0, 1). Move right _____ unit(s) and move _____ _____ unit(s).

What letter represents this point on the coordinate plane? _____

11 The ordered pair (1, 1) tells you to start at the origin and move right _____ unit(s) and up _____ unit(s). What letter names this point on the coordinate plane? _____

12 Plot a point at (3, 2) on the coordinate plane. Label this point "*E*."

▶ Try It Another Way Work with your group to show the coordinates for each point on the coordinate plane on the previous page.

13 Complete the table for each point on the coordinate plane.

Point	A	B	C	D	E	F
x	1				3	4
y	0				2	0

14 The table gives the location of point *F*. Plot and label point *F* in the coordinate plane.

Connect ▶ **Ideas About Points on a Coordinate Plane**

Talk through these problems as a class. Then write your answers below.

15 Show Look at the table below. Plot and label points M and N on the coordinate plane below. Then write ordered pairs for points M and N and describe how to move from (0, 0) to each point.

Point	x	y
M	1	4
N	5	2

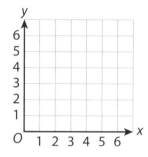

_____

_____

16 Analyze Irvin wrote the ordered pair (4, 3) for the location of point J in the coordinate plane at the right. Explain why Irvin's ordered pair is incorrect for point J.

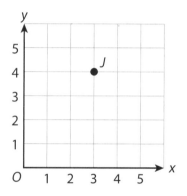

_____

_____

_____

_____

17 Create Choose 3 points on the coordinate plane at the right and draw a triangle. Label the points with letters.

Below, write the letters and ordered pairs you used to draw your triangle.

_____

_____

_____

Ideas About Points on a Coordinate Plane 289

18 Put It Together Use what you have learned to complete this task.

Part A Use the coordinate plane below to complete the table.

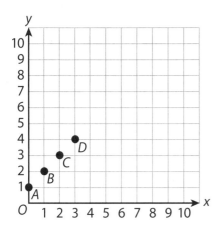

Point	x	y
A		
B		
C		
D		

Part B Identify a pattern you see formed by the points in the coordinate plane above. Then, explain the pattern using the points in the table above.

_____

_____

_____

_____

_____

Part C Plot 3 other points that follow this pattern. Label them with letters and write the ordered pair for each point below.

_____

_____

_____

Ⓖ Use What You Know

In Lesson 28, you learned about the coordinate plane. Now you will use the coordinate plane to solve problems. Take a look at this problem.

The coordinate plane at the right shows the layout at a country fair. Some of the booths are labeled. Meg is at Ring Toss. She wants to go to Face Painting. Suppose Meg can only walk along the grid lines. Describe two different paths she can take.

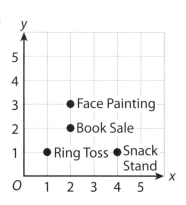

a. What ordered pair represents Ring Toss? _____

b. What ordered pair represents Face Painting? _____

c. Describe one way to move from Ring Toss to Face Painting by first moving to the right.

_____

_____

_____

d. Now describe a different path to get from Ring Toss to Face Painting.

_____

_____

_____

On the previous page you used the coordinate plane to help you describe how to move between points. But you can do this without using the coordinate plane. You can use ordered pairs to describe how to move between points.

Use the ordered pairs (1, 1) and (2, 3) to describe how to move between the points. To describe the horizontal move, look at the change in the *x*-coordinates.

(**1**, 1)   (**2**, 3)
Ring Toss   Face Painting

2 − 1 = 1

Since 2 is to the right of 1 on the *x*-axis, the move is 1 unit to the right.

To describe the vertical move, look at the change in the *y*-coordinates.

(1, **1**)   (2, **3**)
Ring Toss   Face Painting

3 − 1 = 2

Since 3 is above 1 on the *y*–axis, the move is 2 units up.

You can describe the move from point (1, 1) to point (2, 3) as 1 unit right and 2 units up.

▶ Reflect

1 Pick two other points on the coordinate plane on the previous page. Use the coordinates of the points to describe a path from one point to the other.

_____

_____

_____

_____

_____

Learn About ▶ Relationships in the Coordinate Plane

Read the problem below. Then explore different ways to represent and use relationships between quantities to solve problems.

Gabe has $8. He goes to an arcade where each game costs $1. Use equations, a table, and the coordinate plane to represent the relationship between how many games Gabe plays and how much money he has left. How many games can Gabe play if he wants to have exactly $2 when he leaves the arcade?

▶ **Model It** **You can use equations to represent the relationship between the quantities in the problem.**

Gabe starts with $8. Each game costs $1.

$8 − ($1 × **number of games**) = **dollars left**

$8 − ($1 × **1**) = **$7** left

$8 − ($1 × **2**) = **$6** left

$8 − ($1 × **3**) = **$5** left

$8 − ($1 × **4**) = **$4** left

$8 − ($1 × **5**) = **$3** left

$8 − ($1 × **6**) = **$2** left

▶ **Model It** **You can use a table to model the relationship between the quantities.**

The table shows how much money Gabe has left after playing different numbers of games.

Number of Games Played	0	1	2	3	4	5	6
Amount of Money Left ($)	8	7	6	5	4	3	2

Connect It Now you will solve the problem from the previous page by representing the relationship between the quantities using the coordinate plane.

2 What quantity in the problem stays the same? _____

What two quantities change? _____

3 Look at the coordinate plane. What quantity is represented on the *x*-axis?

_____ What quantity is represented on the *y*-axis? _____

4 How much money does Gabe have after he plays 0 games? Complete the ordered pair.

(0 games, $_____)

Plot the point in the coordinate plane.

5 Complete these ordered pairs, where *x* is games played and *y* is dollars left.

(1, _____), (2, _____)
(3, _____), (4, _____)
(5, _____), (6, _____)

Plot each ordered pair in the coordinate plane.

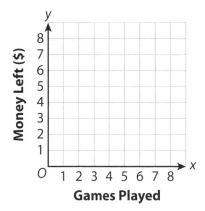

6 How many games can Gabe play and have exactly $2 when he leaves? Which ordered pair shows that? _____

7 How can you use a graph to represent relationships between two sets of numbers?

_____

_____

Try It Use what you just learned about representing relationships between two quantities using the coordinate plane to solve this problem. Show your work on a separate sheet of paper.

8 Suppose that the games at the arcade cost $2 each instead of $1. Write ordered pairs to represent the amounts of money left after playing different numbers of games. Use an "X" to plot each point on the coordinate plane above. How many of these games can Gabe play and have exactly $2 left when he leaves the arcade?

_____

Learn About Solving Problems on a Coordinate Plane

Read the problem below. Then explore different ways of using the coordinate plane to solve a problem.

> Mrs. Sautter writes the following ordered pairs on the board: *M*(2, 1), *A*(2, 5), *T*(5, 5), and *H*(5, 1). The point represented by each ordered pair is a vertex of a rectangle. She lists the vertices in order to name the figure "rectangle *MATH*." What is the perimeter of rectangle *MATH*?

▶ **Picture It** You can picture the rectangle on a coordinate plane.

Plot the points for the vertices of the rectangle. Connect the points to draw the sides of the rectangle. Then shade the rectangle.

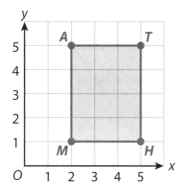

To find the perimeter, count the number of units on each side to find the side lengths.

▶ **Model It** You can find the perimeter of a rectangle with a formula.

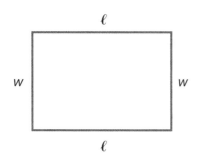

$P = 2\ell + 2w$ or $P = 2 \times (\ell + w)$

Connect It Now you will solve the problem from the previous page using your understanding of distance between two points on a number line.

9 What are the ordered pairs for points *A* and *T*? _____

Which are different, the *x*-coordinates or the *y*-coordinates? _____

Write an expression to find the distance between the points *A* and *T*. _____

What is the length of $\overline{AT}$? _____ units

10 Consider how you found the length of $\overline{AT}$ above.

What is the length of $\overline{MA}$? _____ units

Explain how you found this length. _____

_____

_____

11 What is the perimeter of the rectangle? _____ units

Explain how you found the perimeter. _____

_____

12 How can you find the vertical distance between two points on a coordinate plane?

_____

_____

13 How can you find the horizontal distance between two points on a coordinate plane?

_____

_____

Try It Use what you just learned about finding the distance between two points on a number line to solve these problems.

14 What is the vertical distance between (3, 8) and (3, 4)? _____

15 What is the horizontal distance between (4, 2) and (4, 5)? _____

Practice ▶ **Solving Problems on a Coordinate Plane**

Study the example below. Then solve problems 16–18.

Example

The graph shows how Jaina's parents determine her weekly allowance. What is the meaning of (3, 5)?

Look at how you can use the graph to solve this problem.

The x-axis is labeled "Chores Completed." The x-coordinate in (3, 5) is 3. The y-axis is labeled "Weekly Allowance." The y-coordinate in (3, 5) is 5.

Chores Completed

Solution ___If Jaina completes 3 chores, she will earn $5.___

> The labels on the axes tell me what the numbers mean.

> **Pair/Share**
> Explain how to use the graph to find how many chores Jaina must complete to earn $4.

---

16 Plot the points (4, 4), (8, 4), (3, 1), and (7, 1) on the coordinate plane. Use the points to draw two parallel, horizontal segments. Label the endpoints of one segment *A* and *B*. Label the endpoints of the other segment *C* and *D*. What is the distance between points *A* and *B*? What is the distance between points *C* and *D*?

Solution _____

> Do parallel lines ever intersect?

> **Pair/Share**
> What shape could have the 4 points as vertices? Draw the shape on the coordinate plane.

17 What is the area of rectangle *EFGH* shown on the coordinate plane?

The formula for the area of a rectangle is $A = \ell \times w$.

Show your work.

Solution _____

---

18 Mr. Palmer uses the coordinate plane to design his bulletin board.

He moves *Rules* 2 units right and 3 units down. What ordered pair represents the new location of *Rules*? Circle the letter of the correct answer.

What is the ordered pair for the starting point?

A (5, 3)

B (1, 9)

C (1, 3)

D (5, 9)

Maya chose **C** as the correct answer. How did she get that answer?

_____

_____

_____

_____

Practice ▸ **Solving Problems on a Coordinate Plane**

Solve the problems.

1 Look at triangle *ABC*.

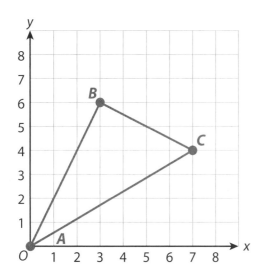

What are the coordinates of points *A*, *B*, and *C*?

A *A*(1, 1), *B*(6, 3), *C*(4, 7)

B *A*(1, 1), *B*(3, 6), *C*(7, 4)

C *A*(0, 0), *B*(6, 3), *C*(4, 7)

D *A*(0, 0), *B*(3, 6), *C*(7, 4)

2 The coordinate plane below shows rhombus *RHOM* with lines of symmetry.

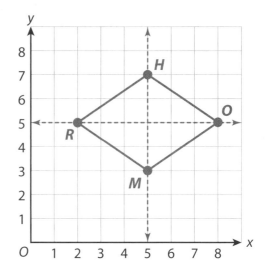

What is the horizontal distance between points *R* and *O*?

_____ units

3 Plot the following three points on the coordinate plane below.

(2, 6)   (7, 4)   (4, 0)

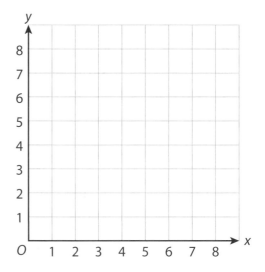

4 The coordinate plane shows the relationship between the amount of water in the bathtub and the amount of time the faucet has been turned on.

How many minutes must the faucet be turned on for the bathtub to hold 8 gallons of water?

A 16 minutes

B 8 minutes

C 4 minutes

D 2 minutes

5 **Part A** The area of rectangle *RSTU* is 20 square units. Draw rectangle *RSTU* on the coordinate plane below with one vertex at the origin.

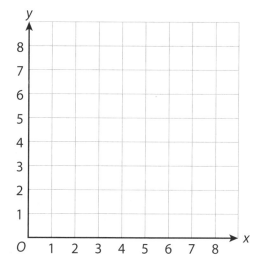

Part B Write the ordered pairs for the points *R, S, T,* and *U.* _____

_____

Part C How do you know that the area of rectangle *RSTU* is 20 square units?

_____

_____

_____

_____

 Self Check **Go back and see what you can check off on the Self Check on page 283.**

Classify Two-Dimensional Figures

5.G.B.4

🄖 Use What You Know

In this lesson, you will classify polygons based on their properties. Take a look at this problem.

Arrange the polygons below so that a polygon can also be called by the name of the polygon before it. Order them from left to right.

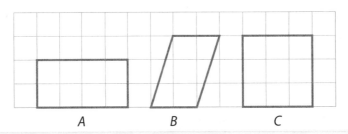

A   B   C

a. Complete the table below. Put a check in each box if the polygon has the property listed.

Property	Polygon A	Polygon B	Polygon C
4 sides			
2 pairs of parallel sides			
2 pairs of sides of equal length			
4 right angles			
4 sides of equal length			

b. Write the most specific name for each polygon from the list below.

quadrilateral   parallelogram   rectangle   square

A: _____   B: _____   C: _____

c. How would you arrange the polygons so each shape has all the properties of the shape(s) before it? _____

Shapes can be classified according to their properties. When you order categories of polygons by their properties, you put them in a **hierarchy**. A hierarchy organizes categories from the most to least general. One model you can use to show a hierarchy is a Venn diagram.

A Venn diagram can show categories and subcategories. This Venn diagram shows that squares have all the properties that rectangles have, plus more. This means all squares are also rectangles. A square is also a parallelogram and a quadrilateral.

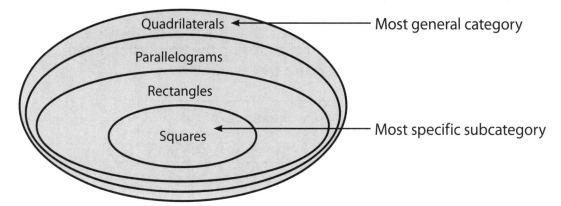

You can also use a flow chart to show the hierarchy of quadrilaterals. The most general category is at the left, while the most specific is at the right. This means that a figure that belongs in one category also belongs in all categories to the left.

▶ Reflect

1 How are the flow chart and the Venn diagram alike? How are they different?

_____

_____

_____

_____

_____

Read the problem below. Then explore different ways to classify figures in a hierarchy.

> Classify the following triangles from the most general to the most specific: scalene triangle, isosceles triangle, and equilateral triangle. Use a tree diagram to classify them as types of triangles.

▶ **Model It** **You can understand the problem by listing the properties of the triangles in a table before arranging them in a tree diagram.**

Types of Triangles	Properties of Sides
Isosceles	2 or 3 sides of equal length
Scalene	no sides of equal length
Equilateral	3 sides of equal length

▶ **Model It** **You can represent the problem with a tree diagram.**

A tree diagram can also be used to show a hierarchy. Put the most general category as the top branch. Then put the more specific subcategories as the branches.

Connect It Now you will solve the problem from the previous page by using the table to complete a tree diagram.

2 Why is "Triangles" in the top row of the tree diagram? _____

_____

3 Write "Scalene" and "Isosceles" in the second row of the tree diagram at the right.

Why are those categories separate?

_____

_____

_____

Triangles

4 Write "Equilateral" beneath "Isosceles."

Why can all equilateral triangles be classified as isosceles triangles?

_____

5 How can you use a tree diagram to order figures? _____

_____

_____

Try It Use what you learned about ordering figures in a hierarchy to solve this problem.

6 Complete the Venn diagram below to show the hierarchy of isosceles, scalene, and equilateral triangles.

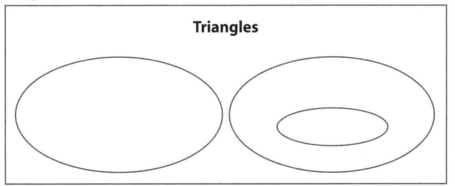

Study the example below. Then solve problems 7–9.

Example

Create a Venn diagram to show the hierarchy of quadrilaterals, polygons, trapezoids, and hexagons.

Look at how you could show your work using a Venn diagram.

A shape can never be both a hexagon and a quadrilateral. So these regions do not overlap.

 Pair/Share
Recreate the hierarchy with a tree diagram.

---

7 Look at the tree diagram below. Write a statement about the relationship between acute triangles and equilateral triangles.

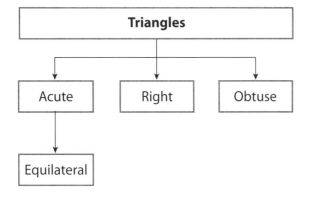

Which type of triangle is the most specific?

Pair/Share
Write a statement about the relationship between acute triangles and obtuse triangles.

Solution _____

_____

8 Create a Venn diagram to show the hierarchy of the polygons described in the chart.

Polygon	Description
Trapezoid	quadrilateral with at least 1 pair of parallel sides
Square	parallelogram with 4 sides of equal length
Parallelogram	quadrilateral with 2 pairs of parallel sides

"At least 1" means 1 or more.

Pair/Share
Draw one example of a polygon in each separate category of your Venn diagram.

---

9 Look at the flow chart below.

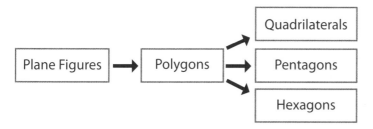

Which statement is true? Circle the letter of the correct answer.

A A plane figure is always a polygon.

B All polygons are plane figures.

C All hexagons are also pentagons and quadrilaterals.

D A hexagon is not a plane figure.

Brad chose **C** as the correct answer. How did he get that answer?

The flow chart is like a tree diagram. But the arrows show that the hierarchy moves from left to right instead of top to bottom.

_____

_____

_____

Pair/Share
Does Brad's answer make sense?

Practice Classifying Two-Dimensional Figures

Solve the problems.

1 Look at the shape below.

Which is a correct classification for this shape from LEAST specific to MOST specific?

A polygon, quadrilateral, rectangle

B quadrilateral, parallelogram, square

C polygon, quadrilateral, square

D quadrilateral, rectangle, square

2 Classify the triangles shown below as "scalene," "isosceles," or "obtuse." Sides that are the same length are marked with a slash. Draw the triangles in the correct column of the table. If a triangle fits more than one classification, draw it in all the columns that apply.

Scalene	Isosceles	Obtuse

3 Look at the flow chart below.

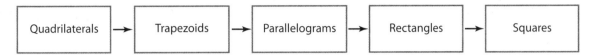

Part A Draw an example of a trapezoid that is not a parallelogram.

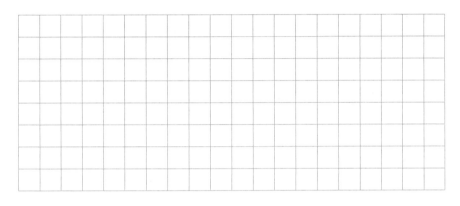

Part B Explain how trapezoids relate to parallelograms.

_____

_____

_____

_____

Part C Can you use the term "parallelogram" to describe a rectangle? Explain your reasoning.

_____

_____

_____

_____

✓ **Self Check** **Go back and see what you can check off on the Self Check on page 283.**

Lesson 30 Classify Two-Dimensional Figures   **307**

Understand Properties of Two-Dimensional Figures

Think It Through

How do we group polygons into categories?

Polygons are grouped into categories by their **attributes**, or properties, such as the number of sides or angles, the side lengths, and the angle measures. All polygons in the same category share certain properties. Some properties of polygons are described in the table below.

Property	Description	Example
Scalene	no sides of equal length	
Isosceles	at least 2 sides of equal length	
Equilateral	all sides of equal length	
Regular	all sides of equal length and all angles of equal measure	
Irregular	at least 1 side and 1 interior angle are not equal in measure to the other sides and angles	
Right	at least 1 pair of perpendicular sides	
Parallel sides	at least 1 pair of opposite sides that will never intersect, no matter how far they are extended	

Think Can a polygon be categorized in more than one way?

Think about how a quadrilateral is defined. It is a polygon with 4 sides. So any shape with 4 sides can be called both a polygon and a quadrilateral. If the quadrilateral has two pairs of parallel sides, then it can also be called a parallelogram.

Every parallelogram is a quadrilateral because every parallelogram has 4 sides. But not all quadrilaterals are parallelograms because not all quadrilaterals have two pairs of parallel sides.

Shade a polygon above that can be named both a quadrilateral and parallelogram.

Think How can you show the relationships among polygons with a diagram?

A Venn diagram is a useful tool for organizing categories of polygons that share properties.

The Venn diagram shows a triangle can never be both right and obtuse.

Notice the "Right" category partly overlaps the "Isosceles" category. This means a right triangle may also have all the properties of an isosceles triangle. Also notice that the "Right" category does not overlap the "Obtuse" category. That means a right triangle can never have all the properties of an obtuse triangle.

The "Equilateral" category is nested completely inside the "Isosceles" category. This shows that equilateral triangles are a subcategory of isosceles triangles. So all equilateral triangles share all the properties of isosceles triangles.

▶ Reflect

1 What does it mean that the Venn diagram shows "Obtuse" partially overlapping "Isosceles?"

_____

_____

_____

Think About ⟩ **Properties Shared by Polygons**

🔍 **Let's Explore the Idea** **A Venn diagram can help you understand what properties are shared by categories of polygons.**

2 The Venn diagram shows categories of quadrilaterals with different properties. Write the name of each category that fits the description.

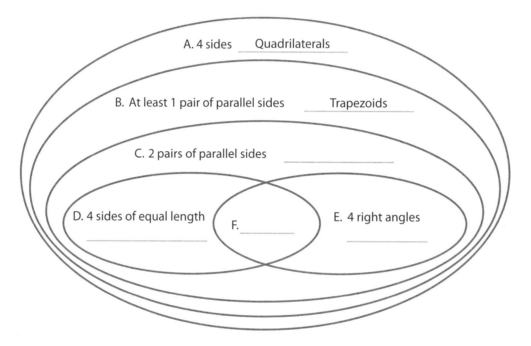

A. 4 sides   <u>Quadrilaterals</u>

B. At least 1 pair of parallel sides   <u>Trapezoids</u>

C. 2 pairs of parallel sides   <u>   </u>

D. 4 sides of equal length   <u>   </u>

F. <u>   </u>

E. 4 right angles   <u>   </u>

3 Use the Venn diagram to fill in the table below.

Category	Properties	Name
A	4 sides	Quadrilaterals
B	4 sides, at least 1 pair of parallel sides	Trapezoids
C	4 sides, 2 pairs of parallel sides	
D	4 sides, 2 pairs of parallel sides, 4 sides of equal length	
E		
F		

Let's Talk About It Use the Venn diagram to help you understand how properties are shared by categories of quadrilaterals.

4 Is every property of parallelograms also a property of all rectangles? _____

Is every property of rectangles also a property of all parallelograms? _____

Explain what the Venn diagram shows about the relationship between rectangles and parallelograms. _____

_____

_____

Classify each inference statement as *true* or *false*. If false, explain.

5 The opposite angles of any parallelogram have the same measure. Therefore, the opposite angles of any rhombus have the same measure. _____

_____

6 The diagonals of any square are the same length. Therefore, the diagonals of any rhombus are the same length. _____

_____

Try It Another Way The flow chart below shows another way to think about how quadrilaterals are categorized.

Use the flow chart to describe the statements as *true* or *false*.

7 In every rectangle the two diagonals have the same length. Therefore, in every

parallelogram the two diagonals must have the same length. _____

8 Every rhombus has at least 2 lines of symmetry. Therefore, every square has at least

2 lines of symmetry. _____

Talk through these problems as a class. Then write your answers below.

9 Categorize All polygons are either **convex** or **concave**. A convex polygon has all interior angles less than 180°. A triangle is an example of a convex polygon. A concave polygon has at least 1 interior angle greater than 180°. The quadrilateral below is an example of a concave polygon.

Categorize concave polygons, convex polygons, triangles, quadrilaterals, and rectangles in a Venn diagram. Draw an example of each polygon in the diagram.

10 Explain Nadriette said that a rectangle can never be called a trapezoid. Explain why Nadriettte's statement is incorrect. _____

_____

11 Create Describe the properties of a shape that is both a rectangle and a rhombus. Name the shape and use the grid below to draw an example.

_____

_____

_____

©Curriculum Associates, LLC   Copying is not permitted.

Apply ▶ **Ideas About Properties of Polygons**

12 Put It Together Use what you have learned about classifying polygons to complete this task.

Part A Create a tree diagram to show the following types of triangles: acute, obtuse, right, isosceles, and equilateral. Make sure to include the category "Triangle." Use information in the table to help you.

Triangle	Types of Angles
Acute	all acute angles
Right	2 acute angles and 1 90° angle
Obtuse	2 acute angles and 1 obtuse angle
Scalene	acute, right, or obtuse
Isosceles	acute, right, or obtuse
Equilateral	all acute angles

Part B Write a statement that is always true about the relationship between obtuse triangles and equilateral triangles.

Part C Write a statement that is sometimes true about the relationship between acute triangles and isosceles triangles.

Work with Geometry and Coordinates

Study an Example Problem and Solution

In this lesson, you will use what you know about shapes and coordinate grids to solve real-world problems. Look at this problem and one solution.

Octagon Trap

Max is working on a new video game, Shape Shake-Up. He uses a coordinate grid to represent the screen. It helps him decide where to place graphics. Read one of Max's ideas.

Game Idea

· A shape that looks like a C traps players.

· The shape's perimeter is 14 to 16 units. Its area is 6 to 8 square units.

· The shape is located more than 2 units above the x-axis and more than 2 units to the right of the y–axis.

Draw a shape on a coordinate grid that works with Max's game idea and explain why it works. Label each vertex with a coordinate pair.

Read the sample solution on the next page. Then look at the checklist below. Find and mark parts of the answer that match the checklist.

✏️ Problem-Solving Checklist

☐ Tell what is known.

☐ Tell what the problem is asking.

☐ Show all your work.

☐ Show that the solution works.

a. **Circle** something that is known.

b. **Underline** something that you need to find.

c. **Draw a box around** what you do to solve the problem.

d. **Put a checkmark** next to the part that shows the solution works.

Max's Solution

Hi, I'm Max. Here's how I solved this problem.

▷ **I know** the choices for area and perimeter of the shape. I need to find the lengths of sides that can make an area and perimeter that work.

▷ **I can try different lengths for the sides.**
There are 8 sides.
Their lengths must have a sum of 14 to 16.
It looks like I should try numbers close to 2.

First I tried a shape that was 5 units wide and 5 units tall, but that was much too big.

▷ **I'll check** that the perimeter works.
4 + (3 x 2) + (1 x 4) = 14

▷ **I'll check** that the area works.
(2 x 1) + (2 x 1) + (2 x 1) = 6

The shape has a perimeter of 14 units and an area of 6 square units.

▷ **Now I can plot the shape on a coordinate grid.**
I'll put the bottom left vertex at (3, 3) so I know it's more than 2 units from each axis.

After I put a corner at (3,3) I counted right 2, up 1, left 1, up 2, and so on to draw the whole shape.

Try ▶ Another Approach

There are many ways to solve problems. Think about how you might solve the Octagon Trap problem in a different way.

Octagon Trap

Max is working on a new video game, Shape Shake-Up. He uses a coordinate grid to represent the screen. It helps him decide where to place graphics. Read one of Max's ideas.

Game Idea

· A shape that looks like a C traps players.

· The shape's perimeter is 14 to 16 units. Its area is 6 to 8 square units.

· The shape is located more than 2 units above the *x*-axis and more than 2 units to the right of the *y*-axis.

Draw a shape on a coordinate grid that works with Max's game idea and explain why it works. Label each vertex with a coordinate pair.

▶ **Plan It** **Answer these questions to help you start thinking about a plan.**

A. How can you make a different "C" shape?

_____

_____

B. What are some different locations you can use on the grid?

_____

_____

Solve It Find a different solution for the Octagon Trap problem.
Show all your work on a separate sheet of paper.

You may want to use the problem-solving tips to get started.

▶ Reflect
Use Mathematical Practices As you work through the problem, discuss these questions with a partner.

- **Use Models** How can a sketch help you solve this problem?

- **Use Tools** Will a ruler be helpful for this problem? Explain how it can help, or explain why not.

Discuss ▸ **Models and Strategies**

Read the problem. Write a solution on a separate sheet of paper.
Remember, there can be lots of ways to solve a problem!

Rectangle Maze

One screen in Max's game has a maze of rectangles. Players try to move through the maze. The rectangles start in a certain location, but they move both left and right and up and down. Max will decide the starting location for each rectangle.

Max's Notes

· Show 5 rectangles.

· Put one rectangle near the middle of the screen.

· Put other rectangles on all 4 sides of the middle rectangle.

· Other rectangles must have an area that is $\frac{1}{2}$ of the area or perimeter that is $\frac{1}{2}$ of the perimeter of the middle rectangle.

· Each shape must be a distance of at least 1 unit from the middle rectangle on all sides.

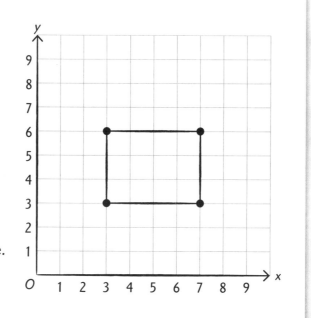

Where should Max put the other 4 rectangles?

▶ Plan It and Solve It Find a solution to the Rectangle Maze problem.

Use the Rectangle Maze Activity Sheet and the information in Max's notes.

- Draw the other 4 rectangles.
- Label the vertices of all shapes with coordinate pairs.
- Explain why your shapes work with Max's notes.

Problem-Solving Tips

- **Questions**
  - What areas can your rectangles have?
  - What perimeters can your rectangles have?

- **Word Bank**

area	distance	coordinate pair
perimeter	unit	coordinate grid

Problem-Solving Checklist

Make sure that you . . .

- ☐ tell what you know.
- ☐ tell what you need to do.
- ☐ show all your work.
- ☐ show that the solution works.

▶ Reflect

Use Mathematical Practices As you work through the problem, discuss these questions with a partner.

- **Be Precise** How can you find the area and perimeter of a rectangle on a coordinate grid?

- **Use Models** What expressions can you write to find half of the perimeter and half of the area of the given rectangle?

Persevere ▸ **On Your Own**

Read the problems. Write a solution on a separate sheet of paper.
Remember, there are many different ways to solve a problem.

The Plunging Parallelogram

In Max's game, a parallelogram starts at the top of the screen and zigzags
down to the bottom. Read Max's design notes.

Max's Design Notes

· The parallelogram has all right angles.

· The sides are at least 2 units long.

· At the start, one vertex is located
at (10, 10).

· At the end, one vertex is located
at (0, 0).

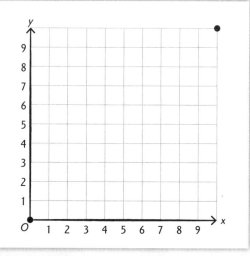

What points should Max use as the parallelogram's vertices?
What path can the shape take to get to the bottom of the screen?

▶ Solve It Help Max draw the parallelogram.

• Plot points and draw the parallelogram at its starting point.
• Give the coordinates of each vertex.
• Plot points and draw the parallelogram at its ending point.
• Describe a path the shape could follow to get to the bottom of the screen.
  Use directional words and numbers of units in your description.

▶ Reflect

Use Mathematical Practices After you complete the task, choose one
of these questions to discuss with a partner.

• **Critique Reasoning** Does the path your partner described work? Why or
  why not?

• **Be Precise** What are all the different names that can be used to describe
  Max's shape?

Hierarchy Hit

At three times in Max's game a quadrilateral appears on the screen. Players smash the quadrilateral to score bonus points. When a shape is hit, it morphs into a different quadrilateral. It continues to morph into other quadrilaterals according to the rules below.

Hierarchy Hit Rules

· The morphing can go from the more general to more specific shape. Or it can go from the more specific to more general shape.

· There are at least three different quadrilaterals in the morphing sequence.

▶ Solve It Help Max design the hierarchy.

• Find quadrilaterals that will fit with the rules.

• Make a flow chart that shows a hierarchy of quadrilaterals and their names.

• Draw an example of each quadrilateral.

• Explain why the order of shapes shows a hierarchy.

▶ Reflect

Use Mathematical Practices After you complete the task, choose one of these questions to discuss with a partner.

• **Use Models** How does the flow chart you made show the hierarchy of shapes? Explain.

• **Be Precise** How does the most specific shape you drew fit in all of the other categories? Explain.

Solve the problems.

1 Jack, Chris, Ryan, Peter, and Sam all attend Laurelleaf Elementary School. The coordinate plane below shows the locations of their houses and the school.

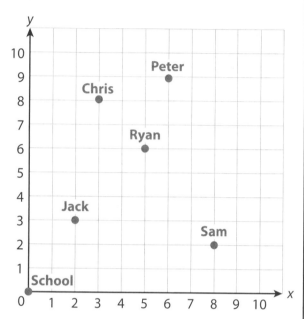

What *x*-coordinate describes the location of Ryan's house?

A 2   **C** 5

B 3   **D** 6

2 Which figure shown below is a rectangle?

3 Look at rectangle *ABCD* on the coordinate plane below.

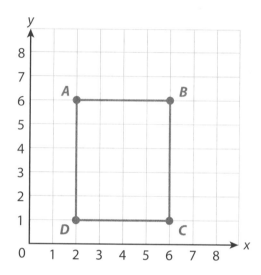

Choose *True* or *False* for each statement.

a. The coordinates of point *A* are (6, 2).

☐ True   ☐ False

b. The coordinates of point *D* are (2, 1).

☐ True   ☐ False

c. The area of rectangle *ABCD* is 36 square units.

☐ True   ☐ False

d. The perimeter of rectangle *ABCD* is 18 units.

☐ True   ☐ False

4 Which statement is true based on the diagram at the right? Circle the letter for all that apply.

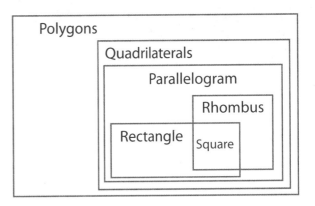

Polygons
Quadrilaterals
Parallelogram
Rhombus
Rectangle Square

A All squares are rhombuses.

B All rectangles are squares.

C All quadrilaterals are parallelograms.

D All squares are parallelograms.

E All polygons are quadrilaterals.

5 Part A Circle the quadrilaterals below that are rectangles.

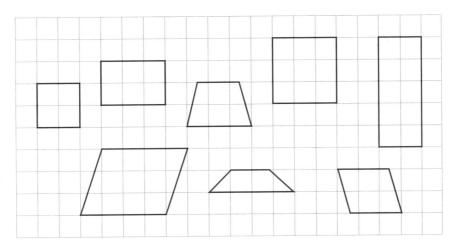

Part B The table shows properties of parallelograms and rhombuses.

All parallelograms have:	All rhombuses have:
4 sides	4 sides of equal length
4 vertices	4 vertices
2 pairs of parallel sides	2 pairs of parallel sides

Use the information in the table to complete the sentence below.

All _____ are _____, but not all _____

are _____ .

Performance Task

Answer the questions and show all your work on separate paper.

Ben and Cari are trying to solve the puzzle below.

Name That Shape

1. The figure is a quadrilateral.

2. The figure has a pair of parallel sides.

3. Three of the vertices are located at (1, 2), (3, 5), and (7, 5) on a coordinate plane.

What type of figure is it? Where is the fourth vertex?

Ben thinks there's only one solution to the puzzle. Cari says there's more than one possible answer. Who do you think is right? Explain your reasoning. Then solve the puzzle. If you agree with Cari, find at least two possibilities for the fourth vertex.

Now create your own geometry puzzle with 3 clues. Make sure your puzzle has only one answer and that it cannot be answered with only 2 clues.

▶ Reflect

Use Mathematical Practices After you complete the task, choose one of the following questions to answer.

- **Use Structure** How did you use the clues to solve the puzzle?

- **Be Precise** What did you think about when writing your own puzzle?

Glossary

AM morning, or the time from midnight until noon.

acute angle an angle with a measure less than 90°.

acute triangle a triangle that has three acute angles.

addend a number being added.

angle two rays that share an endpoint.

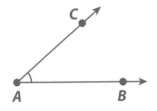

area the amount of space inside a closed, two-dimensional figure. Area is measured in square units such as square centimeters.

array a set of objects grouped in equal rows and equal columns.

☆ ☆ ☆ ☆ ☆
☆ ☆ ☆ ☆ ☆
☆ ☆ ☆ ☆ ☆

associative property of addition Changing the grouping of three or more addends does not change the sum.

••• • • •• = • • •• ••
(2 + 3) + 4 = 2 + (3 + 4)

associative property of multiplication Changing the grouping of three or more factors does not change the product.

(2 × 4) × 3   2 × (4 × 3)

attribute a characteristic of an object. Attributes of a shape include the number of sides and the length of the sides.

base ten the number system we use everyday using ten digits. The value of a digit depends on its place value. The value of each place is 10 times the value of the place to the right.

benchmark fraction a common fraction that you might compare other fractions to.

For example, $\frac{1}{2}$ can be used as a benchmark.

capacity the amount of liquid a container can hold. Capacity is measured in the same units as liquid volume.

centimeter (cm) a unit of length in the metric system. Your little finger is about 1 centimeter across. 100 centimeters is equivalent to 1 meter.

Glossary

closed figure a two-dimensional figure that begins and ends at the same point.

Closed   Open
Figure   Figure

column a top-to-bottom line of objects in an array.

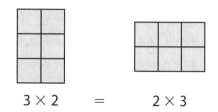

common denominator a number that is a common multiple of the denominators of two or more fractions.

commutative property of addition Changing the order of the addends does not change the sum.

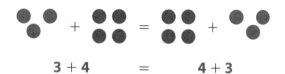

3 + 4   =   4 + 3

commutative property of multiplication Changing the order of the factors does not change the product.

3 × 2   =   2 × 3

compare to decide if one number is greater than (>), less than (<), or equal to (=) another number. Also, to tell how much more one number is than another number, or how many times as many one number is than another number.

compose to make by combining parts.

composite number a number greater than 0 that has more than one pair of factors.

concave polygon a polygon with at least one inside angle with a measure greater than 180°.

convert to change from one measurement unit to another.

convex polygon a polygon with all inside angles with measures less than 180°.

coordinate plane a two-dimensional space formed by two perpendicular number lines called axes.

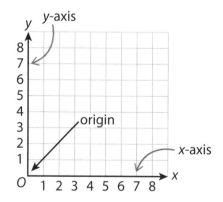

corresponding terms (in two related patterns) the numbers that have the same position. For example, the second term in one pattern and the second term in a related pattern are corresponding terms.

cubic unit a cube with edge lengths of 1 unit. Cubic units are used to measure the volume of a solid figure.

cup (c) a unit of liquid volume in the customary system. Four cups is equivalent to 1 quart.

customary system the measurement system commonly used in the United States. It measures length in inches, feet, yards, and miles; liquid volume in cups, pints, quarts, and gallons; and weight in ounces and pounds.

data information, often numerical information such as a list of measurements.

decimal a number containing a decimal point that separates the ones place from the tenths place.

decimal point the period or dot used in a decimal that separates the ones place from the tenths place.

decompose to break up into parts.

degree (°) a unit used to measure angles. There are 360° in one circle.

denominator the number below the line in a fraction. It tells how many equal parts are in the whole.

$$\frac{2}{5} \longleftarrow \text{denominator}$$

difference the result of subtraction.

digit a symbol used to write numbers. The digits are 0, 1, 2, 3, 4, 5, 6, 7, 8, and 9.

dimension length in one direction. A figure may have one, two, or three dimensions.

distribution (of data) how spread out or clustered pieces of data are.

distributive property When one of the factors of a product is written as a sum, multiplying each addend by the other factor before adding does not change the product.

$$2 \times (3 + 6) = (2 \times 3) + (2 \times 6)$$

divide to separate into equal groups.

dividend the number that is divided in a division problem.

division an operation used to separate a number of items into equal-sized groups.

divisor the number you divide by in a division problem.

elapsed time the time that has passed between a start time and an end time.

equal (=) having the same value, same size, or same amount.

equation a mathematical statement that uses an equal sign (=) to show that two expressions have the same value.

Glossary

equilateral triangle a triangle that has all three sides the same length.

equivalent fractions two or more fractions that have the same value. They name the same part of a whole and the same point on a number line.

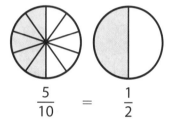

$$\frac{5}{10} = \frac{1}{2}$$

estimate (noun) a close guess made using math thinking.

estimate (verb) to make a close guess based on math thinking.

evaluate to find the value of an expression.

even number a whole number that ends in the digit 0, 2, 4, 6, or 8. Even numbers have 2 as a factor.

expanded form the way a number is written to show the place value of each digit.

$$254.3 = 200 + 50 + 4 + \frac{3}{10}$$

exponent the raised number in an expression such as 10^3. The exponent tells you how many times to use the base as a factor.

10^3 ⟵ exponent

$10^3 = 10 \times 10 \times 10$, or 1,000

expression numbers or unknowns combined with operation symbols. For example, $5 + a$ or 3×6.

fact family a group of related math facts that all use the same numbers. The group of facts shows the relationship between addition and subtraction, or between multiplication and division.

$5 \times 4 = 20$

$4 \times 5 = 20$

$20 \div 4 = 5$

$20 \div 5 = 4$

factor a number that is multiplied.

factor pair two numbers that are multiplied together to give a particular product. For example, 1 and 12, 2 and 6, and 3 and 4 are all factor pairs of 12.

factors of a number whole numbers that multiply together to get the given number.

foot (ft) a unit of length in the customary system. One foot is equivalent to 12 inches.

formula a mathematical relationship that is expressed in the form of an equation. For example, the formula for the area of a rectangle is $A = \ell \times w$.

fraction a number that names equal parts of a whole; a fraction names a point on the number line and can also represent the division of two numbers.

$\dfrac{3}{4}$

gallon (gal) a unit of liquid volume in the customary system. One gallon is equal to 4 quarts.

gram (g) a unit of mass in the metric system. A paper clip has a mass of about 1 gram. 1,000 grams is equivalent to 1 kilogram.

greater than symbol (>) a symbol used to compare two numbers when the first has greater value than the second.

hexagon a polygon with exactly six sides and six angles.

hierarchy a ranking of categories based on properties.

hour (h) a unit of time. One hour is equivalent to 60 minutes.

hundredths the parts formed when a whole is divided into 100 equal parts.

inch (in.) a unit of length in the customary system. A quarter is about 1 inch across. Twelve inches is equivalent to 1 foot.

inverse operations operations that undo each other. For example, addition and subtraction are inverse operations, and multiplication and division are inverse operations.

isosceles triangle a triangle that has at least two sides with the same length.

8 in. 8 in.

6 in.

kilogram (kg) a unit of mass in the metric system. One kilogram is to equivalent to 1,000 grams.

kilometer (km) a unit of length in the metric system. One kilometer is equivalent to 1,000 meters.

Glossary

length a measurement that tells the distance from one point to another, or how long something is.

less than symbol (<) a symbol used to compare two numbers when the first has less value than the second.

line (in geometry) a straight row of points that goes on forever in both directions.

line of symmetry a line that divides a shape into two mirror images

line plot a data display that uses a number line to show measurement data.

line segment a straight row of points that starts at one point and ends at another point, or, a part of a line.

liquid volume the amount of space a liquid takes up.

liter (L) a unit of liquid volume in the metric system. One liter is equivalent to 1,000 milliliters.

mass the amount of matter in an object. Measuring the mass of an object is one way to measure how heavy it is. Units of mass include the gram and kilogram.

meter (m) a unit of length in the metric system. One meter is equivalent to 100 centimeters.

metric system the measurement system that measures length based on meters, liquid volume based on liters, and mass based on grams.

mile (mi) a unit of length in the customary system. One mile is equivalent to 5,280 feet.

milliliter (ml) a unit of liquid volume in the metric system. 1,000 milliliters is equivalent to 1 liter.

minute (min) a unit of time equivalent to 60 seconds.

mixed number a number with a whole part and a fractional part.

$$4\frac{1}{2}$$

multiple the product of a number and any other whole number. For example, 4, 8, 12, 16, and so on, are multiples of 4.

multiplication an operation used to find the total number of items in equal-sized groups.

multiplicative comparison a comparison that tells how many times as many. For example, $7 \times 3 = 21$ means 21 is 3 times as many as 7, and 21 is 7 times as many as 3.

multiply to find the total number of items in equal-sized groups.

numerator the number above the line in a fraction. It tells how many equal parts are described.

$$\frac{2}{5} \longleftarrow \text{numerator}$$

obtuse angle an angle that measures more than 90º but less than 180º.

obtuse triangle a triangle that has one obtuse angle.

odd number a whole number that ends in the digit 1, 3, 5, 7, or 9. Odd numbers do not have 2 as a factor.

operation a mathematical action such as addition, subtraction, multiplication, and division.

ordered pair a pair of numbers, (x, y), that describes the location of a point on a coordinate plane. The first number tells the point's horizontal distance from the origin, and the second number tells the point's vertical distance from the origin.

origin the point (0, 0) where the x-axis and the y-axis intersect on a coordinate plane.

ounce (oz) a unit of weight in the customary system. A slice of bread weighs about one ounce. Sixteen ounces are equivalent to 1 pound.

PM the time from noon until midnight.

parallel lines two or more lines that are always the same distance apart and will never cross.

parallelogram a quadrilateral with opposite sides parallel and equal in length.

parentheses () a grouping symbol; they group parts of an expression that should be evaluated before others.

Glossary

partial products a strategy used to multiply multi-digit numbers. The products you get in each step are called "partial products".

$$
\begin{array}{r}
218 \\
\times \quad 6 \\
\hline
48 \\
60 \\
1200 \\
\hline
1308
\end{array}
$$

48 (6 × 8 ones)
60 (6 × 1 ten)
1200 (6 × 2 hundreds)

partial quotients a strategy used to divide multi-digit numbers. The quotients you get in each step are called "partial quotients".

pattern a series of numbers or shapes that follow a rule to repeat or change.

pentagon a polygon with exactly five sides and five angles.

perimeter the distance around a two-dimensional shape. The perimeter is equal to the sum of the lengths of the sides.

period a group of three related place values, usually separated by commas. Examples are the ones period, the thousands period, and the millions period.

Thousands Period			Ones Period		
Hundred Thousands	Ten Thousands	Thousands	Hundreds	Tens	Ones
4	6	7	8	8	2

perpendicular lines two lines that meet to form a right angle, or a 90° angle.

pint (pt) a unit of liquid volume in the customary system. One pint is equivalent to 2 cups.

place value the value of a digit based on its position in a number. For example, the 2 in 324 is in the tens place and has a value of 2 tens, or twenty.

plane figure a two-dimensional figure, such as a circle, triangle, or rectangle.

point a single location in space. Two lines cross at a point, and two sides of a triangle meet at a point.

polygon a two-dimensional closed figure made with three or more straight line segments that do not cross over each other.

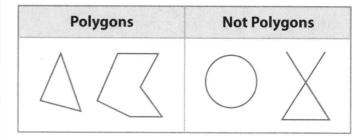

Polygons	Not Polygons

pound (lb) a unit of weight in the customary system. One pound is equivalent to 16 ounces.

power of ten a number that can be written as a product of tens. For example, 100 and 1,000 are powers of ten because $100 = 10 \times 10$ and $1,000 = 10 \times 10 \times 10$.

prime number a whole number greater than 1 whose only factors are 1 and itself. For example, 2, 3, 5, 7, and 11 are prime numbers.

product the result of multiplication.

protractor a tool used to measure angles.

Q

quadrilateral a polygon with exactly four sides and four angles.

quart (qt) a unit of liquid volume in the customary system. One quart is equivalent to 4 cups.

quotient the result of division.

R

ray a straight row of points that starts at one point and goes on forever in one direction.

A B

rectangle a parallelogram with four right angles. Opposite sides of a rectangle are the same length.

rectangular prism a solid figure with six rectangular faces.

regroup to compose or decompose tens, hundreds, thousands, and so forth. For example, 10 tenths can be regrouped as 1 whole, or 1 tenth can be regrouped 10 hundredths.

remainder in division, the amount left over after equal groups have been made.

Remainder

$17 \div 5 = 3 \text{ R2}$

rhombus a parallelogram with four equal sides.

right angle an angle that looks like a square corner and measures $90°$.

right triangle a triangle with one right angle.

Glossary

round to find a number that is close in value to the given number by finding the nearest ten, hundred, or other place value.

row a side-to-side line of objects in an array.

rule in a pattern, a procedure that describes the relationship between one number or shape and the next.

scale on a graph, the difference between numbers labeling points on the axes.

scalene triangle a triangle that has no two sides with the same length.

scaling resizing a quantity by multiplying.

second (s) a unit of time. Sixty seconds is equivalent to 1 minute.

side one of the line segments that form two-dimensional figures.

solid figure a three-dimensional figure.

square a shape that has four sides of equal length and four right angles.

square unit a square with a side length of 1 unit that is used to measure area.

standard form the way a number is written using digits. For example, the standard form of *twelve* is 12.

sum the result of addition.

symbol any mark or drawing with a particular meaning, including numbers, letters, and operation signs. A symbol can be used to stand for an unknown number in an equation.

tenths the parts formed when a whole is divided into ten equal parts.

thousandths the parts formed when a whole is divided into one thousand equal parts.

three-dimensional solid, or having length, width and height. For example, cubes are three-dimensional.

trapezoid a type of quadrilateral. A trapezoid always has a pair of parallel sides.

triangle a polygon with exactly three sides and three angles.

two-dimensional flat, or having measurement in two directions, like length and width. For example, a rectangle is two-dimensional.

unit fraction a fraction with a numerator of 1. Other fractions are built from unit fractions.

For example, $\frac{1}{4}$ and $\frac{1}{10}$ are unit fractions.

unknown the piece or pieces of a problem that you are not given or do not know.

Venn diagram a drawing that shows how sets of numbers or objects compare.

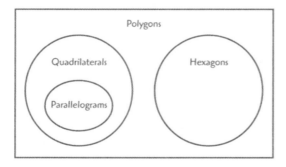

vertex the point where two rays or line segments meet to form an angle.

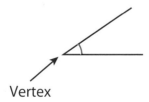

volume the amount of space inside a solid figure. Volume is measured in cubic units such as cubic inches.

weight the measurement that tells how heavy an object is. Units of weight include ounces and pounds.

word form (of a number) the way a number is written with words, or said aloud. For example, the word form of 105.7 is *one hundred five and seven tenths*.

***x*-axis** the horizontal number line in the coordinate plane.

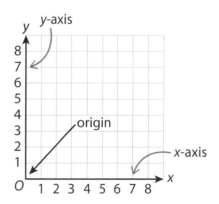

***x*-coordinate** the first number in an ordered pair. It tells the point's horizontal distance from the origin

Glossary

y-axis the vertical number line in the coordinate plane.

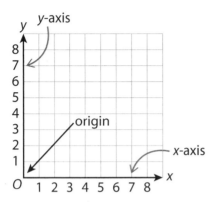

y-coordinate the second number in an ordered pair. It tells the point's vertical distance from the origin.

yard (yd) a unit of length in the U.S. customary system. One yard is equivalent to 3 feet.

TNCore State Standards Coverage by *Ready* Instruction

The chart below correlates each TNCore State Standard to the *Ready® Instruction* lesson(s) that offer(s) comprehensive instruction on that standard. Use this chart to determine which lessons your students should complete based on their mastery of each standard.

TNCore State Standards for Grade 5 Mathematics Standards	Content Emphasis	*Ready® TNCore* Instruction Lesson(s)
Operations and Algebraic Thinking		
Write and interpret numerical expressions.		
5.OA.A.1 Use parentheses, brackets, or braces in numerical expressions, and evaluate expressions with these symbols.	Supporting/ Additional	19
5.OA.A.2 Write simple expressions that record calculations with numbers, and interpret numerical expressions without evaluating them. *For example, express the calculation "add 8 and 7, then multiply by 2" as 2 × (8 + 7). Recognize that 3 × (18932 + 921) is three times as large as 18932 + 921, without having to calculate the indicated sum or product.*	Supporting/ Additional	19
Analyze patterns and relationships.		
5.OA.B.3 Generate two numerical patterns using two given rules. Identify apparent relationships between corresponding terms. Form ordered pairs consisting of corresponding terms from the two patterns, and graph the ordered pairs on a coordinate plane. *For example, given the rule "Add 3" and the starting number 0, and given the rule "Add 6" and the starting number 0, generate terms in the resulting sequences, and observe that the terms in one sequence are twice the corresponding terms in the other sequence. Explain informally why this is so.*	Supporting/ Additional	20
Number and Operations in Base Ten		
Understand the place value system.		
5.NBT.A.1 Recognize that in a multi-digit number, a digit in one place represents 10 times as much as it represents in the place to its right and $\frac{1}{10}$ of what it represents in the place to its left.	Major	1
5.NBT.A.2 Explain patterns in the number of zeros of the product when multiplying a number by powers of 10, and explain patterns in the placement of the decimal point when a decimal is multiplied or divided by a power of 10. Use whole-number exponents to denote powers of 10.	Major	2

The Standards for Mathematical Practice are integrated throughout the instructional lessons.

Number and Operations in Base Ten *continued*

Understand the place value system. *continued*

TNCore State Standards for Grade 5 Mathematics Standards	Content Emphasis	Ready® TNCore Instruction Lesson(s)
5.NBT.A.3 Read, write, and compare decimals to thousandths.	Major	3, 4
5.NBT.A.3a Read and write decimals to thousandths using base-ten numerals, number names, and expanded form, e.g., $347.392 = 3 \times 100 + 4 \times 10 + 7 \times 1 + 3 \times \left(\frac{1}{10}\right) + 9 \times \left(\frac{1}{100}\right) + 2 \times \left(\frac{1}{1000}\right)$.	Major	3
5.NBT.A.3b Compare two decimals to thousandths based on meanings of the digits in each place, using $>$, $=$, and $<$ symbols to record the results of comparisons.	Major	4
5.NBT.A.4 Use place value understanding to round decimals to any place.	Major	4

Perform operations with multi-digit whole numbers and with decimals to hundredths.

TNCore State Standards for Grade 5 Mathematics Standards	Content Emphasis	Ready® TNCore Instruction Lesson(s)
5.NBT.B.5 Fluently multiply multi-digit whole numbers using the standard algorithm.	Major	5
5.NBT.B.6 Find whole-number quotients of whole numbers with up to four-digit dividends and two-digit divisors, using strategies based on place value, the properties of operations, and/or the relationship between multiplication and division. Illustrate and explain the calculation by using equations, rectangular arrays, and/or area models.	Major	6
5.NBT.B.7 Add, subtract, multiply, and divide decimals to hundredths, using concrete models or drawings and strategies based on place value, properties of operations, and/or the relationship between addition and subtraction; relate the strategy to a written method and explain the reasoning used.	Major	7, 8, 9

Number and Operations—Fractions

Use equivalent fractions as a strategy to add and subtract fractions.

TNCore State Standards for Grade 5 Mathematics Standards	Content Emphasis	Ready® TNCore Instruction Lesson(s)
5.NF.A.1 Add and subtract fractions with unlike denominators (including mixed numbers) by replacing given fractions with equivalent fractions in such a way as to produce an equivalent sum or difference of fractions with like denominators. *For example, $\frac{2}{3} + \frac{5}{4} = \frac{8}{12} + \frac{15}{12} = \frac{23}{12}$. (In general, $\frac{a}{b} + \frac{c}{d} = \frac{(ad + bc)}{bd}$.)*	Major	10
5.NF.A.2 Solve word problems involving addition and subtraction of fractions referring to the same whole, including cases of unlike denominators, e.g., by using visual fraction models or equations to represent the problem. Use benchmark fractions and number sense of fractions to estimate mentally and assess the reasonableness of answers. *For example, recognize an incorrect result $\frac{2}{5} + \frac{1}{2} = \frac{3}{7}$, by observing that $\frac{3}{7} < \frac{1}{2}$.*	Major	11

The Standards for Mathematical Practice are integrated throughout the instructional lessons.

Number and Operations—Fractions *continued*

Apply and extend previous understandings of multiplication and division to multiply and divide fractions.

		Content Emphasis	Ready® TNCore Instruction Lesson(s)
5.NF.B.3	Interpret a fraction as division of the numerator by the denominator $\left(\frac{a}{b} = a \div b\right)$. Solve word problems involving division of whole numbers leading to answers in the form of fractions or mixed numbers, e.g., by using visual fraction models or equations to represent the problem. *For example, interpret $\frac{3}{4}$ as the result of dividing 3 by 4, noting that $\frac{3}{4}$ multiplied by 4 equals 3, and that when 3 wholes are shared equally among 4 people each person has a share of size $\frac{3}{4}$. If 9 people want to share a 50-pound sack of rice equally by weight, how many pounds of rice should each person get? Between what two whole numbers does your answer lie?*	Major	12
5.NF.B.4	Apply and extend previous understandings of multiplication to multiply a fraction or whole number by a fraction.	Major	13, 14
5.NF.B.4a	Interpret the product $\left(\frac{a}{b}\right) \times q$ as a parts of a partition of q into b equal parts; equivalently, as the result of a sequence of operations $a \times q \div b$. *For example, use a visual fraction model to show $\left(\frac{2}{3}\right) \times 4 = \frac{8}{3}$, and create a story context for this equation. Do the same with $\left(\frac{2}{3}\right) \times \left(\frac{4}{5}\right) = \frac{8}{15}$. (In general, $\left(\frac{a}{b}\right) \times \left(\frac{c}{d}\right) = \frac{ac}{bd}$.)*	Major	13
5.NF.B.4b	Find the area of a rectangle with fractional side lengths by tiling it with unit squares of the appropriate unit fraction side lengths, and show that the area is the same as would be found by multiplying the side lengths. Multiply fractional side lengths to find areas of rectangles, and represent fraction products as rectangular areas.	Major	14
5.NF.B.5	Interpret multiplication as scaling (resizing), by:	Major	15
5.NF.B.5a	Comparing the size of a product to the size of one factor on the basis of the size of the other factor, without performing the indicated multiplication.	Major	15
5.NF.B.5b	Explaining why multiplying a given number by a fraction greater than 1 results in a product greater than the given number (recognizing multiplication by whole numbers greater than 1 as a familiar case); explaining why multiplying a given number by a fraction less than 1 results in a product smaller than the given number; and relating the principle of fraction equivalence $\frac{a}{b} = \frac{(n \times a)}{(n \times b)}$ to the effect of multiplying $\frac{a}{b}$ by 1.	Major	15
5.NF.B.6	Solve real world problems involving multiplication of fractions and mixed numbers, e.g., by using visual fraction models or equations to represent the problem.	Major	16

The Standards for Mathematical Practice are integrated throughout the instructional lessons.

Number and Operations—Fractions *continued*

Apply and extend previous understandings of multiplication and division to multiply and divide fractions. *continued*

	Content Emphasis	Lesson(s)
5.NF.B.7 Apply and extend previous understandings of division to divide unit fractions by whole numbers and whole numbers by unit fractions.	Major	17, 18
5.NF.B.7a Interpret division of a unit fraction by a non-zero whole number, and compute such quotients. *For example, create a story context for* $\left(\frac{1}{3}\right) \div 4$, *and use a visual fraction model to show the quotient. Use the relationship between multiplication and division to explain that* $\left(\frac{1}{3}\right) \div 4 = \frac{1}{12}$ *because* $\left(\frac{1}{12}\right) \times 4 = \frac{1}{3}$.	Major	17
5.NF.B.7b Interpret division of a whole number by a unit fraction, and compute such quotients. *For example, create a story context for* $4 \div \left(\frac{1}{5}\right)$, *and use a visual fraction model to show the quotient. Use the relationship between multiplication and division to explain that* $4 \div \left(\frac{1}{5}\right) = 20$ *because* $20 \times \left(\frac{1}{5}\right) = 4$.	Major	17
5.NF.B.7c Solve real world problems involving division of unit fractions by non-zero whole numbers and division of whole numbers by unit fractions, e.g., by using visual fraction models and equations to represent the problem. *For example, how much chocolate will each person get if 3 people share* $\frac{1}{2}$ *lb of chocolate equally? How many* $\frac{1}{3}$-*cup servings are in 2 cups of raisins?*	Major	18

Measurement and Data

Convert like measurement units within a given measurement system.

	Content Emphasis	Lesson(s)
5.MD.A.1 Convert among different-sized standard measurement units within a given measurement system (e.g., convert 5 cm to 0.05 m), and use these conversions in solving multi-step, real world problems.	Supporting/ Additional	21, 22

Represent and interpret data.

	Content Emphasis	Lesson(s)
5.MD.B.2 Make a line plot to display a data set of measurements in fractions of a unit $\left(\frac{1}{2}, \frac{1}{4}, \frac{1}{8}\right)$. Use operations on fractions for this grade to solve problems involving information presented in line plots. *For example, given different measurements of liquid in identical beakers, find the amount of liquid each beaker would contain if the total amount in all the beakers were redistributed equally.*	Supporting/ Additional	23

Geometric measurement: understand concepts of volume and relate volume to multiplication and to addition.

	Content Emphasis	Lesson(s)
5.MD.C.3 Recognize volume as an attribute of solid figures and understand concepts of volume measurement.	Major	24
5.MD.C.3a A cube with side length 1 unit, called a "unit cube," is said to have "one cubic unit" of volume, and can be used to measure volume.	Major	24
5.MD.C.3b A solid figure which can be packed without gaps or overlaps using *n* unit cubes is said to have a volume of *n* cubic units.	Major	24

The Standards for Mathematical Practice are integrated throughout the instructional lessons.

Measurement and Data *continued*

Geometric measurement: understand concepts of volume and relate volume to multiplication and to addition. *continued*

5.MD.C.4 Measure volumes by counting unit cubes, using cubic cm, cubic in, cubic ft, and improvised units.	Major	25
5.MD.C.5 Relate volume to the operations of multiplication and addition and solve real world and mathematical problems involving volume.	Major	26, 27
5.MD.C.5a Find the volume of a right rectangular prism with whole-number side lengths by packing it with unit cubes, and show that the volume is the same as would be found by multiplying the edge lengths, equivalently by multiplying the height by the area of the base. Represent threefold whole-number products as volumes, e.g., to represent the associative property of multiplication.	Major	26
5.MD.C.5b Apply the formulas $V = l \times w \times h$ and $V = b \times h$ for rectangular prisms to find volumes of right rectangular prisms with whole-number edge lengths in the context of solving real world and mathematical problems.	Major	26
5.MD.C.5c Recognize volume as additive. Find volumes of solid figures composed of two non-overlapping right rectangular prisms by adding the volumes of the non-overlapping parts, applying this technique to solve real world problems.	Major	27

Geometry

Graph points on the coordinate plane to solve real-world and mathematical problems.

5.G.A.1 Use a pair of perpendicular number lines, called axes, to define a coordinate system, with the intersection of the lines (the origin) arranged to coincide with the 0 on each line and a given point in the plane located by using an ordered pair of numbers, called its coordinates. Understand that the first number indicates how far to travel from the origin in the direction of one axis, and the second number indicates how far to travel in the direction of the second axis, with the convention that the names of the two axes and the coordinates correspond (e.g., *x*-axis and *x*-coordinate, *y*-axis and *y*-coordinate).	Supporting/ Additional	28
5.G.A.2 Represent real world and mathematical problems by graphing points in the first quadrant of the coordinate plane, and interpret coordinate values of points in the context of the situation.	Supporting/ Additional	29

Classify two-dimensional figures into categories based on their properties.

5.G.B.3 Understand that attributes belonging to a category of two-dimensional figures also belong to all subcategories of that category. *For example, all rectangles have four right angles and squares are rectangles, so all squares have four right angles.*	Supporting/ Additional	31
5.G.B.4 Classify two-dimensional figures in a hierarchy based on properties.	Supporting/ Additional	30

The Standards for Mathematical Practice are integrated throughout the instructional lessons.

Acknowledgments

Illustration Credits

page 34: Fian Arroyo

page 50: Rob McClurkan

page 98: Fian Arroyo

All other illustrations by Sam Valentino.

Photography Credits

page 86: M88/Shutterstock (goat)

page 86: Tsekhmister/Shutterstock (pig)

page 88: 3drenderings/Shutterstock

page 89: Africa Studio/Shutterstock

page 168: Romas_Photo/Shutterstock

page 172: Maksym Bondarchuk/Shutterstock

page 174: LianeM/Shutterstock

page 175: Madlen/Shutterstock

page 200: Stephen Mcsweeny/Shutterstock

page 206: Cool Vector Maker/Shutterstock (sandwich)

page 206: Macrovector/Shutterstock (pizza and hot dog)

page 207: Zeljko Radojko/Shutterstock

page 272: Miro Novak/Shutterstock

page 276: Iryna Rasko/Shutterstock

page 278: stockcreations/Shutterstock

Background images used throughout lessons by Ortis/Shutterstock, irin-k/Shutterstock, and Kritsada Namborisut/Shutterstock.